RICHARD III's 'BELOVED COUSYN'

RICHARD III's 'BELOVED COUSYN'

JOHN HOWARD
AND THE
HOUSE
OF YORK

JOHN
ASHDOWN-HILL

The
History
Press

To my friends, the Canonesses Regular of the Holy Sepulchre in Colchester, who helped me to commemorate John Howard and his men at St John's Abbey, and especially to Sister Stephanie, who took a special interest in my progress, and Sister Mary Stephen, who is one of John Howard's descendants.

Front cover illustrations
Top: An engraving of John Howard. *Bottom:* Richard III. (© World History Archive)

First published 2009
This edition published 2015

The History Press
The Mill, Brimscombe Port
Stroud, Gloucestershire, GL5 2QG
www.thehistorypress.co.uk

© John Ashdown-Hill, 2009, 2015

The right of John Ashdown-Hill to be identified as the Author
of this work has been asserted in accordance with the
Copyright, Designs and Patents Act 1988.

British Library Cataloguing in Publication Data.
A catalogue record for this book is available from the British Library.

ISBN 978 0 7509 6129 5

Typeset in Bembo 11/13pt
Printed and bound in Great Britain by TJ International Ltd, Padstow, Cornwall

Contents

Acknowledgements

My grateful thanks for their kind and invaluable assistance are due to the staff of the Essex Record Office, the Suffolk Record Office (Ipswich branch), the British Library, the archival and library staff of His Grace the Duke of Norfolk at Arundel Castle, and the library staff of the Society of Antiquaries of London. I also owe a considerable debt of gratitude to Dr Chris Thornton, who supervised my PhD research, and to the members of my supervisory board: Dr Joan Davies and Dr Herbert Eiden. My thanks also go to Annette Carson and Dave Perry, who kindly read draft versions of the text, and corrected typographical and other errors; and likewise to Cath D'Alton and Geoff Wheeler who supplied illustrations. I should also like to thank my PhD examiners, Professor Anne Curry and Professor John Walters, without whose encouragement I might never have attempted to make parts of my thesis more widely available in the form of this book.

List of Abbreviations and Symbols

BL	British Library
BM	British Museum
B.OB	W.G. Benham, ed., *Colchester Oath Book*
CCCC	Corpus Christi College, Cambridge
CHM	*Calendar of Muniments, Harwich*
CP	G.E. Cockayne, *The Complete Peerage*, London, 1910–59
CPR	*Calendar of Patent Rolls*
Cr. Chr.	N. Pronay and J. Cox, eds, T*he Crowland Chronicle continuations 1459–1486*, London, 1986
ERO	Essex Record Office
Gothic	R. Marks & P. Williamson, eds, *Gothic, Art for England 1400–1547*, London: V&A, 2003
HHB	A. Crawford, ed., *Howard Household Books*, Stroud, 1992
HM	Harwich Muniments
HP Biog.	J.C. Wedgwood and A.D. Holt, *History of Parliament 1439–1509 – Biographies of the Members of the Commons House*
IRO	Suffolk Record Office (Ipswich Branch)
J.Ch.	I.H. Jeayes, ed., *Descriptive Catalogue of a Collection of Charters sometime preserved at Gifford's Hall in Stoke-by-Nayland, Co. Suffolk*, unpublished, IRO, S 347

Mancini C.A.J. Armstrong, ed., Dominic [*sic*] Mancini, *The Usurpation of Richard III*, Gloucester, 1984

MEJ R.W. Lightbown, *Mediaeval European Jewellery*, London:V&A, 1992

NPG National Portrait Gallery

ODNB *Oxford Dictionary of National Biography*

PL N. Davis, *Paston Letters and Papers of the fifteenth century*, 2 vols, Oxford, 1971; 1976

PPE N.H. Nicolas, ed., *Privy Purse Expenses of Elizabeth of York & Wardrobe Accounts of Edward IV*, London: W. Pickering, 1830; reprinted London: F. Muller, 1972

R3MK A. Carson, *Richard III, the Maligned King*, Stroud 2008

Ric. *The Ricardian*

Road P.W. Hammond and A.F. Sutton, *Richard III – the Road to Bosworth Field*, London, 1985

Soc.Ant. The Society of Antiquaries of London

TNA The National Archive [formerly PRO]

V&A Victoria and Albert Museum

VCH Victoria County History

WRO Warwickshire Record Office

Θ J. Ashdown-Hill, 'The client network, connections and patronage of Sir John Howard (Lord Howard, first Duke of Norfolk) in north-east Essex and south Suffolk', unpublished PhD thesis, University of Essex, 2008

Introduction

This book arose largely out of research for my PhD thesis. The latter was essentially local in its focus, concentrating in detail upon John Howard's client network and patronage in north Essex and south Suffolk. But inevitably it also considered John Howard's national importance. Reviewing Howard's service to and relationship with the Yorkist kings produced new evidence, new interpretations and new perspectives, and these form the basis of the present study.

Although the presentation of material is sequential within each chapter – and in general terms, within the book as a whole – a complete chronological account of John Howard's career was not my aim. The individual chapters are thematic in their approach, while the overarching purpose of the book is to examine every aspect of John Howard's relationship with the ruling house of York.

Studying those men and women who were key figures in the entourage of the Yorkist kings is of interest in its own right, but it also has the potential to shed new light upon the enigmas of the period. Certainly, through this study, we discover much about John Howard himself: his technological awareness, the state of his health, his leisure activities, his government service, his relationship with the royal family and others, his beliefs, and perhaps something of his character. But at the same time hopefully a clearer picture also emerges of the Yorkist era as a whole. As a result of the evidence presented here we can now accord due credit (perhaps for the first time) to Edward IV's role in building up the navy, and the reader is invited to reconsider the standard assessment of Edward's character.

At the same time, new light is shed on the key events of 1483 and the accession of Richard III, as these are re-examined in minute detail in the light of John Howard's day-to-day experience of the course of events.

All my references to John Howard's surviving household accounts give details of the original manuscript source as well as the more readily accessible 1992 published transcripts. This is because the latter contain a few errors of transcription, a number of discrepancies in folio numbering, and a few omissions (full details of which can be found in Θ, appendix 1).

Conventions

The following conventions have been adopted:

Spelling
In quotations from medieval sources, unless othersise stated, original spellings have been retained, including use of yogh (3 = g or y) and thorn (þ = th). The third defunct Old- and Middle-English letter, eth (ð = th), does not occur in any of the quoted texts. Standard abbreviations have been expanded without comment. Some punctuation has been modernised.

Dates
In the fifteenth century the calendar year in England began on Lady Day (25 March), and not on 1 January. Therefore, for dates falling between 1 January and 24 March the usual convention is followed. February 1464/5 means February 1464 (medieval calendar) or February 1465 (modern calendar).

A Suffolk Gentleman

... they seid to me they wolde have [Chaumberleyn], but not
Howard, in asmeche as he hadde no lyvelode in [Norfolk].
John Jenney, 1455

On 10 December 1455 an untitled and relatively obscure
Suffolk gentleman received for the first time an official commission from the government of Henry VI.[1] His name was
John Howard and, since he was the fifth known member of
his family to bear that name, we shall call him John Howard V.
Although Howard's family origins amongst the Suffolk gentry
clearly made him eligible to serve on government commissions of the peace, or of array, and although he had for some
years been old enough for such nominations, none had ever
previously been addressed to him by the crown. From the
point of view of the Lancastrian regime, Howard was tainted
by the wrong associations. In the ongoing dispute between
the Mowbray dukes of Norfolk and the de la Pole dukes of
Suffolk, John Howard's family connections and personal commitment placed him on the wrong side.[2]

Thirty years later, on 22 August 1485, John Howard V was
killed at the battle of Bosworth, fighting for the house of York
against the Tudor invader who pretended, not very convinc-
ingly, to represent the claims of the house of Lancaster.[3] By
then, Howard was a wealthy man.[4] Under the Yorkist dynasty
he had risen through the ranks of knight, admiral and baron.
He was several times a peer, Earl Marshal of England and Duke

of Norfolk, and he died commanding the vanguard of his sovereign's army. In the course of those thirty years the change in Howard's status had been tremendous, and his influence and patronage had grown enormously.

Those years had witnessed Howard's transformation into a 'new magnate'. In the power vacuum left by the ineffectuality of his Mowbray kinsmen, the dukes of Norfolk, the eclipse of the de la Poles (earls and dukes of Suffolk), and the ultimate flight of the de Veres (earls of Oxford),[5] Sir John Howard first became the dominant lord in Suffolk (rather as Sir Thomas Montgomery did in neighbouring Essex). However, Howard ultimately rose even higher. From a position in which he played a key but regional role in the eastern counties, he became a figure of national importance. In serving the house of York, John Howard also became one of the principal figures shaping that dynasty's future: he built Edward IV's navy; lawyers whom Howard retained subsequently went on to serve the royal family; he acted as a diplomat between Edward IV and the Burgundian and French courts; he even touched on the most private aspects of Edward IV's life, serving as an intermediary for the enigmatic Eleanor Talbot, and having close links with the Shore family.

Enjoying the trust of both Edward IV and Richard III, and closely linked by ties of blood and friendship with both the Mowbray and Talbot families, Howard ultimately became a leading player in the dramatic events which marked the final years of Yorkist rule in England. The decision which he made in the summer of 1483 to support the accession of Richard III in the face of the rival claims of Edward IV's children, the probable reasons for that decision, and Howard's role in the events which followed, are all vital pieces of evidence in a complex jigsaw puzzle, the complete pattern of which has yet to be fully comprehended. The true significance of Howard's part in these dramatic happenings has never hitherto been properly documented or understood.

John Howard V's date of birth is not recorded, but when he received his first commission in 1455 he was at least thirty years old, and had been married for twelve years or more to Catherine de Moleyns, a baron's daughter[6] who had already borne him six children. During the course of the thirteenth and fourteenth centuries his Howard forebears had risen from humble beginnings in north Norfolk. Like the Pastons later, their route to worldly success was initially via a legal career. From simple beginnings the early fourteenth-century Howards established themselves in a small way as members of the local landed gentry. It had been John Howard III who, as a result of his second marriage to Alice, daughter and heiress of Sir William Tendring of Stoke-by-Nayland, settled the family in Suffolk.

John Howard V was something of a hybrid. His grandfather, Sir John Howard III, had made a very good first marriage, and a second marriage which at least left its descendants (of whom John Howard V was ultimately the chief) in possession of a little landed property. Sir John Howard III figures in the Suffolk records of the first decades of the fifteenth century as a man of some local consequence. However, his second son, Sir Robert Howard II, was a relatively minor knight of no great lineage or achievements, who died comparatively young and who figures scarcely at all in national and local records – though like some of his ancestors and successors, he was a naval commander.[7] In fact, Robert Howard II's one towering achievement in terms of his family's future was his marriage. His wife, the mother of John Howard V, was Lady Margaret Mowbray, one of the daughters of Thomas Mowbray, first Duke of Norfolk, and descendant of Edward I.[8]

We know neither the date of Margaret's birth nor that of her marriage to Robert Howard. However, Margaret's father died in 1399, so she must have been over twenty years old when she married Robert, who was her first husband.[9] It seems certain that she married relatively late and somewhat beneath her. It has been asserted that there is some evidence of a frosty relationship between Lady Margaret and her mother, Elizabeth Fitzalan, the dowager Duchess of Norfolk, and that this may well indicate that Margaret married against her mother's wishes. In fact, the evidence for this assertion is somewhat controversial.[10] But Robert Howard's inferior status cannot be questioned. It is not even certain that he had received knighthood prior to his marriage, for he appears in the Colchester Borough records in 1418–19 untitled.[11] Indeed, his elder half-brother, John Howard IV, seems never to have attained knightly rank.[12] Robert's father, Sir John Howard III, figures frequently in deeds of the 1430s from Stoke-by-Nayland.[13] Although details of the collateral Howard pedigree are not clear, Sir Robert Howard probably had cousins in varying degrees, whose descendants play a minor role in the story of the dynasty.[14] A William Howard is mentioned at Stoke-by-Nayland in 1471,[15] and a John Howard, who is not one of those shown on the family trees published here, occurs in Colchester records of about the same period.[16] There is also one obscure mention of a priest, 'Howard's son', where it is not clear which Howard is meant.[17]

Robert Howard's and Margaret Mowbray's son, the young John Howard V, was probably born in or around 1422. He gravitated naturally into the entourage of his maternal uncle, John Mowbray, second Duke of Norfolk. Later he also served his cousin, the third Mowbray duke, and finally his cousin's son, the fourth (last) Mowbray duke. Despite the fact that he occupied a position of power and influence in the Mowbray retinue during the minority and young adulthood of the fourth Mowbray duke, the thought can scarcely have entered his head that one day the Mowbray line would be extinct, and that he himself would succeed to the dukedom of Norfolk. Nevertheless, John Howard's life story represents a tale of steady, if somewhat slow progress to that unexpected pinnacle.

For many years he was a simple esquire. Being in the orbit of the Mowbrays, he was drawn with them into the service of their cousin, Richard of Cambridge, Duke of York. One can therefore argue that John Howard was virtually born a Yorkist. At any rate, neither he nor anyone else (including the government of Henry VI) seems ever to have been in much doubt as to where his probable loyalties would lie. By 1460, if not before, John Howard was personally acquainted with York's eldest son, the young Edward, Earl of March. Their names occur together as feoffees in a deed of 27 August 1460, relating to a messuage and lands in Higham and Stratford St Mary, Suffolk.[18] Shortly after the date of this feoffment, when the Earl of March attained the throne as Edward IV, it was only natural that John Howard, as one of the supporters of the new dynasty, should also rise in rank. On 28 June 1461, at Edward IV's coronation, Howard was knighted.[19] Edward IV, who employed him regularly, would later (late 1469 or early 1470) create him Baron Howard. Later still, in 1483, Edward's brother, Richard III, raised him to the dukedom of Norfolk, thereby founding a new ducal dynasty which has lasted to the present day.

It is tempting to speak of the relationship which grew up between Howard and the Yorkist princes as one of friendship, and this is a point to which we shall return later. There is certainly evidence that Edward IV generally favoured him, though the relationship was perhaps not without its ups and downs, as we shall discuss in due course. For the moment, however, let us merely observe that Howard and the king were by no means of an age. Howard was twenty years Edward's senior, and although he was some ten years younger than the Duke of York, Howard was certainly old enough to have been Edward IV's father, since his own eldest son, Thomas Howard, was about Edward's age. We shall return to this age gap in Chapter 4, when its possible implications will be more fully explored.

The relationship between Howard and Edward's younger brother, the future Richard III, has also been spoken of in terms of friendship, and again, there is certainly evidence of the trust reposed in Howard by Richard. But here too, it is very important to bear in mind the age gap between the two men. As we shall see in Chapter 4, in Richard's case Howard may well have been perceived by the young royal duke as something of a surrogate father-figure – a role strengthened, perhaps, by Howard's close ties of service to Richard's mother, Cecily Neville, Duchess of York.

It was probably early in the 1460s that John Howard was appointed Cecily Neville's steward in respect of the honour of Clare. There was a significant degree of overlap between those who served Cecily Neville, those who served the Mowbrays, and those who served John Howard. This is particularly notice-able in respect of the retention of legal advisers. Although it is difficult to be certain which of the three first employed (and subsequently recommended) such lawyers and other servants, it is clear that exchanges and recommendations did take place. These issues are examined more fully in Chapter 3.

Sir John Howard V remained intimately linked with the house of York and its fortunes throughout the Yorkist period. In 1470, when Edward IV was forced to seek refuge in the Low Countries during the Lancastrian Readeption, Howard's power and influence in the eastern counties was at its nadir. Some of his close associates from the Mowbray entourage accompanied Edward IV into exile,[20] however, Howard himself remained behind in England, taking sanctuary at St John's Abbey in Colchester, together with one of Lord Hastings' brothers.[21] Neither Howard nor his cousin the Duke of Norfolk (who was forcibly detained at this time in London by the Earl of Warwick) was on hand to offer personal support when Edward IV and his brother, the Duke of Gloucester, tried to land at Cromer, in Norfolk, on Tuesday evening, 12 March 1471.[22] Nevertheless, the Duke of Norfolk slipped out of London and made his way back to the eastern counties, to raise support for the house of York in Norfolk. Howard meanwhile emerged from his sanctuary at Colchester Abbey and in April 1471 it was reported 'that þe Lord Howard hath proclaimed Kyng E[dward] Kyng of Inglond in Suffolk'.[23] Howard rejoined Edward in person soon after the king's return to London.

What was John Howard really like? We shall, of course, return to this point later, but it may be helpful to begin with some impression of his appearance and character. In terms of his physical appearance there are no surviving fifteenth-century representations, so for an idea of his looks we are dependent upon the work of later artists. However, the so-called 'portrait' of Howard displayed at the present Duke of Norfolk's home, Arundel Castle, is a sixteenth-century representation, and there is no reason whatever to suppose that it accurately depicts Howard's features or colouring.

Contemporary representations of Howard did once exist, but they are lost. Nevertheless, two such representations were recorded before the originals disappeared. One of these was a stained-glass representation at Stoke-by-Nayland, and the second, a similar figure at Long Melford. The original location of the Stoke- by-Nayland glass is variously reported in the surviving sources. John Weever, who in 1631 published an inaccurate engraving of this figure, described it as being in 'the east window of the private chapel of Tendring Hall'.[24] George Vertue (1684–1756), who produced a painting of the same glass, said that it was in the parish church at Stoke-by-Nayland.[25] It is, of course, conceivable that the glass was moved at some stage. Alternatively it may have been in the east window of the south chapel of the parish church which, to this day, houses burials of the Tendring and Howard families, and which may have been regarded as 'the Tendring Hall chapel'. A later engraving of the same Stoke-by-Nayland glass was published in James Dallaway's *A History of the Western Division of the County of Sussex* (1815– 30). However, there is no reason to suppose that the glass itself still existed as late as the early nineteenth century, and it is therefore probable that Dallaway (or his engraver) worked at second hand, from Vertue's painting.

A second stained-glass figure of John Howard V was once among the fifteenth- century donor portraits in the windows of Long Melford Church, to the rebuilding of which Howard contributed. A lithograph of this figure, taken from an apparently seventeenth-century drawing or engraving, is reproduced in G.H. Ryan and L.J. Redstone, *Timperley of Hintlesham, a Study of a Suffolk Family* (London, 1931). Unfortunately, Ryan and Redstone give no earlier source for their illustration. However, the original of their lithograph so obviously reflects the style and fashions of the reign of Charles I that its value is somewhat questionable.

Previous writers seeking a representation of John Howard V have tended to favour Dallaway's nineteenth-century engraving of the Stoke-by-Nayland stained glass. However, as we have seen, it is unlikely that Dallaway (or his engraver) ever saw the original window. Vertue, on the other hand, clearly did see the original fifteenth-century stained glass at Stoke-by-Nayland. Since the earlier (seventeenth-century) copies of Howard's figure both from Stoke-by-Nayland and from Long Melford are of dubious accuracy, it seems likely that Vertue's 'John Howard' is the nearest we can now get to a contemporary representation. It is therefore George Vertue's visual image of the mature but still slim and youthful-looking Howard of the 1460s, with fair or light-brown hair, which is illustrated here.

As for John Howard's character, he undoubtedly had a sense of his own rank and importance. He was capable of displaying both pride and anger at times. In 1455 his cousin, the third Mowbray duke, put Howard's name forward as a prospective candidate for election to Parliament as a knight of the shire for Norfolk. This recommendation was opposed by the local gentry on the grounds that Howard 'hadde no lyvelode in the shire'. John Jenney, a member of the Duke of Norfolk's council, reported that when he heard of this opposition 'Howard was as wode [mad] as a wilde bullok'.[26]

His most obvious characteristic, however, seems to have been his loyalty. Recently 'the point has been made that individual aristocrats were guided by concepts of honour and loyalty' in the fifteenth century, and that self-aggrandisement and self-interest were not their only possible motivations.[27] Howard was consistently loyal to the last two Mowbray dukes of Norfolk and trusted by his cousins. He showed the same loyalty also to the house of York, as personified successively by Richard, Duke of York, and his sons, Edward IV and Richard III. As we shall see later, the divisions within the house of York after the death of Edward IV confronted Howard – and others – with a choice which some found difficult, between the previously accepted heir, Edward V, who was now found to be illegitimate, and his uncle, Richard, Duke of Gloucester (Richard III). Howard's associate and former superior in Calais, Lord Hastings, certainly had problems with it. However, for reasons which we shall explore in due course, Howard never seems to have hesitated over whether Edward V or Richard III was the true heir of the dynasty. His loyalty seems to have been accorded to Richard from the moment of the latter's arrival in London, and was thereafter unswerving. It extended ultimately to dying at Richard's side on the battlefield of Bosworth in 1485. Howard's courage cannot be questioned. It is also clear that he was an effective military leader, diplomat and government representative at local level.

Later generations of the Howard dynasty would be noted for their religious commitment, maintaining their Catholic faith in an England which had become Protestant, at no small cost to themselves. Some have sought to argue that there is no evidence of anything more than conventional piety on the part of John Howard V.[28] Nevertheless, there is clearly evidence of some religious commitment on his part – for example in his patronage of churches and in his record of pilgrimages. While the latter certainly conforms to the norms expected of a man of his rank and time, in Howard's case it perhaps goes beyond the minimum requirements, and may be evidence of genuine faith. It is surely not without significance that, as we shall see in Chapters 13 and 15, there was to be an overt religious motivation at the very heart of Howard's formal, public celebration of his elevation to the dukedom of Norfolk in the summer of 1483. The evidence on this point has not hitherto been noticed or explored.

2

Black and Blue

Item, my Lord bout v. yerdes of blak velvet, prise of the yerd xij s.
whereof my Lord sent to Mastres Jane Tymperley, by his servaunt
Laurence, a lyvere iiij yerdes.
Howard Accounts

In this chapter we shall briefly examine John Howard V's power base in the eastern counties, considering its origin, its expansion, and the manner in which its existence was proclaimed and demonstrated in visual and tangible form. It was the existence and ongoing expansion of Howard's local power-base which made his support desirable to the house of York; a thing to be wooed and solicited by the dynasty by means of grants of lands, offices, favours and honours, all of which will be explored later (see Chapter 5).

The first year of the fourteenth century had found the Howard family based in Norfolk, where it held two manors: East Winch and Fitton (Wiggenhall St Germain).[1] By purchase and by a series of astute marriages the family subsequently accumulated a substantial patrimony, comprising manors in Norfolk, Essex, Hertfordshire, Cambridgeshire, and Suffolk. Of this patr imony, John Howard V would eventually inherit only two manors: Tendring Hall (Stoke-by-Nayland) and Fersfield (near Diss). The reason for this meagre inheritance was simple: John Howard V's father, Sir Robert Howard II, was a younger son. Most of the Howard estates were inherited by

Robert's elder half-brother, who left them to his only child, Elizabeth Howard, Countess of Oxford.

Thus, at the start of his career John Howard V was merely a minor Suffolk gentleman. His Suffolk base remained important throughout his life, and although Howard subsequently obtained estates in many parts of the country, his principal seat up until two years before his death remained Tendring Hall at Stoke-by-Nayland. In June 1483, upon his elevation to the dukedom of Norfolk, the focus shifted to Framlingham Castle, also in Suffolk.

For the greater part of his life a significant proportion of his political, social, economic and cultural activity was firmly based within approximately a twenty-mile (thirty-two kilometre) radius of Stoke-by-Nayland, taking in Colchester and Ipswich, and extending as far as Harwich in the east and Bury St Edmunds in the north-west. Of course Howard travelled, and had interests much farther afield. For most of his life, however, this comparatively compact region represented his 'home range'.

The origins of John Howard V's gentry connections and client network were various, and not all of them can be traced or fully reconstructed. Nevertheless, it is possible to discern and document amongst those names which have been preserved in relation to John Howard V as a young man (prior to his aggrandisement under the Yorkist dynasty) men and women who came from families which had previously served Howard's paternal grandfather, and who therefore had a hereditary link with the Howard family. Robert Mannok seems to be a case in point, for the Mannock family had also been linked with Sir John Howard III. Next, we find examples of people who entered Howard's orbit as a result of his own connection with the Mowbray network. The Tymperley family of Hintlesham is one instance. In the first half of the fifteenth century they were Mowbray clients, but from the 1470s they became closely linked with John Howard, and the Tymperley heir married one of Howard's daughters. In fact, it is clear that after the family line of the Mowbray dukes of Norfolk died out, a number of former Mowbray clients were attracted to Howard's service as the natural successor of the Mowbray dukes. Others among Howard's early associates were apparently attracted to his service as a result of his first marriage. An obvious example of this phenomenon is Thomas Moleyns, a presumed cousin of Howard's first wife, Catherine.[2]

'The corporate sense of the household was reinforced by marks of identification.'[3] Thus a lord's clients received and wore his distinctive livery, which might also be given, as a sign of friendship, to colleagues. Livery comprised clothing of a distinctive colour or colours; a kind of uniform,[4] which the lord might require his retainers to wear on specific occasions. Thus, in 1240–42 the Countess of Lincoln stipulated that her livery should be worn at mealtimes.[5] To briefly summarise the history of livery, its evolution was intimately connected with the growth of paid retinues and factional rivalry. In 1390, Parliament had perceived the issuing of livery as an abuse which it petitioned Richard II to curb. In April 1400, Henry IV specifically prohibited the distribution and wearing of any livery within his kingdom, except that of the king himself.[6] Yet this enactment quickly proved a dead letter. By the second half of the fifteenth century any lord with a claim to status had his own livery, and was issuing it to his supporters and friends.

A lord's retainers received and wore his livery as a sign of their allegiance to him. Some of his colleagues might also wear it on suitable occasions as a token of friendship. The giving and receiving of livery was an important part of the service obligation. Indeed, for a lord to withhold from a retainer the gift of his livery, though possibly of rare occurrence, was highly significant, as can be seen in 1469, when the last Mowbray Duke of Norfolk refused his livery to John Paston III and others with whom he was in dispute over the possession of Caister Castle.[7]

The distribution and wearing of livery was the principal means by which a fifteenth-century lord made manifest his 'worship'. Howard, therefore, naturally made use of livery and badges in his household and retinue throughout his career, though, as we shall shortly see, the precise details of his livery changed as his career progressed. The Howard accounts and other fifteenth-century sources record numerous gifts of cloth or clothing to retainers. Not all of these constituted formal livery. Dr Carol Chattaway has proposed certain criteria for distinguishing formal livery from other, more general gifts of clothing or fabric.[8] These include regular distribution, to a defined group, of fabric or clothing of a standard colour, and the distribution of standard badges where the colour and the design are clearly linked to the distributor. To Chattaway's criteria we should add, as an alternative possibility, gifts of fabric the colour of which is specifically related to the recipient. It is clear, for example, that on occasions Edward IV presented to members of his retine cloth of their own livery colours.[9]

Details of the livery colours and badges of some noble families are known. Surviving evidence indicates that the Talbots of Shrewsbury had a dark green livery,[10] while the Mowbray livery colour was 'crymeson engreyned', or 'cremyson owt of greyn', the 'greyn' or grain being an insect which was used to produce a high quality crimson dye.[11] One previous writer has suggested that the Howard livery colours were red and blue.[12] This is clearly an error, and one which we shall presently correct. Murray and blue were actually the livery colours of the house of York.[13] The wearing of one particular livery did not exclude the possibility that others might also be worn on occasions. Client networks overlapped, and even rival service ties were not necessarily mutually exclusive. John Howard himself certainly wore the crimson livery of his Mowbray cousins, and the numerous references in the Howard accounts to the purchase of red and blue fabric are examples of Howard dressing himself and members of his household in the Yorkist royal livery, thus publicly proclaiming his Yorkist allegiance.

'By the end of the fourteenth century ... it became fashionable to extend the [affinity] group further by the use of livery collars and badges.'[14] Such badges probably had a heraldic origin and may date back as far as the twelfth century, but in the late fourteenth century and the fifteenth century the wearing of badges bearing a lord's device became widespread.[15] The use of flower emblems is well-attested in the fifteenth century, and included the well-known white rose of York.[16] The punning Mowbray 'flower' badge actually comprised sprigs of mulberry leaves,[17] while the personal emblem of Elizabeth Talbot, wife of the last Mowbray Duke of Norfolk, may have been the borage flower.[18]

Not all such livery badges were flowers. The now-extinct talbot hound was the family badge of the Duchess of Norfolk's own Talbot family, and examples of talbot hound livery badges have survived.[19] As an alternative to their mulberry sprig emblem, the Mowbray family had a second livery badge which comprised a white lion rampant.[20] This badge was also used by Sir John Howard as his personal livery badge, but it was 'differenced for Howard with an azure crescent', while the Mowbray dukes were still living.[21] Later, the new Howard dynasty of dukes of Norfolk used the white lion badge undifferenced, just as it had been used by their Mowbray cousins and predecessors prior to 1474. A sixteenth-century livery badge depicting a white lion rampant and inscribed on the reverse for Thomas Howard, fourth Duke of Norfolk, was recently discovered at Cressing Temple, Essex, and is now in the Braintree Museum.

In some cases, lords are known to have given out their badges as gifts to reinforce ties of loyalty.[22] Such gift badges were often intrinsically valuable. Examples survive in silver, and even in gold and enamel.[23] Sir John Howard is known to have proclaimed his Yorkist loyalties by owning and wearing a Yorkist collar 'of gold with 34 roses and suns set on a corse of black silk with a hanger [pendant] of gold garnished with a sapphire'.[24] In 1465 Howard purchased from 'Arnold gooldsmythe a devyse of goold for mastres Margret', and later that year he gave his new wife two sumptuous devices in the form of collars, each of fourteen links, alternately enamelled and set with rubies, diamonds and pearls.[25] The precise design of these collars is not recorded.

As for the livery colour of Sir John Howard V, for most of his career this was black. There is ample evidence in support of this contention.[26] The most important testimony is a long list of recipients of black fabric from Sir John Howard, similar to a list recording his distribution of the Mowbray crimson to the Duke of Norfolk's affinity.[27] Unfortunately this issue of black cloth has hitherto been consistently misinterpreted. As published by Beriah Botfield in 1841,[28] it was dated to November of year five of Edward IV (1465), and assumed to be the issue of mourning for the first Lady Howard, Catherine de Moleyns, who died around 14 November 1465. All subsequent writers have followed Botfield in this assumption, but unfortunately Botfield's reading of the year date of this entry was incorrect. A careful re-examination of the original manuscript has shown that there are at least two strokes after the 'v' of the year number, so that the regnal date is probably year seven of Edward IV. This would date the issue of the black fabric to November 1467.[29]

The list of named recipients of the black fabric itself proves that this cannot have been issued in mourning for Catherine de Moleyns.[30] Briefly, the recipients include 'My Lady; Mastres Jane her dowter; Mastres Isabelle her dowter; Mastres Letuse her dowter [and] Master William hir sones'.[31] 'My Lady' can only be one of Howard's two wives, and in this instance it is obvious that Margaret Chedworth (Howard's second wife) is meant, because the names which immediately follow are those of Margaret's children by her previous husbands: Isabel Wyfold and Lettice and William Norris.[32] 'Mastres Jane her dowter' is probably Margaret Chedworth's youngest Norris stepdaughter.[33] Howard did not marry Margaret until January 1466/7, and since the black fabric list is dated to November, it follows that November 1467 would be the earliest possibility. A comparison between the black fabric distribution list and the two household lists of Howard and his bride-to-be, drawn up in

January 1466/7, a few days before their marriage,[34] also shows that the issue of black fabric cannot have taken place in 1465, because the cloth was distributed to a mixed group of retainers, some of whom had been members of Howard's household prior to his second marriage, while others came from the household of Margaret Chedworth.[35]

The obvious alternative is that the list records a distribution of Howard livery. Clear supporting evidence for this interpretation exists elsewhere in the form of other records of the issue of black fabric by John Howard V, though only in some of the entries is this black fabric specifically stated to be the Howard livery. In the early summer of 1465, while distributing the crimson Mowbray livery fabric to Mowbray clients on behalf of his cousin, the Duke of Norfolk, Howard issued four and a half yards of 'blak a lyr' to Dr Hew.[36] In the same year he issued black fabric to his lawyer, James Hobart, to whom on other occasions he gave the crimson Mowbray livery, or the murray and blue livery of the house of York.[37] On 15 April 1467 Sir John Howard paid Robert Rochester's man 21*s.* for three and a half yards of 'blakke a lyre'.[38]

The wardrobe accounts of Edward IV for 1480, listing the presentation of liveries by the king to officers of his household, specify 'to the Lord Howard ... Blac velvet, ix yerdes'.[39] Sir John's daughter, Jane, who received an allocation of black cloth with other members of her family and the household in 1467, went on to marry John Tymperley,[40] who then entered the service of his father-in-law, both in the Howard household and in the navy. In November 1482 Lord Howard sent his daughter Jane Tymperley four yards of what is specifically stated to be Howard livery cloth of black velvet.[41]

Later in his career, probably when he was raised to the dukedom of Norfolk, John Howard seems to have changed his livery colour. He did not, however, adopt the crimson of his cousins, the former Mowbray dukes. Instead his new livery as Duke of Norfolk was blue – the same colour that he had used during the lifetime of the Mowbrays to difference

their white lion livery badge for the use of his own retainers. Again, the evidence for this change is quite clear from the
Howard accounts. In 1482, as we have seen, Lord Howard had
still been issuing black livery. Indeed, as late as 17 April 1483
a purchase of eleven yards of black cloth is recorded, though
this might possibly have been in connection with the death
of Edward IV.[42] In 1483, however, the cloth purchased 'for my
lordes leverey' was not black but blue.[43]

3

'The High and Mighty Princess'

*… the hy an myty prynses, my lady, the Kenges moder, to wome
I hame steward.*
Sir John Howard

The cause in which Howard used the men who elected him to serve him, and who wore his livery and badges, was sometime his own, and sometime that of his cousin the Duke of Norfolk, but first and foremost, that of the royal house of York. Broadly speaking, adherence to the cause of a dynasty can express itself in two possible ways. First it may be manifested through military or administrative service to the regime which the dynasty represents. Alternatively, it may manifest itself through personal ties of loyalty and service to a leading individual member or members of the ruling family itself. In the case of John Howard's Yorkism, evidence of both kinds of service can be found. We shall begin to explore Howard's military and administrative service to the Yorkist regime in Chapters 5 and 6. Before that, however, in this and the following chapter, we shall consider evidence of the personal ties which linked John Howard to leading individual members of the dynasty.

Even in the days of his obscurity Howard, through his Mowbray cousin, the third Duke of Norfolk, had certainly known, and been known to, Richard of Cambridge, Duke of York (1411–60). Evidence of this fact survives amongst the Paston correspondence.[1] This evidence also shows that as early as about 1450 Howard was viewed by the Duke of York as a trustworthy potential servant, whose loyalty was already engaged. Yet it was after the Duke of York's death and the accession of his eldest son, Edward IV, that one of Howard's most important ties of loyalty and service to the house of York arose. This was the link which bound him to the Duke of York's widow, Cecily Neville, the matriarch of the dynasty, the mother of Edward IV and the 'Queen of right'. Richard, Duke of York and his wife, Cecily Neville, were of more or less the same generation as Howard himself. They were also his distant relatives. In particular, Howard and Cecily were quite close contemporaries. Born at Raby Castle on 3 May 1415, Cecily Neville was the youngest daughter of Ralph Neville, Earl of Westmorland, by his second wife, Joan Beaufort. Joan had been the daughter of John of Gaunt and Catherine de Roët,[2] so Cecily was a great-granddaughter of Edward III. She, the Duke of York and John Howard, therefore, had King Edward I as their common ancestor. In 1424 the nine-year-old Cecily had been betrothed to her father's ward (and her own second cousin) Richard, Duke of York. The young couple had married five years later. Theirs seems to have been a very successful union, and was patently a very fruitful one.

Cecily's precise role within the house of York is in itself an interesting topic for debate, and one to which we shall return later, both at the end of the present chapter and when we come to consider the reign of Richard III. It was a role which doubtless underwent various changes during the twenty-five-year duration of the Yorkist era. Presumably when her husband laid claim to the throne in the autumn of 1460 this did not take Cecily by surprise, and she almost certainly accompanied his triumphal entry into London. Yet while he abandoned, at that point, the heraldic label which until then had differenced his arms from those of the sovereign, curiously Cecily retained this label until 1463.[3] What factors caused her to modify her coat of arms only at that stage, and as a widow, we shall consider presently. But at all events, when her eldest son, the Earl of March, was proclaimed king as Edward IV, Cecily – initially the first

lady of the land since the new king was as yet unmarried –
automatically acquired semi-regal status. She also enjoyed
the publicly-stated trust of the new king.[4] After his victory
at the battle of Towton, in April 1461, one of the first things
that Edward IV did was to write to his mother, giving her the
good news.[5]

To enhance her status, Cecily was granted manors and castles by her son soon after his accession. Amongst these were
the manor and castle of Clare in Suffolk: part of Edward's
patrimony which had descended to him via his paternal
grandmother, Anne Mortimer, Countess of Cambridge. It was
on 1 June 1461 that 'the castle, manor, lordship and honour of
Clare, with the borough of Clare, with appurtenances in the
counties of Suffolk, Essex, Norfolk, Hertford and Cambridge
and other counties, the manors of Erbury and Hundon, co.
Suffolk ... [and] the town of Sudbury, co. Suffolk' were gifted
to Cecily by the king.[6] And although no record survives of
the appointment, it was probably very soon after 1 June 1461
that Cecily named as her steward of the honour of Clare,
her Suffolk neighbour, the then recently knighted Sir John
Howard of Tendring Hall, Stoke-by-Nayland. As a result of
this appointment Howard formally became a member of the
Duchess of York's client network.

Edward IV's relationship with his mother was close during
the early years of his reign (closer than it would be later),
and at this period Cecily seems to have spent a significant
proportion of her time actually dwelling with her son.[7] Since
she also held numerous other properties (including the York
family's London home, Baynard's Castle) she certainly did not
live permanently at Clare Castle. Nevertheless, there can be
no doubt that she did regularly reside there during the 1460s.
Her visits to Clare may have constituted part of an established
cycle of moves from one residence to another through the
course of the year. She was undoubtedly living at Clare Castle
in October 1463, when her son the king visited her there.[8]
She was also in residence in June 1465.[9] In August 1465 John

Howard travelled from Colchester to Lavenham, and had dealings with Cecily's secretary.[10] Given the route Howard was travelling this meeting is quite likely to have taken place in Clare, though that is not explicitly stated in the surviving record. Nor is it necessarily the case that Cecily herself was in residence at the time (though she may have been). Evidence will be presented in Chapter 4 to indicate that Cecily was at Clare Castle during July of either 1467 or 1468. In short, we can be confident that Cecily was living at Clare on various occasions in summer and autumn during the period 1463 to 1468. She is also likely to have been there on other occasions, of which no record has survived. Tangible testimony of her presence at Clare Castle may survive in the form of a small enamelled gold reliquary crucifix set with pearls, found at the castle site in 1866. This jewel belongs to the second half of the fifteenth century and was therefore almost certainly lost during Cecily's tenure of Clare. This fact, together with the quality of the workmanship and Cecily's well-known religious devotion, make her its most likely former owner.[11] The reliquary crucifix contains small, carefully wrapped fragments of wood and stone, which are assumed to be a relic of the True Cross, and of the rock of Calvary. This suggests that Cecily Neville may have cultivated a particular devotion to the Holy Cross – a devotion which John Howard appears to have shared.[12]

In the early years of the reign of Edward IV, Cecily was reported to enjoy considerable influence over him. In April 1461 the Bishop of Elphin said that she could 'rule the king as she pleases'.[13] During this period her close relationship with the king may perhaps have been helpful to Sir John Howard on occasions, as when he found himself embroiled in disputes with the Paston family and the Earl of Oxford. However, the relationship between mother and son apparently changed following the announcement of Edward IV's marriage in 1464. Medieval literature was already familiar with the cliché of conflict between a newly wedded wife and her mother-in-law: a

conflict which, in the case of a king's mother, was exacerbated
by the mother-in-law's implied loss of status:

> If it so is
> Mi Sone him wedde in this manere,
> Than have I lost my joies hiere,
> For myn asat so scahl be lassed.

The poet John Gower caused his Sultan's mother to cry out
in one of his verses. She was bemoaning the fact that since her
son had taken a wife he had thereby demoted her from the
rank of first lady.[14]

Cecily Neville certainly suffered something of an eclipse
following the public announcement of Edward IV's secret
marriage to Elizabeth Woodville. Nothing bears more elo-
quent testimony to this than the records of royal grants to
religious houses in return for prayers for the royal family.
The first such grant recorded from Edward IV's reign is dated
6 September 1461, and was in favour of St Mary's Abbey, Trym,
Meath. It endowed a votive light to burn before the image
of the Blessed Virgin Mary in the abbey church at mass, and
during the singing of the appropriate Marian antiphon for
the liturgical season at the end of vespers.[15] In return for this
endowment, the abbey was to pray for 'the good estate of the
king and Cicely his mother and his heirs, and the souls of his
progenitors'.[16] The wording of this quid pro quo was more or
less a standard formula, maintained with only minor variations
throughout the early years of Edward IV's reign. After 1465,
however, the standard wording was changed, to include reference to Elizabeth Woodville, the king's consort.[17] Elizabeth's
name immediately follows that of the king himself, pushing
the name of Cecily Neville into third place.

Significantly, perhaps, it was at about this time that
Cecily began to stress her own rightful queenship.[18] It has
been noted that she 'responded to her eldest son's marriage
by adopting a new title which stressed her dead husband's

regal claim, thereby attempting to reassert her proximity to queenship now that another woman had a better claim to be identified with the king'.[19] Cecily's role in the disputes relating to Edward IV's marriage, and during the dramatic events of the summer of 1483, together with her relationship with her youngest son, Richard III, are issues to which we shall return in a later chapter, but it is pertinent to remark at this point that all the evidence suggests that Cecily Neville completely supported Richard III's claim to the throne and retained a close relationship with her youngest son during his brief reign.[20]

No record survives telling us why Cecily Neville chose to appoint Sir John Howard her steward of the honour of Clare but, as we have already seen, Howard had known the York family even before Cecily's husband formally claimed the crown as the heir-general of Richard II in October 1460. In addition to the Duke of York's letters, written in favour of Howard's election as knight of the shire for Norfolk in the 1450s, we know that Howard also had established Yorkist links within his own county of Suffolk before Edward IV achieved the crown. Thus we have found him already associated with the future king (then Edward, Earl of March) by the summer of 1460 at the latest.[21] Moreover, from early in 1458 (when she married John de la Pole, second Duke of Suffolk and set up home at Wingfield Castle) Cecily Neville's daughter, Elizabeth of York (1444–1503) was another member of the dynasty who was among John Howard's Suffolk neighbours.[22]

Howard's surviving household accounts specifically refer to his visits to Cecily Neville at Clare, as for example in 1465:'Item, the xj day of June my mastyr spent for costys at Clare, whan he rode to my Lady of Yorke, viij s.'[23] Elsewhere, Howard proudly alluded to his role as steward to this 'high and mighty princess'. In about 1466 Sir John Howard drafted a letter, in which he defended the interests of a widow of Sudbury (tenant of his employer, Cecily Neville) and of her intended husband, his own servant and tenant.[24]

One of the most interesting ways in which John Howard's connection with Cecily Neville impinged upon his links with the house of York as a whole emerges through records of the names of the lawyers whom Howard employed. Some of these men then went on to serve Cecily and other members of the ruling house. Some of them also subsequently received legal appointments of high status at the hands of the Yorkist regime.[25]

A good example of this phenomenon is the career of John Sulyard (later of Wetherden, Suffolk). Sulyard studied at Lincoln's Inn, where in 1454–55 he was admitted as a fellow. He remained closely connected with Lincoln's Inn for much of his career.[26] The outline of Sulyard's career is traceable via the Patent rolls. His name is first found there on 12 November 1459, when he acquired land in Mendlesham. He was not then a knight, or even an esquire. Probably already linked to the Mowbray client network, rather like John Howard, Sulyard received no commissions from Henry VI's government. Following the accession of Edward IV, the picture changed dramatically. He is first mentioned in a commission of 12 February 1462. Subsequently his name often occurs in association with known Mowbray clients. On 11 June 1464 he was a member of a commission headed by John Mowbray, fourth Duke of Norfolk. By the 1470s he is described as 'esquire', and a patent of Edward IV dated 16 February 1479 reveals that he was by then a serjeant-at-law.

There are numerous records of payments to and on behalf of John Sulyard in the Howard accounts.[27] The two men were probably much of an age, and Sulyard's direct service to Howard seems to date from the 1460s, when Howard was rising from relative obscurity and beginning to become a figure on the national stage. Chronologically, the evidence seems to imply that Sulyard was first employed by the Mowbrays, and then began to work directly for John Howard. Consequently he came to the attention of Howard's employer, Cecily Neville, and that of the young Duke of Gloucester, in whom Howard took some interest.[28]

Between December 1464 and April 1465, Howard made frequent payments and gifts to John Sulyard, and his 'man', John Butler.[29] Subsequent references are less frequent, but the fact that Sulyard was paid 4s. on 13 May 1467 'for inrollynge of ij wryttes, one ageyn Sulyard and a noder ayeyn my mastyr' indicates that he continued to be closely associated with John Howard and his interests.[30] By the late 1460s Howard was becoming a presence in Colchester, and it is possible that his influence there lay behind John Sulyard's appointment as Legisperitus for the borough in 1473.[31] Although there are some gaps in the Colchester records, Sulyard's tenure of this office was probably continuous from 1473 until about 1482. Significantly, he was eventually succeeded as legisperitus by another of Howard's lawyers, Thomas Appleton.[32]

From serving John Howard, Sulyard went on to enjoy the favour of the royal family. In February 1474 he was chosen to act on behalf of Richard, Duke of Gloucester, of whose 'learned council' he is plainly stated to have been a member. The case is recorded in draft letters from Cecily Neville, who was involved in it, and who clearly knew Sulyard personally. These hitherto unpublished letters concern a dispute over an estate called 'Gregory's' which, according to Cecily, properly belonged to her servant John Prince.[33] A certain Thomas Wethiale had seized it, and in an attempt to bolster his dubious claim had tried to enlist the support of the Duke of Gloucester. This was probably a mistake on his part, because Gloucester and his mother had then 'comuned togiders' and agreed to refer the dispute to the arbitration of their respective legal representatives: John Catesby and Roger Townshend for the Duchess of York, and Guy Fairfax[34] together with either John Sulyard or Richard Pigot[35] for the Duke of Gloucester. The existence of a draft bond in the sum of £200 from John Catesby and Roger Townshend confirms that the adjudication did take place as planned by Cecily Neville, and that John Sulyard, 'gentleman', together with Guy Fowler [sic], 'serjeant-at-law', did act in the matter for Cecily's son, the Duke of Gloucester.[36]

Sulyard's service to the Duke of Gloucester bore fruit when the latter achieved the crown. In 1483 Richard III appointed Sulyard to a commission headed by John Howard (then newly created Duke of Norfolk). At the same time Richard numbered Sulyard among the notables of Suffolk, in a list which also included John Howard, Duke of Norfolk, and his son Thomas, Earl of Surrey.[37] In the same year Sulyard went on the Home Circuit with Chief Justice Bryan.[38] On 22 October 1484 Richard III appointed Sulyard one of the Justices of the King's Bench.[39]

The draft letters from Cecily Neville concerning the 'Gregory's' dispute also name four other lawyers in addition to John Sulyard. Three of these four men – Guy Fairfax (Ferfox/ Fawefox/Fowler), John Catesby and Roger Townshend – had also worked for John Howard, and we shall review them briefly. Fairfax received payments from Howard in the 1460s, and then went on to become a member of the Duke of Gloucester's council.[40] As in the case of John Sulyard, the associations of Fairfax with Yorkist royalty seem to come later, chronologically, than his service to John Howard, and may have arisen as a result of Howard's recommendation. John Catesby also received payments from Howard in the 1460s. Later we find him as a member of the council of Cecily Neville.[41] However, he continued to have links with John Howard and his client network.[42] His name is also associated with that of the better-known William Catesby, to whom John was perhaps related.[43] Catesby's links with Howard continued into the 1480s, and Lord Howard bought Catesby a drink on 14 March 1481, when both men were in Colchester.[44]

As for Roger Townshend, like John Sulyard, he had trained at Lincoln's Inn, of which he was an active fellow.[45] No record survives of Townshend's direct employment by John Howard, but Howard certainly knew him. On 18 February 1465/6 Sir John Howard delivered three and a half yards of Mowbray livery cloth to Townshend,[46] and on the following day Howard paid Townshend 35s.[47] On 7 October 1466 he gave Townshend

four ells of fine holland cloth worth 20d. an ell, together with a
dagger worth 3s. 4d.48 On 19 November 1467 Howard wrote
a memo to remind himself that he owed Townshend £100 on
behalf of the Duke of Norfolk,[49] 40 marks of which he then
paid him.[50] It seems that Townshend was chiefly in the service
of Howard's young cousin, the last Mowbray Duke of Norfolk.
As we have seen, he was also a member of the 'learned council'
of Cecily Neville.[51] He was later appointed one of the king's
serjeants-at-law by Richard III.[52]

John Howard's amicable connections with Cecily certainly
continued into the 1480s, by which time both parties were in
their sixties. On 14 February 1481/2, for example, 'my Lord
[Howard] gaf my Lady [the Kinges Moder] iij yerdes and di.
white russet, that cost x corounes and di'.[53] Regrettably, no
specific evidence survives to document Cecily's relationship with John Howard during the key period 1483 to 1485.
However, since the dowager Duchess of York seems to have
backed Richard III's claim to the throne,[54] and since Howard
was one of Richard's key supporters at that time, it is legitimate to assume that Howard must have been in close contact
with her during the difficult months of the summer of 1483.
One must therefore deduce that (like those of Richard III
himself) John Howard's links with Cecily Neville remained
significant right to the end of his life. At that period Cecily had
not yet ceased to take an interest in secular matters. Although
she became an oblate of the Benedictine order in 1480, she
'did not retire altogether from the world' at that stage.[55] It was
only after the death of her youngest son, Richard III – and
that of his leading supporter, John Howard – at the battle of
Bosworth in August 1485, that Cecily Neville finally became
reclusive, adopting 'a semi-monastic lifestyle'.[56]

Curiously, her relationship with her own supplanter, Lady
Margaret Beaufort, may offer one small shred of tangible evidence as to Cecily's attitude to Richard III – and therefore by
implication her attitude to John Howard – after Edward IV's
death. Margaret Beaufort was Cecily's first cousin, at a remove

of one generation, and she occupied a position in relation to Henry VII which closely parallels Cecily's role in relation to Edward IV. Both women seem to have been conscious of this similarity, and Cecily's relationship with Margaret was strangely ambiguous. The two matriarchs must have known one another well, but instead of the hostility which one might have expected, in fact a kind of sympathetic understanding seems to have existed between them. Thus, when she died, Cecily bequeathed one of her two prayer books to Margaret, who seems by that time to have overtly adopted Cecily as a role-model for her own religious life.[57]

The prayer book which Cecily left to Margaret has not hitherto been traced. However, there is one prayer book in existence which undoubtedly belonged to Margaret Beaufort, and which is known to have previously belonged to a key member of the house of York. This is the well-known Hours of Richard III.[58] The intriguing possibility thus arises that the prayer book mentioned in Cecily's will was actually the Hours which had belonged to her youngest son. Although there is no direct proof that Richard's Book of Hours passed through the hands of his mother, it is perfectly possible that the Duchess of York had treasured this prayer book after Richard's death, as a memento of a son whom she had held very dear.[59]

4

Father Figure?

*The final end of a Courtier, wher to al his good condicions and
honest quelities tende, is to become an Instructor and Teacher of
his Prince.*
Count Baldassare Castiglione

Howard hath with the Kinge a great fellowship.
Catherine de Moleyns, Lady Howard

Yesterday my lord of Gloucester came to Colchester ...
Sir John Howard

From our consideration of his links with Cecily Neville, it has
emerged that Howard and she were more or less of an age.
Thus one significant factor in Sir John Howard's involvement
with Edward IV, with the Duke of Gloucester (Richard III),
and with his own young cousin, John Mowbray, fourth Duke
of Norfolk, is the age gap which existed between them. This
point is often overlooked, but John Howard was not of the
same generation as these young men. Indeed, all three of them
were quite literally young enough to have been Howard's
sons. Edward IV was born in 1442; the Duke of Norfolk in
1444 and Richard, Duke of Gloucester in 1452. The birth
of Howard's own children by his first wife, Catherine de
Moleyns, covers the same span of years. Howard's eldest child,
his son Thomas, was probably born in 1443, and his youngest child by his first wife, his daughter Jane, was born in the

1450s. We must therefore take on board the fact that to John Mowbray or to Richard, Duke of Gloucester, John Howard would have appeared in the guise not of a friend and companion of the same age, but rather of a father or uncle figure. His relationship with Edward IV is more difficult to categorise, and we shall defer consideration of it until the end of this chapter, merely remarking for the moment that although he too was young enough to have been Howard's son, Edward IV was apparently not intimidated by the older man, and seems to have had the strength of character to stand up to Howard if he felt the occasion demanded.[1]

That Howard may have played something of a paternal or avuncular role can be documented most clearly in the case of John Mowbray; although we can also find some hints that he assumed a similar role in relation to Richard, Duke of Gloucester. In the case of John Mowbray, Howard frequently came to the rescue with financial assistance. One small instance is particularly revealing. On Friday 24 May 1465 Sir John Howard lent 20*s* to his young cousin, 'whan he lay at the stewe'.[2] *Stews* were medieval brothels. Since both Howard and the duke were resident in London at the time, the reference in this instance is almost certainly to the well-known Southwark brothels.

The term 'Middle Ages' covers quite a long period, and medieval attitudes to prostitutes seem to have undergone certain changes as time went by. The better preserved French and Italian source material on this subject suggests that during the twelfth and thirteenth centuries prostitution gradually became accepted, following which, during the fourteenth and fifteenth centuries, it was institutionalised and subject to regulation. Thus we find French and Italian towns authorising brothels in defined locations outside the town, and then prosecuting illicit prostitutes (including married women) who carried on their business within the town walls. The process began with negative enactments 'defining places where prostitutes should *not* work'. Later 'places of prostitution were reduced to one house

... often the property of the municipality ... where houses remained private they were often in the hands of the great *Bourgeois* or nobles'.[3]

Some English towns and cities followed the continental example in delimiting specific areas within which prostitutes might operate. London and Colchester certainly did so, and Ipswich seems to have similar regulations, though it remains unclear to what extent this was the general practice in England.[4] In London the intention was to confine prostitution to Cock Lane and Southwark. In doing this, 'the city authorities were not so much concerned with personal morality as with keeping the peace'.[5] The Southwark brothels (situated on land owned by the Bishop of Winchester) dated back to at least the twelfth century, when they were the subject of ordinances laid down by Henry II.[6]

The Duke of Norfolk (and probably also his young duchess) was staying at the Mowbrays' townhouse at Broken Wharf, on the north bank of the Thames just south of St Paul's Cathedral, at the time when John Howard financed his visit to a brothel. The Southwark brothels were located almost directly opposite the Mowbrays' house, on the south bank of the Thames.[7] Given this fact and the further information that Norfolk was undoubtedly in Southwark two weeks later, on Thursday 6 June, visiting Sir William Brandon, a Mowbray client,[8] it is reasonable to conclude that his brothel expedition was to Southwark. Probably the duke stayed at the brothel until the following morning, since 'rowing across the river to and from these houses after sunset was discouraged by the London authorities, and it was generally felt that a professional woman should keep her visitor all night'.[9]

The fact that the Duke of Norfolk was frequenting the Southwark prostitutes was, in itself, not remarkable. In the fifteenth century 'the pleasure of sex was ... taken as so self-evident as to require no particular comment. Sexual activity in the form of prostitution was thought to be an evil thing, but at the same time necessary to keep sinful men driven by lust from corrupting respectable women, including their own wives, or from turning to homosexuality'.[10] Then, as at most other periods of history, sexual morality discriminated strictly between genders. Girls were expected to remain chaste, while young (and not so young) men were free to sow wild oats if the fancy took them.

The interesting features of the transaction between Sir John Howard and the duke on 24 May are, first, the fact that Sir John clearly condoned and financed his young cousin's extramarital sexual activity, and second, that Howard was apparently with his cousin on this occasion. This suggests that Howard was also in Southwark, and perhaps was therefore frequenting the stews himself, as well as underwriting Norfolk's visit. At this period Sir John Howard was about forty-five years old, and still married to his first wife, Catherine de Moleyns, although she was already suffering from the unknown illness – possibly tuberculosis or 'consumption' – which would lead to her death later the same year.[11] John Mowbray was aged about twenty years and six months.[12] He had been married to Elizabeth Talbot since both of them were children,[13] but the marriage, though apparently happy, was first and foremost a dynastic alliance and would not have precluded the duke from finding other sexual outlets. In John Howard's own case, however, our only other possible hint that he may have engaged in extramarital relationships comes in the equivocal form of an obscure reference to 'þe prest, Howardys sone' in April 1453.[14] It is possible – but by no means certain – that the Howard in question was John V, and that the anonymous priest was his illegitimate son.

Howard does also seem to have condoned sexual activity outside marriage on the part of his own sons. A list of Sir John's household, drawn up on 22 January 1466/7,[15] mentions 'Richard, mast[er] Thomas' child'. Master Thomas was Sir John's eldest son and heir, the future second Howard Duke of Norfolk and victor of the battle of Flodden. As we have seen, Thomas was probably born in about 1443.[16] In 1472 he would marry his first wife, Elizabeth Tilney,[17] but in January

1466/7 he was as yet a bachelor, so if this use of the word 'child' imputes paternity, Richard must have been Thomas Howard's illegitimate son.[18]

Since Sir John Howard was also taking an avuncular interest in the young Duke of Gloucester at this period, we can well imagine that in his case too, youthful sexual activity may have been condoned. There is no specific evidence surviving on this point, but certainly Gloucester fathered at least two illegitimate children: John of Gloucester and Lady Catherine Plantagenet. The date of birth of neither child is recorded, but John was under the age of twenty-one in March 1485, and was therefore not born before 1465. Catherine married the Earl of Pembroke in 1484. Although child marriages were not uncommon amongst the fifteenth-century aristocracy, Catherine would only really have become an attractive marriage proposition for an earl when her father mounted the throne, so it is probably safe to guess that she may have been fourteen or fifteen years old at the time of her wedding. Both children were therefore probably engendered in the late 1460s.[19] This was a period when Howard had begun to cultivate the Duke of Gloucester's acquaintance.[20] Howard's certain involvement in the Duke of Norfolk's extramarital sexual activity, and his possible knowledge of the Duke of Gloucester's early sexual experiments, raises the intriguing and possibly important further question of whether he also had any special involvement in Edward IV's amorous affairs. We shall explore this point in a later chapter.

Howard may have had some involvement with the Duke of Gloucester earlier in the 1460s, since the duke held the office of Admiral of England, and Howard was his deputy in respect of the North Sea. However, the first surviving firm evidence of Howard's interest in, and relationship with, the young Duke of Gloucester comes in the form of a draft of a letter preserved among Howard's household documents and referring to Gloucester's visit to Colchester. This visit has hitherto been largely ignored, and its precise timing has previously been entirely conjectural, since the letter bears no year date.[21]

Nevertheless, careful study by the present writer has suggested
that the visit can only have taken place either in the summer
of 1467 or the summer of 1468.[22]

The text of the Howard letter, in which the punctuation has
been modernised, is as follows:

> My ryte espesyal good lord (after al dew rekomendasyon)[23]
> plese 3owe to wete
> 3esterday my lord a Glowseter kame to Kolchester, and as
> I was in kome-nykasyon wethe is lordesche[p] of dyvers
> materes, amonge hoder I dede[24] remember 3ower lord-
> eschepe to my lord, prometenge 3owe I fowend my lord
> as wel desposed toward 3owe as any lord may be to anoder;
> safe my lord spekethe it largely,[25] wereof I was[26] ryte glad to
> here it.
>   Ferther mor, my lord hathe desyred me to be wethe
> heme at Sodebery, Lanom and Seynte Hemondesbery, and
> ferther 3effe I myte; bote I dorste promese heme no ferther,
> fore I was nor hame nat in serten howe hastely 3e wold have
> me: werefore I pray 3owe sende me worde be wate day 3e
> wol have me ther, and I schal nat breke itc, be the grase of
> God, ho have my ryte good lord in is blesed safegard.
> Wreten on Mary Mawdelen day [22 July].[27]

Since it is preserved among the Howard papers, Sir John
Howard was logically either the sender of the letter, or its
recipient. Neither individual is actually named in the text;
although the recipient is addressed as 'lord', and this was a title
which Howard did not hold in the 1460s.[28] Moreover, the
letter as it survives is manifestly a draft rather than a finished
version. It would be extraordinary to find the draft of a letter
to Howard among his household papers. One must therefore
conclude that the letter was sent by Howard, and the original editor of the Howard accounts has proposed plausibly that
its intended recipient was Howard's cousin, John Mowbray,
fourth Duke of Norfolk.[29]

Both the summer of 1467 and that of 1468 witnessed significant royal events in London at which Sir John Howard and Richard Duke of Gloucester could have met. In 1467 Howard stood in for the Duke of Norfolk (who was first indisposed himself, and subsequently in mourning for his mother-in-law) at the great tournament between Lord Scales and the Bastard of Burgundy at Smithfield. The young Duke of Gloucester must surely have been at the tournament, and this was very probably the first occasion on which Howard really encountered the adolescent prince, then aged fifteen. The following summer saw the start of Margaret of York's wedding journey to Flanders. Howard is known to have crossed the Channel with Margaret, while her brothers accompanied the early stages of her journey from London towards the Kent coast, so on this occasion, too, Howard and Gloucester are almost certain to have met. In either year, therefore, Howard could plausibly have issued the invitation which brought Gloucester to Colchester.

By 1467 Howard was a trusted servant of Richard's brother, the king, and a long-standing employee of Richard's mother, Cecily Neville. Doubtless he was well known to all the members of the royal family, at least by reputation. Howard was also well used to dealing with young men. He had sons of his own, and had personally overseen their development through adolescence into early adulthood;[30] and we have already seen that he played a significant role in the life of his young cousin, Norfolk. It is, of course, impossible at this late date to recapture the underlying motivation of either Howard or Gloucester, but there is every reason to suppose that Richard would have found the older man a congenial companion. Probably he got on well with Howard from the outset. As for Howard, it is entirely possible that he genuinely liked the young royal duke. At the same time, however, he can hardly have missed the potential advantages which would stem from cultivating this young man's friendship, particularly given his own naval involvement and the duke's tenure of the office of admiral.

In July 1467 or 1468 Richard of Gloucester set off along the route of the present A12. It was perhaps the first time he had enjoyed the freedom of choosing his destination for himself. His journey would have taken him via Chelmsford, and a vague and ill-documented report survives of a brief visit to Chelmsford by Richard, which may relate to this journey. 'There is a tradition that Richard III caused his hunting party much concern. Thinking him lost in the forest, they searched high and low, to discover him eventually passing his time pleasantly ... in the Black Boy.'[31] Although the only source I have found for this story refers to 'Richard III' (as though the Chelmsford visit had taken place in the 1480s), in fact the Richard of the Chelmsford story seems to have been a rather young and thoughtless individual, suggesting that if the tale has any basis it may well relate to an earlier period. Moreover, Richard never visited Chelmsford as king, so the story could only relate to the period before his accession.

On 21 July the prince reached Colchester where he spent at least one night, almost certainly at St John's Abbey. He was met by Sir John Howard, who hastened to pass on the news of the prince's arrival to his cousin the Duke of Norfolk. Together with Howard, Richard then rode on to Sudbury, probably calling on his mother at Clare Castle. A week later Howard and Richard were in Bury St Edmunds, where they doubtless paid their respects at the shrine of St Edmund. Richard's visit to Essex and Suffolk also included a hunting holiday, based in Lavenham. This was no doubt organised for him by Howard, taking advantage of the hunting park of his cousin, the 13th Earl of Oxford. Howard himself had enjoyed hunting there with John de Vere on previous occasions. It may also be worth noting in passing the unusual purchase of quantities of green fabric by Sir John Howard in the summer of 1467, both for himself and for distribution to others in the manner of a livery.[32] This fabric, of a colour not otherwise associated with Howard himself, may have been to provide Richard of Gloucester with attendants suitably arrayed during his visit.[33]

Given John Howard's apparently close connection with Richard, Duke of Gloucester, one is entitled to wonder also about Howard's relationship with Richard's elder brother, George, Duke of Clarence. Clarence was only a few years older than Richard and one might have expected that Howard would have cultivated similar relationships with both the young royal dukes. In fact, there is no evidence that this was the case. The Duke of Clarence certainly knew (and was possibly quite friendly with) Howard's young cousin, the last Mowbray Duke of Norfolk.[34] He also undoubtedly knew John Howard, but the two seem not to have been especially close. While the surviving Howard accounts mention Gloucester a total of seventeen times, there are a mere four mentions of the Duke of Clarence. Nor can this be due solely to the fact that Clarence's interests lay partly in other geographical areas, since the surviving correspondence of the Paston family (based, like John Howard, in the eastern counties) contains fifteen references to Clarence and eleven references to Gloucester.[35] For some reason Howard clearly had far less to do with Clarence than with his younger brother. Perhaps it was the fact that Clarence was sometimes at odds with his own family which made John Howard somewhat wary of associating too closely with him.[36] All we really know is that on 1 January 1464/5 Clarence sent Howard a New Year's Day gift, but that towards the end of that year Howard, who had owned a gown in the livery colours of the Duke of Clarence, gave it away.[37]

As for Howard's relationship with Edward IV, more will be said on this in the following and later chapters. For the moment we shall simply make two points. First, the fact that Howard was older than Edward was by no means atypical amongst the coterie of Edward's advisers; Lord Hastings, the Earl of Warwick and Lord Stanley were all older than the king.[38] Second, Howard and Edward seem generally to have been close, although there may possibly be occasional hints of stress in the very early years. In October 1461 the first Lady Howard (Catherine de Moleyns) is said to have boasted

that her husband 'hath with the Kinge a great fellowship'.[39]
However, Howard's high-handed attempt to seize the manor
of Winch from the 12th Earl of Oxford, and the brawling of
his servants with John Paston I, in the course of which an
attempt was made to stab Paston, may have led Edward to
conclude that Sir John Howard needed to be put in his place.[40]
By November 1461 Howard was reportedly under arrest, and
in the following spring the Pastons were spreading rumours
that he was about to lose his head.[41] The precise details of what
followed are not recorded, but clearly Howard weathered this
temporary setback. Indeed, following the Earl of Oxford's
execution in February 1462, he made an attempt to seize the
manor of Lavenham, together with one other unnamed manor
previously held by his dead cousin.[42] Nevertheless, from 1462
Howard seems to have consistently enjoyed the royal favour.

5

'Trusty and Well-Beloved'

Trusty and right welbeloved, we grete yow well
Letter from Edward IV[1]

We have now noted a number of features of John Howard's
'Yorkism' in relation to, and during the reign of, the first
Yorkist monarch. We have documented Howard's early association with Edward in Suffolk, prior to the king's accession.
We have reviewed evidence of Howard's public stance as a
Yorkist, as witnessed by his various uses of livery and badges.
We have explored his close links with the king's mother, both
in his capacity as steward of the honour of Clare, and through
links with high status lawyers, and we have noted his apparent
interest in cultivating the friendship of Edward IV's youngest
brother, Richard.

We shall now begin to review the record of Howard's service
to, and recognition by, the first king of the house of York. The
relevant material can conveniently be summarised under five
headings. First, there is the record of Howard's role as a local
representative of the Yorkist regime in the eastern counties and
elsewhere. This includes his appointment to royal commissions,
and his activity in connection with elections. Next we shall
consider the rewards which Howard received from Edward IV
in various forms. Third, we shall review evidence of Howard's
foreign and diplomatic missions. A fourth category of evidence comprises Howard's military service from 1461 to 1483.
Of course, a further highly relevant and significant category

of evidence is that which relates to Howard's involvement with Edward IV and his affairs on a more private and personal level. That topic, however, will be reserved for consideration in Chapter 10.

Howard as a Local Representative of Edward IV's Government

On 10 April 1461 the new King Edward IV issued a commission to John Howard, Gilbert Debenham and others to seize various rebels and their goods.[2] If this was the first indication that the new monarch trusted Howard and intended to employ him in his own region of influence (and indeed, beyond it), it was certainly not to be the last. On 12 May 1462 Howard was commissioned to make further arrests,[3] and he subsequently served on numerous commissions of the peace and of array, relating to the counties of Suffolk, Norfolk and Berkshire during the period 1462–67.[4]

On 8 June 1468 Howard was serving on a commission of enquiry in Norfolk,[5] and on 22 May 1469 he was appointed to a general commission of oyer and terminer in the northern counties.[6] Early in 1470 he served on a commission of array.[7] A few weeks later Edward IV granted a general pardon to 'John Howard, knight, Lord Howard', lately one of the king's commissioners in Calais. The pardon presumably related to the completion of Howard's tour of service in Calais. Pardons were often granted when officials ended a particular tour of duty, to safeguard them from subsequent litigation. This reference is particularly interesting, however, since among other things, it proves that by March 1470 Edward IV had raised John Howard to the peerage.[8]

Shortly after this the Lancastrian Readeption intervened. Yet by 15 September 1471 Lord Howard was back in Calais with Lord Hastings.[9] On 1 April 1473 a further pardon was granted to Lord Howard, curiously described on this occasion as 'late of Stoke by Nelond Suffolk'.[10] He served on various further commissions of the peace for Berkshire, Essex, Norfolk and Suffolk during 1467–76.[11] One commission of enquiry, addressed to him on 13 March 1476, related to alleged piracy off the Suffolk coast, at 'Kyrklod'.[12] Another commission of 1476, for the county of Essex, linked Howard's name with that of Richard, Duke of Gloucester and others.[13] Howard continued to be appointed to commissions periodically to the end of Edward IV's reign.[14] His record in this respect (while quite impressive, and in marked contrast to the lack of such service that he had experienced under the government of Henry VI) is more or less what might be expected for a person of his local prominence and dynastic loyalty.

Meanwhile, in addition to his service as a representative of the national government, Howard was also exerting his own influence in the region around his eastern counties home base. One way in which he did so was in connection with the election of parliamentary representatives. Parliamentary representatives (called 'knights of the shire', though often they were esquires by rank, rather than knights) were elected at two levels. First, there were the representatives of the various counties, and second, the representatives of the boroughs. Thus, within Howard's immediate area of influence representatives were elected by the counties of Essex and Suffolk, and also by the boroughs of Colchester and Ipswich.

In the choice of representatives as knights of the shire for the counties it was normal for local magnates to exert influence. Thus we have already seen that in the 1450s John Mowbray, third Duke of Norfolk, had sponsored the candidature of John Howard himself for election as one of the knights of the shire for Norfolk. Although this had occasioned local protests, because Howard held no land in the county of Norfolk at that time, letters had been written by both the Duke and the Duchess of Norfolk promoting Howard's candidature, and the Duke of York had also been enlisted to support him.[15] The outcome had been that John

Howard had indeed been elected one of the knights of the shire for Norfolk in 1455.

An examination of the lists of candidates elected during the Yorkist period as knights of the shire for the counties of Essex and Suffolk shows that a similar state of affairs pertained in those areas. In fact, a study of known MPs returned for Suffolk and Essex, during roughly the third quarter of the fifteenth century, establishes clearly that it was probably the norm for patronage to be exerted by magnates in respect of the election of the knights of the shire.

In Essex, to which the influence of the Mowbrays did not really extend, and where the de Vere family was in an eclipse throughout the greater part of the Yorkist period, we find the powerful and influential Essex-based Yorkist Sir Thomas Montgomery of Faulkbourne, returned as MP for Essex in 1463, 1467, 1478, June 1483 and 1484. Various members of the important Tyrell family, which held lands in both Essex and Suffolk, were also returned for Essex,[16] while another member of the same family was returned for Suffolk in 1449.[17]

Other Suffolk MPs at this period included Sir Gilbert Debenham (1442, 1449, 1453, 1483, 1484), John Tymperley of Hintlesham (1445), Sir Thomas Brewes (1445, 1467), Thomas Danyell (1447), Sir John Howard himself (1449, 1463, 1467), William Jenney, J.P. (1455, 1470) and Sir William Brandon (1472, 1483).[18] Thus Howard himself served as the Suffolk parliamentary representative on three occasions, while at other times the men elected had well-known links both to Howard and to his Mowbray cousins. In the choice of Suffolk representatives the influence of Howard and his patrons certainly seems to have made itself felt.

The selection of Ipswich representatives seems to have followed a somewhat similar pattern. Ipswich, situated between the Duke of Norfolk's power base at Framlingham Castle and his cousin Howard's power base at Stoke-by-Nayland, regularly chose MPs who were closely linked to the Mowbray and Howard client networks. The list of known Ipswich MPs for the Yorkist period is reproduced in Appendix 2. It is apparent that by no means all the Ipswich MPs were actually residents of the town. The non-resident Tymperleys were very closely linked to John Howard and the Mowbrays – though at least one of them was a freeman of Ipswich.[19] Similarly, Fellow, Wymondham, Hobart (who served three times), Sampson and Wentworth were all Mowbray and Howard servants.

Intriguingly, the pattern of men elected to represent the borough of Colchester during this time presents quite a different picture.[20] There is no evidence of the influence of any magnate; the men returned as Colchester MPs were consistently local residents. They were also frequently experienced in local government, and almost all were former or future bailiffs. Generally they returned to the post of bailiff after (or between) terms of serving as MP for Colchester. This is in marked contrast both with the knights of the shire elected for the counties of Essex and Suffolk, and with those returned by the borough of Ipswich. One possible explanation may be that Colchester, located between rival magnates – the Mowbrays at Framlingham and the de Veres at Hedingham Castle – was able to escape the influence of both and exercise some freedom of choice. At the start of the Yorkist period, at least, John Howard's personal influence in Colchester was probably slight.

Nevertheless, there is one known way in which Howard exerted his influence in Colchester. The important Benedictine Abbey of St John's was a mitred abbey with impressive rights of chartered sanctuary, identical to those enjoyed by Westminster Abbey.[21] Also the Abbot of Colchester had a seat in Parliament. When the long abbacy of Abbot Ardeley ended with his death in 1464, he was succeeded by John Canon (1464–68), who was a Howard protégé.[22] In theory the choir monks of the abbey had freedom to elect their father abbot, but evidently in this instance John Howard had exerted some influence in the matter, since he himself recorded that he had secured Canon's election as abbot.

When Abbot Canon died after only four years of office it seems probable that Howard would also have sought to influence the choice of his successor. No direct evidence survives of Howard's involvement in the election of 1468, which brought to power Walter Stansted (1468–97).[23] However, Abbot Stansted gave Lord Howard sanctuary at his abbey during the Lancastrian Readeption, and the abbot seems not to have attended the Lancastrian Parliament of 1470–71. If he was known as a Howard nominee, the Earl of Warwick may have wished to avoid summoning him.[24] It does seem likely that Stansted shared Howard's political loyalties.

After the battle of Bosworth, the abbot received Yorkist fugitives at the abbey, most notably Francis, Lord Lovell.[25] The abbey may subsequently have been implicated in the Yorkist risings which focused on 'Lambert Simnel' and 'Perkin Warbeck'. Later, it received indirect bequests from Cecily Neville, dowager Duchess of York.[26] Interestingly, when Abbot Stansted died no election was permitted. Instead, the new abbot was directly appointed by the Bishop of London. This procedure was unusual, and may represent an attempt on the part of King Henry VII (through the bishop) to bring the abbey to heel. Another innovation at that time was the fact that Henry VII had subsequently to be paid in order to secure restoration of the abbey's temporalities![27]

Howard's Rewards at the Hands of Edward IV

Throughout his reign Edward IV augmented John Howard's tenure of manors, either by direct gift, or indirectly (for example, by granting him an office which he was then allowed to exchange for land). Howard also received honours at the hands of the king, and grants of income in various forms. This pattern commenced very soon after the new king's accession. Thus Howard was one of the men knighted by Edward IV at his coronation on 21 June 1461.[28] Three further appointments quickly followed his knighthood. On 6 July 1461 Sir John was granted custody of Colchester Castle (together with appropriate revenues).[29] Two weeks later, on 21 July 1461, he was appointed constable of Norwich Castle,[30] and a week after that, on 28 July, he was given the post of king's carver.[31] Later in the 1460s he also received various grants of manors from the crown. The manors were located in the counties of Dorset, Essex, Norfolk, Suffolk and Wiltshire. He was also given two houses in London.[32]

According to the correspondence of the Pastons (not always his greatest friends) Howard was not content with the lands he had been given, and was also intent at this period on augmenting his holdings by seizing property of his attainted cousin the Earl of Oxford.[33] This confronts us with the perennial historical problem of how to evaluate the evidence. Contemporary writers sometimes made mistakes. They also sometimes deliberately distort the picture they present for their own ends. While it is not possible to conclude that the Paston correspondence misrepresents John Howard and his actions, the picture it offers of Howard at this time, and of his relationship with the government of Edward IV, does seem to contrast markedly with the impression which we derive from official records of the same period such as the Patent rolls.

On 5 February 1467 Howard was granted custody of additional manors during the minority of Edmund Gorges.[34] Edmund Gorges and his brother John were the sons of Walter Gorges of Wraxall, Somerset. Both were being educated in the Howard household when their father died and they then became John Howard's wards. Eventually Edmund also became Howard's son-in-law by marrying his second daughter, Anne. In fact it is probable that by 1467 this marriage had already taken place.

By 1468 Howard was Edward IV's Treasurer of the Household, and towards the end of that year he was granted emoluments which included the profits from the mint and a share (together with Richard Neville, Earl of Warwick) of the profits of mines.[35] As we have already noted, before the end of Edward IV's first reign Howard was granted a barony.[36]

Following Edward IV's return from his brief exile in the Low Countries, Howard profited from the discomfiture of his de Vere relations, being granted former de Vere manors in the counties of Cambridgeshire, Essex and Suffolk, together with the stewardship of the Earl of Oxford's seat at Hedingham Castle.[37] In 1472 he was installed as a Knight of the Garter.[38] Subsequently Howard also benefited slightly from the attainder and execution of the king's brother, George, Duke of Clarence, but only to the extent of a single manor.[39] In 1479 the Patent rolls record the grant to Lord Howard of the reversion of office of constable of the Tower of London. In the event, however, he did not live long enough to profit from this.[40]

Although Edward IV's grants to John Howard may have seemed generous at the time, they pale into insignificance when compared with the grants which came Howard's way during the much shorter reign of Richard III. To emphasise this point we shall go on to summarise briefly Richard's munificence. In 1483 he granted Howard forty-six former de Vere manors. This was followed by the gift of twenty-one manors confiscated from the attainted Earl Rivers, while a further twenty-two manors of divers provenance were granted in 1485. Richard also gave Howard the lordship of Hungerford, and the castle and lordship of Farleigh (both formerly held by the Earl of Oxford), a house in London (once owned by the Duke of Somerset), the profits from the fisheries of Wignall, the hundred of Free Bridge, and the tolls of Bishop's (now King's) Lynn, together with grants from fee farms in Warwickshire, Essex and Suffolk. He also created him Duke of Norfolk, and gave him the offices of Earl Marshal and Admiral of England. In addition he created Howard Steward of England (to officiate as such at Richard's coronation). Howard also received grants of wardships and marriages from Richard III,[41] not to mention powers of supervision and array in no fewer than thirteen counties.

Thus, while there is no reason to doubt that Edward IV trusted John Howard and wished to advance his status, it is clear beyond any possible question that Richard III reposed enormous trust in him and promoted him very markedly.

Howard's Diplomatic Missions for Edward IV

While foreign contacts are mentioned in the surviving Howard accounts, not all of them were diplomatic, and not all of them involved John Howard in person. Thus Howard's involvement in Scotland (then a foreign country) in 1481 was as a participant in Edward IV's Scottish campaign. It was therefore military rather than diplomatic in nature. His involvement in the French campaign of 1475 was also initially military, but later became diplomatic.[42] Howard's involvement in Edward IV's rather desperate (and ultimately ill-fated) negotiations to prevent a rapprochement between Louis XI of France and the Archduke Maximilian of Austria in 1482, is a further example of his employment in diplomacy.[43]

We have already noted that Howard was serving the king in Calais both early in 1470 and in 1471. He was also in Calais on a number of other occasions, but his earliest trips were almost certainly commercial ventures rather than diplomatic missions. Records survive of a voyage by 'my mastyrys balynger ... to Caleyys ward' during the late summer (12 August–5 September) of 1463. This represents Howard's earliest known connection with Calais, though from the surviving evidence it is not certain that he made the trip in person on that occasion.[44] In much the same way, Howard's only recorded sending of one of his ships to Spain seems to have been a commercial enterprise, and Howard himself seems not to have made that voyage himself.[45] In 1466, on the other hand, it is specifically recorded that 'my master was at Calais from the 15 day of May to the 17 day of September'.[46] Several records remain of this prolonged visit of four months duration, during which numerous purchases were made requiring the use of Flemish currency.[47]

The following summer was the time of the Smithfield Tournament between Lord Scales (Anthony Woodville) and the unfortunately named 'Great Bastard of Burgundy'. The tournament began on Thursday 11 June 1467 and, in the absence of the young Duke of Norfolk (who had himself been unwell, and whose mother-in-law, the dowager Lady Shrewsbury, was on her death bed), Howard officiated at this tournament as deputy Earl Marshal. On about Wednesday 17 June, news reached London of the death of the 'Bastard's' father, the Duke of Burgundy. Shortly thereafter Howard left London for Dover, accompanying the Burgundian delegation. On either Saturday 20 or Sunday 21 June he embarked with the Bastard of Burgundy for Calais, and a week later, on Saturday 27 June, Howard re-embarked at Calais to begin the return journey to England.[48] He arrived back in England on about Sunday 28 June. This trip to Calais, undertaken as the escort of a high-ranking foreign visitor, clearly counts as 'official business' rather than the pursuit of Howard's own commercial interests.

In 1468 the king's sister, Margaret of York, married Charles the Bold, the new Duke of Burgundy. On 18 June Margaret's wedding party left London for Flanders.[49] Large numbers of the nobility and gentry had been commanded by the king to attend her, and we know for certain that John Howard, a prominent supporter of the dynasty and the holder of a senior naval appointment, was a member of the princess's official entourage. His name stands in fifth place amongst the male English wedding guests listed by Olivier de la Marche.[50] The festivities in the Low Countries lasted nearly a month, and it was not until about 13 July that the English wedding guests began to leave Bruges, homeward-bound.[51] They arrived back in Kent on about 15 July.

There are traces of other visits to Calais at about this period. On 19 July of a year not recorded in the accounts, Howard purchased a bow in Calais.[52] This date does not seem to quite fit with either the visit of 1467 or that of 1468. Also, between 10–13 December of an unspecified year in the later 1460s Howard was again in Calais, and wrote some letters home from there.[53] The purpose of these visits is unknown.

Howard's Military Service

The surviving Howard accounts give their fullest details of his military service towards the end of his life (by which time he was a very important figure). However, in the early years of the reign of Edward IV, Sir John Howard saw military service in England on Edward's behalf. Thus, for example, at the end of 1462 Howard was serving with the Duke of Norfolk at Newcastle.[54]

At the same time, as we saw in the last chapter, Howard was involved in various violent activities which were no part of the king's service. In May 1461 his men set upon Thomas Denys (a servant of the Earl of Oxford). This seems to have been part of the ongoing conflict between Howard and Oxford over possession of the ancestral Howard manor of Winch in Norfolk.[55] It was followed in August by a violent attack by Howard's men on John Paston which included an attempted stabbing,[56] all of which left Howard in trouble with the king. He was reportedly arrested and early the following year the Pastons were spreading rumours of his impending execution. In the event, though, these rumours came to nothing.[57]

On 4 March 1470 Edward IV appointed the newly ennobled Howard 'governor of the armed power prepared by the king for the custody of the sea'.[58] Although Howard took sanctuary during Edward's exile later in 1470, the fact that the following April (1471) he proclaimed Edward IV King of Engand in Suffolk suggests that at that point, if not earlier, he may have taken up arms on Edward's behalf, or at least was prepared to do so.[59] Subsequently Howard accompanied Edward IV on his expedition to France (1475).

Quite detailed records of Howard's military service agreements survive from 1480/1.[60] These relate to the Scottish campaign. Following the death of Charles the Bold, Duke of Burgundy, leaving no direct male heir, his dukedom reverted to the French crown.[61] During Burgundy's re-absorption, Louis XI was anxious to avoid English interference.[62] He therefore encouraged James III of Scotland to break his truce with England. James raided the English border counties in the spring of 1480 and Edward IV appointed his brother, the Duke of Gloucester, as his lieutenant-general in the north. Lord Howard indented with Edward IV to serve the king for sixteen weeks with 3,000 men who were to receive 15d per man per week as wages, and an allowance of 12½d for food. Lord Howard then entered into a series of agreements with others in order to provide the required total of 3,000 men.[63] Records survive of his indentures with Lord Cobham, Sir Harry Wentworth, Clyfford, Alfred Corneborough, Edward Brampton, John Waynflete and John Williams. Together these produced a total of 2,300 men. However, some leaves are missing from the Howard accounts, which would presumably have accounted for the remaining 700.

Later, Howard performed important military services for Richard III. The first was his part in suppressing 'Buckingham's Rebellion'. One record of this survives in the form of his letter summoning John Paston III to his array in October 1483.[64] There are also brief references in Howard's accounts to movements in Kent during that autumn.[65] Two years later he fought at the king's side at the battle of Bosworth, in which engagement Howard lost his life. In this case, once again, his letter to John Paston survives, sent on about 12 August 1485, summoning Paston to his array at Bury St Edmunds. Although no specific records survive of the names of the men from the eastern counties who served with the Duke of Norfolk at Bosworth, it is possible tentatively to reconstruct such lists, at least in part.[66]

Records of payments survive, made to men who served Howard on a regular basis in a mainly military capacity. An interesting example which we shall examine in some detail is a set of payments made at Colchester's port of the New Hythe. These payments were as follows:

Wady 5ˢ
James Baker, Harbronde, John Steward the Barber, Klegge, Borges, Frosdam, Becham and Erdiswyk 3s 4d each
Christopher Cresford, John Mersch and Edward Johnson 6s 8d each

At the same time 8d was paid to Mortimer for bringing a present, and 4d was paid to Nicholas Bloke. These last two items look like payments for specific tasks performed, rather than regular wages, and we shall ignore them here.[67]
Although all these payments were made at the Hythe, most of the recipients were not Hythe residents. Only John Steward the Barber, who is not named elsewhere in the surviving Howard accounts, is known to have lived at the Hythe. However, the majority of the other men were regular Howard servants.[68] They are an interesting group of men from the north Essex or south Suffolk region, most of whom comprised part of Howard's military forces. John Wady was a yeoman in Howard's service. Wages were paid to him from at least 1465.[69] In January 1467 he received livery.[70] Sometimes he served Howard at sea.[71] The fact that he was supplied with bows shows that his service was military.[72] Presumably he was therefore an archer rather than a sailor. In 1471 he is named in John Howard's own handwriting in a list of retainers, who are thought to have served with Howard at the battles of Barnet and Tewkesbury, and he is also listed amongst the men-at-arms who put to sea with Lord Howard in 1481 during the Scottish campaign.[73] At this time he was equipped with 'a peir brygandines, a standart, a salate ... a pair splentes, a cheff of arowes and his jaket'.[74] Although Wady was sometimes paid in London and elsewhere, there are also indications that he was frequently in the Colchester area.[75] He was probably a native

of north Essex or south Suffolk. Still listed amongst the men of this region who were serving Howard in 1483–84,[76] Wady probably accompanied the new Duke of Norfolk to the battle of Bosworth in 1485.

Like Wady, John Klegge (Clegg) served John Howard for at least fifteen years. His name first appears in the accounts as one of the men-at-arms serving Howard in 1471, so it is likely that he too fought at Barnet and Tewkesbury.[77] Later he served in the Scottish Campaign,[78] and since he was still providing military service in 1483/4,[79] he too probably fought at Bosworth. There are numerous records of payments of wages to him,[80] and he was supplied with military equipment.[81] He also undertook errands to Colchester, and from Stoke to London.[82]

Several other men in the Hythe list had similar career patterns to those of Wady and Clegg. James Baker, Becham (Beauchamp) and Erdiswyk served with Howard in the Scottish campaign, regularly received wages, and were supplied with clothing and basic military equipment.[83] All three men, like Wady, were still serving Howard as men-at-arms in 1484,[84] and may have accompanied him to Bosworth. Erdiswyk was clearly an archer. Edmund Harbronde was another archer,[85] who also served at sea, and who regularly received wages, clothing and equipment.[86] In addition to the Hythe, Harbronde is recorded in Howard's accounts at Stoke, at Nayland, at Chelmsford and Brentwood, at London, and at Windsor.[87] He also accompanied Howard on his triumphal tour as Duke of Norfolk in 1483, and may well have fought at Bosworth.[88]

Edward Johnson was with Howard during the Scottish campaign,[89] and was regularly in receipt of wages.[90] On one occasion his wages were paid by the steward at Stoke-by-Nayland.[91] He carried out varied missions for Howard: errands to the parker at Greenstead (near Colchester) and to Lord Cobham; buying gear for Lord Cobham's man; and an errand from Stoke to London (12 September 1483).[92] About the time of Richard III's coronation, Howard reimbursed Johnson for money laid out at Ludgate, and he had made similar payments on Howard's behalf on other occasions.[93] He received military equipment very similar to that of John Wady,[94] and was still serving Howard in a military capacity in 1483/4, so he too probably fought at Bosworth.[95]

John(?) Burgess appears to have come from Harwich.[96] He received regular wages and perhaps livery, and appears to have served Howard in a military capacity. However, he also acted as Howard's messenger on occasions. He also seems to have supplied naval materials.[97] Christopher Cresford, who possibly had connections with Dovercourt,[98] enjoyed a similarly mixed career.[99] Nor are Burgess and Cresford the only men in Howard's service to have known origins in the Harwich area.

On 6 May in the seventeenth year of the reign of Edward IV (1477) Richard Lullay, his wife Alice and others were involved in the transfer of a tenement in Harwich abutting Middle Street [High Street] and West Street.[100] Three years later, in the spring of 1480, Richard Lullay of Harwich was serving Lord Howard aboad the *Mary Howard*.[101] Nevertheless, he is not listed among the *maryners*, and he is named as a trumpeter in Lord Howard's service during the Scottish campaign of 1481.[102] On 10 March 1481 he accompanied Lord Howard and Giles St Clare abroad to buy *pypes*.[103] Several records survive of payments of his wages, and it is not impossible that Richard Lullay's trumpet sounded for Howard at the battle of Bosworth.

The connections of Burgess, Cresford and Lullay with Harwich and Dovercourt lead us to consider next John Howard's links with the Harwich area, and most particularly his important role in building up Edward IV's navy.

6

The First English Carvel

... and the Kenge howethe me xxx li. for mony leyd dowen for the
kervel of Donwesche ...
Sir John Howard, 1464

The importance of naval power to England was already recognised in the fifteenth century. Henry V possessed a fleet of
thirty ships by 1417, and in 1454 Edward IV's father, the Duke
of York, had argued in Parliament the importance of proper
naval provision. Richard Neville, Earl of Warwick, was also
well aware of the potential power inherent in the possession
of a fleet of ships.[1] But in naval affairs, as arguably in other
matters, the change of ruling dynasty in England in 1485 seems
to have led to a certain amount of editing of history in favour
of the newcomers. As a result, the foundations of the English
navy are usually ascribed to the Tudors, and the shipbuilding
activity of Edward IV tends to be overlooked or undervalued.
Thus Colin Richmond, while referring to John Howard's role
as admiral, largely ignores Edward IV's contribution to the
creation of the navy. Likewise Mackie, while conceding that
'Edward IV had laid the foundations of a new fleet', fails to
note that Edward's ships included such innovations as multiple
masts and sails, and carvel construction.[2]

John Howard's naval role represents a very important aspect
of his career, and of his service to the house of York. Records
of his agreements to man ships for the king survive.[3] However,
Howard's involvement went far beyond the mere manning

of ships. It comprised also the commissioning and outfit-
ting of vessels for Edward IV. His activity in this field is an
important example of Howard's sponsorship of new technology.[4] Records survive of the construction and commissioning
of the royal carvel, Edward, built at Dunwich and fitted out
at Harwich in the 1460s.[5] A less complete record relates to
Howard's own ship, Barbara, outfitted at Harwich and Ipswich
in the 1480s.

In the ports and shipbuilders he patronised, and in the
type of vessels he commissioned, Howard was innovative.
He promoted Harwich as a naval dockyard,[6] and although
naval historians have previously been unanimous in dating
the English advent of carvel-built ships with multiple masts
and sails to the reign of Henry VIII, incontrovertible evidence
from Howard's surviving accounts proves that he was already
constructing carvels for Edward IV in the 1460s. Hitherto
this fact seems to have passed entirely unnoticed. Thus, in a
recent appraisal, Milne, while acknowledging that the latest
archaeological research in England has 'produced a fascinating
outline picture of medieval boat and shipbuilding which is at
odds with what had traditionally been assumed', continues to
assert that 'before 1500 ... all vessels were built in the clinker
style'.[7] Marsden likewise declares that Edward IV's ships were
clinker-built and seems utterly unaware of the evidence to the
contrary contained in John Howard's accounts.[8]

Howard may have favoured Harwich because he had family
links with the town and with neighbouring Dovercourt
through his de Vere and Mowbray cousins. Dovercourt (the
name of which seems to be a corruption of 'de Vere court') was
the older of the two adjacent settlements, and housed the original parish church.[9] This contained the shrine of the Holy Rood
of Dovercourt, which the Howard family is known to have
patronised (see Chapter 15). The town of Harwich had been a
planned development, and the street pattern of old Harwich can
still be seen to conform to a kind of grid network. Figure 17

shows the plan of the town in the fifteenth century. Towards the end of the fourteenth century Richard II had granted murage to build walls and a castle, and following that Henry IV (1399–1413) granted permission for tolls to be levied for the castle's maintenance.[10] In 1466 John Howard built (or possibly rebuilt) a tower in Harwich.[11] This was perhaps the tall bastion at the south-eastern corner of the town walls, which may have served as a lighthouse. The town's castle stood at the north-eastern corner of the town, close to where the naval dockyards were subsequently developed.

From the castle, the wall ran south-south-east, following the line of the present Kings Quay Street. 'It is possible that some large septaria blocks in cellars along that street may be remnants of the town wall.'[12] In addition one complete slice of the town wall survives above ground level, albeit generally unnoticed, a little further to the south, between the southern side of the churchyard and the alleyway which enters the Hanover public house from the rear (east). This section, which clearly owes its preservation to the fact that a later brick wall was constructed on top of it, shows the medieval town wall of Harwich to have been between 4.5 and 5 metres in width at ground level, and built of rough blocks of a yellowish septaria set in mortar.

At the eastern end of St Austin's Lane the town wall was interrupted by St Austin's Gate, which was clearly a substantial structure since (prior to the building of the seventeenth-century Guildhall) the borough authorities held their meetings there. The entire block between St Austin's Lane and Market Street, adjacent to the town wall, was occupied by the townhouse of John Howard's cousin, the Duke of Norfolk. Substantial cellars of this large building survived until the eighteenth century. At the eastern end of Market Street the wall was again broken, by the East Watergate. This gave access to the quays of the eastern harbour, which medieval documents call 'the Port of Orwell'. In the fifteenth century the water reached practically to the eastern town walls at high tide.

The substantial strip of land which now separates Kings Quay Street from the water is due to later silting and reclamation.

'Outside the wall on the east was the common quay, between the castle and the watergate, whilst the medieval ship-yards (which remained in use until the eighteenth century) lay between the watergate and the church postern.'[13] These were the shipyards which John Howard used, in the 1460s, to outfit the new royal carvel Edward, which was probably destined to be Edward IV's flagship. The silting of the foreshore means that in twenty-first-century Harwich Howard's shipyards now lie buried beneath modern Kings Quay Street and Wellington Road.[14] This land has been built over and is therefore not currently available for archaeological investigation. Nonetheless, excavation of a medieval shipyard at Poole in Dorset suggests that the late medieval Harwich shipyards were probably very simple in appearance. At Poole 'there were no major installations found, no dry docks or slipways – just sixty timbers arranged in groups, laid out over an area that had once been the open foreshore'.[15]

Earlier medieval sailing ships had carried one mast with a single square sail.[16] They had oar ports, and were clinker-built, that is constructed with the planks overlapping, as in weather-boarding. By the thirteenth century such ships had fore-and-aft fighting castles, for use in battle. The earlier examples had steering oars, but later stern-mounted rudders were introduced.[17] Some of the trading vessels owned by John Howard may have been simple, clinker-built, one-masted ships of this type. By the fifteenth century, however, the lateen sail, a triangular fore-and-aft sail which allowed a ship to manoeuvre under sail against the wind, had been borrowed by European mariners from Arab sailors. Initially this was set on the *artemon*, a spar in the front part of the vessel which later gave rise to both the foremast and the bowsprit. In Europe a lateen sail was also set on the mizenmast, when that evolved. The lateen sail spread first in the Mediterranean, but it had reached English

waters by the first half of the fifteenth century, when Henry
V's *Grace Dieu* already possessed two masts, a 'great mast' and
a 'mesan'.[18]

From two masts it was only a short step to three.[19] There
were three-masted ships in northern European waters by the
mid-fifteenth century, and one is illustrated on a seal of 1466.[20]
The *Edward* undoubtedly had three masts: a 'ffuk' or foremast
(the word seems to be Dutch in origin), a mainmast, and a
'musyn' (mizzen, or aftermast). We know this because in 'the
sext yer of Kynge Edward the iiijth and the xvij day of marche,
mastyr brout of Clayse of Herewyche a mast for the musyn
and ij seyle yerdys for the ffuk and the said musyn'.[21] By the
1490s, if not before, a spritsail and a set of topsails were the
norm,[22] and it also seems certain that the Edward carried at
least one topsail, presumably over her mainsail, for an account
of 10 July 1465 records:

Item, paid for the maste of the said shippe,	vli.
Item, my master paid for the yerde	...
Item, my mastyr paid for the toppe	... [23]

Carvel-built ships, constructed with the planks butting one
against another, had much stronger hulls than clinker-built
vessels, and they were therefore better able to bear the weight
of cannons. Thus, naval historians – incorrectly associating the
advent of ships' guns with the sixteenth century – have wrongly
assumed the English introduction of carvel shipbuilding to date
to the first half of the sixteenth century.[24] Fifteenth-century
warships already carried small cannon on the after castle and,
by about 1460, also on the forecastle.[25] John Howard's accounts
prove beyond any question that carvel shipbuilding was practised in England by the 1460s. In addition to the royal carvel
Edward, other carvels are mentioned in Howard's surviving
accounts.[26] John Howard may not personally have been responsible for the introduction to England of carvel shipbuilding and
the use of multiple masts and sails, but there can be no possible

doubt that he promoted and encouraged these developments.[27] Thus, the Yorkist navy that he built up for Edward IV foreshadowed the better-known Tudor navy of the following century. It is regrettable that Howard's very significant contribution to the development of the English navy has hitherto passed totally unrecognised by naval historians.

7

Innovations

Hym thought he rood al of the newe jet.
Chaucer, Canterbury Tales, Prologue: The Pardoner

In addition to his sponsorship of new technology in the field of shipbuilding, there are other features of John Howard's activities which suggest that he was a man interested in exploring new processes and products, and who wished to be as up to date as possible. Curiously there is also some evidence which suggests that this aspiration was not a feature peculiar to Howard as an individual, but one to be found more widely disseminated amongst the servants of the house of York. We shall now briefly explore some examples of Howard's apparent interest in innovation insofar as the building and furnishing of his houses was concerned.

Like carvel shipbuilding, there is a tendency for English domestic brickbuilding to be attributed to the Tudor period – and this attribution is likewise incorrect. The Romans had built in brick in the eastern counties of what would later be England, and there was some building in large white bricks in that region in the thirteenth century. However, the trend for building in small red bricks which grew up in the fifteenth century was a fashion imported from mainland Europe, and probably in the first instance the bricks themselves also had to be imported. Many so-called 'Tudor' red brick buildings in the eastern counties actually date from the Yorkist period, or even a little before. The Duke of York's own house at Hunsdon

(Herts), and the Montgomerys' seat at Faulkbourne (near Witham, Essex) are examples.

By the second half of the fifteenth century red bricks were certainly being produced in north Essex and south Suffolk. John Howard's accounts show that there were brickmakers not far from Colchester, at Great Horkesley. 'One of the kilns may have been at Kiln House, at the western end of Brick Kiln Lane, where sixteenth-century kiln debris has been found.'[1] Bricks were ordered for John Howard from John Perrekyn of Mile End (near Colchester) in April 1481, and there were also payments to John Smith, brickman of Ipswich.[2] On 7 September 1482 Lady Howard paid the 'brykman' 20s.[3]

The use of brick in domestic architecture became well-established in England during the mid to late fifteenth century, notably in the eastern counties. One curious feature of this trend is the suggestion that it was promoted particularly amongst a close-knit group of friends and political allies of Richard, Duke of York.[4] John Howard was, of course, one such. His exploitation of this new building material may therefore have both proclaimed, and been influenced by, his Yorkist connections.

Howard was also up to date in his furnishings. The large mirror which was delivered to him in Colchester in 1482 was probably something of an innovation.[5] It was perhaps a convex glass, similar to that depicted on the rear wall in Van Eyke's *Arnolfini Marriage* portrait. In 1524, when John's son Thomas, the second Howard Duke of Norfolk, died, an inventory of his furnishings at Framlingham Castle was taken. It records that on one wall of the dining chamber hung a large mirror. This may have been that very same 'gret glasse' acquired by Lord Howard in Colchester in December 1482.[6]

Both the Framlingham Castle inventory and the Howard accounts make frequent mention of tapestry (usually as wall hangings, but occasionally as furnishing fabrics – for the covering of cushions and so on). Much rarer is the mention of carpets. During the fifteenth century carpets were status symbols. They might be used on floors on special occasions such as weddings. Small rugs were sometimes placed in bedrooms at the side or foot of the bed.[7] They were also used on tables and cupboards as covers. The display of a carpet on a table before a person, or even more so, on the floor at his feet, reflected that person's dignity and authority. Such honour 'was not to be lightly assumed by those not entitled to it'.[8] Carpets were luxury items. Thus at Framlingham Castle the inventory of 1524 makes it clear that the floor carpets were certainly not left lying about on the ground permanently, but were stored in the wardrobe or the vestry, being set out only as and when the occasion demanded.[9]

Carpets are reputed to have been first brought to England by Edward I's bride, the infanta Eleanor of Castile. Those first carpets were undoubtedly imported, and there is very little surviving evidence of carpet manufacture in England in the Middle Ages. In the 1460s Sir John Howard's floors were probably most often covered not with carpets but with rushes, like those purchased on 25 April 1465.[10] Even in the 1480s, when Howard was a much grander person, supplies of rushes were still being bought.[11]

Nevertheless, John Howard did purchase carpets.[12] No indication of their origin is given in his accounts, but of the five floor carpets recorded as being at Framlingham Castle in 1524, two were specifically described as being from England (the remaining three being presumably imported).[13] This is significant. Not one single medieval English carpet survives, and there has been very little study of carpet manufacture in England at this period, so it is not known exactly where this industry was practised. In other countries, however, its chief prerequisite was an abundance of wool. Since this feature was widely present in the eastern counties, it is possible that the two English carpets at Framlingham Castle were manufactured locally, and that John Howard and his family encouraged the growth of English carpet manufacture.

Howard also appears to have encouraged the development of pewter-making in the eastern counties. On 28 November

1465 he acquired 'a garnish of counterfeit vessels' from Beche of Colchester.[14] John Beche was a member of an established Colchester family which seems to have shared Howard's Yorkist sympathies. John Beche's forebears had been loyal to Richard II, and had been involved in an early plot to dethrone the Lancastrian usurper, Henry IV.[15] Unfortunately, the Beche family's predilection for the first name 'John' makes it rather difficult to distinguish one family member from another,[16] but the John Beche who figures in the Colchester Court Roll in 1466–67 is probably identical with Howard's supplier of pewter (though he is described in the court rolls not as a pewterer, but as a card maker).[17] In fact it is unclear from the Howard accounts whether Beche was himself a pewterer or merely a merchant retailing pewter items. This point is quite significant and requires further exploration.

Earlier evidence of pewter manufacture in Colchester, and of the Beche family's involvement in its production, emerges from records of the Lawhundred held in Colchester on the Monday after the Feast of St Michael the Archangel in the sixth year of the reign of Edward IV (6 October 1466). On this occasion William Beche was fined for selling substandard pewterware.[18] While the court roll does not explicitly state that William Beche had himself made the illicit artefacts, the presumption seems strongly in favour of his having done so. This evidence that the Beche family was probably manufacturing pewterware in Colchester as early as 1465–66 is significant, since it antedates by nine years the earliest previously published evidence of pewter manufacture in the town.[19]

One of Lord Howard's proudest and most notable possessions was his clock. In March 1482 he paid 2s 4d 'to the clokke maker of Kolchester for emendyng the clokke'.[20] The clockmaker is unnamed, but he had received 4d. for similar services a year earlier, when his name was recorded as Wegayn.[21] He can thus be identified as Austyn Wogayn, listed as a 'foreigner' amongst the Colchester inhabitants who did fealty to the restored Edward IV in 1472.[22] In a later era Colchester was to become famous as a centre of clock manufacture, but this early reference is remarkable. The possession of a private timepiece at this period indicates both status and a degree of technological awareness. Lord Howard's timepiece, which evidently required regular maintenance, was probably a wall-mounted, weight-driven clock with a single hand to indicate the hour.[23] Such clocks were generally made of iron.[24]

It is extremely unlikely that John Howard introduced clockmaking to Colchester. Clocks were very useful in monastic houses for calling the inhabitants to prayer, and it was perhaps the presence in Colchester of St John's Abbey, 'a rich and powerful foundation', that was 'responsible for the first Colchester clockmaker'.[25] In 1357–58 John Orlogeer had been admitted a burgess of Colchester, and later, in 1368–69 William Orlogeer was likewise admitted.[26] Since *horloger* is the French for clockmaker, it seems likely that John and William were engaged in this profession.[27] Also the churchwarden's accounts for Saffron Walden record that during the year 1460–61 a 'man of Colchester' repaired the church clock at a cost of 3*s* 4*d*,[28] and although he is not named, he was probably that same clockmaker of Colchester – Austyn Wogayn – who repaired Lord Howard's clock in 1482.[29]

The early evidence for clockmaking in Colchester is tantalisingly incomplete, but one probably fifteenth-century clock from the region survives,[30] and another (now lost) existed until the nineteenth century.[31] The evidence, such as it is, does not therefore appear to suggest that it was John Howard's patronage that brought this craft to the town. It seems much more likely that clockmaking came to Colchester under other auspices (possibly those of the abbey), and somewhat before Howard's lifetime. Nevertheless, the evidence certainly indicates the presence of at least one active clockmaker in Colchester in about the third quarter of the fifteenth century. John Howard (doubtless wishing to keep up with the latest technology) simply availed himself of his services.

8

The Howard Lifestyle

X lyvere gelte boses – xxvj s. viij d.
Item, Blake velavetes upon velavete, x ˙erdes - the ˙erde, xiiij s. vj d.
Sir John Howard: unpublished account for Howard livery

During the 1460s, in addition to modernising and extending
Tendring Hall, John Howard acquired additional residences.
These included townhouses in Colchester, Harwich, Ipswich,
Thetford, Hadleigh and Stepney. These townhouses seem to
have been substantial though not palatial. Howard's Ipswich
property stood on the waterfront (most likely in the parish
of St Mary-at-the-Quay) and had its own landing stage.[1] The
location of the Colchester house, though nowhere explicitly
stated, can also be deduced. Before becoming an inn in the sixteenth century, the present Red Lion Hotel, on the south side
of Colchester's High Street, was the private residence of the
Howard family. Its name, originally 'the White Lion', derives
from their arms and livery badge. 'The building's oldest features are the fourteenth century doorway and some masonry
in the vaulted cellars. ... [It] is mainly fifteenth century with
extensive exposed timbers.'[2] In the early sixteenth century this
building was certainly in the possession of Thomas Howard,
future third Duke of Norfolk (1473–1554), who is named as
its owner in a deed.[3] There is every reason to suppose that it
had earlier belonged to Thomas's grandfather, John Howard.[4]
The expansion of Howard's property holdings reflected his
increasing wealth and importance at this time. They also made

Howard and his family visible and significant members of the local population. A wide variety of goods for the consumption of the household was purchased locally.

Hosiery, gowns and doublets were purchased particularly from Colchester. On one occasion Howard bought a new hat there.[5] We should also note the work of two clothes manufacturers, Cache and Wadselle, both of whom seem to have been based in Colchester. Cache's name is encountered in a variety of spellings in the Howard accounts (including Kache and Schasche), and it seems that these were attempts to spell the foreign name which figures in contemporary Colchester records as Oliver van Cach.[6] Cache supplied hosiery, made gowns and repaired garments for the household over a period of some twenty years.[7] Wadselle's association with the Howard household seems to be confined to the 1460s, but he made a number of gowns, repaired doublets, supplied cloth, made a pair of sleeves for Lady Howard, and even helped her out with the hanging of some tapestries.[8] His Howard association seems to have been closer than that of Cache, for in 1467 he is listed as a member of the household, and included in that year's distribution of the black Howard livery.[9]

There are scant records in the surviving accounts of the provision of armour for Howard and his men. Howard's own plate armour probably came from London, or even further afield. Certainly in the summer of 1483, when he had attained the dukedom of Norfolk, he was dealing with 'the armerer of Flaunderes'.[10] However, what records survive for the 1460s suggest that at this period Howard patronised local manufacturers in the eastern counties when buying defensive attire for his men. This generally consisted of reinforced leather jacks or brigandines. On 7 October 1463 there was a payment of 4*d.* to John Brown, 'armerer', or 'bregander makere'.[11] John Brown worked in Colchester.[12] The payment is small, and the substitution of 'bregander makere' for the more prestigious-sounding 'armerer' in the duplicate copy of this entry implies that Brown's skills were perhaps somewhat basic. On

5 October 1463, more substantial payments are recorded (for twelve days' work in 'fforbeshynge') to Robyn, armourer of Ipswich, together with his 'fellow' and his 'man'.[13] The previous month 'a peyre of breganderys' had been obtained from Clayson of Harwich. He, however, was not even a 'bregander makere', but merely a general retailer.[14]

One curious feature of the consumption of the Howard household was the fact that, during the 1460s at least, the household obtained its footwear exclusively from Colchester and from the London area.[15] Moreover, in Colchester the purchase of footwear involved the Howard household with one single practitioner: James the Cordwainer of Colchester.[16] In the vicinity of London, John Howard patronised Peter Hanse, a Southwark cordwainer, and two London cordwainers: Albryte and Curteys.

While the Howards' Colchester shoemaker was clearly not the only cordwainer in the town, he apparently enjoyed the exclusive patronage of the Howard family. On several occasions Howard must have been particularly pleased with James's work, for not only did the family continue to employ him but he also received small tips.[17] His footwear ranged in price from 4d for a pair of shoes for Isabelle Howard,[18] to 2s 4d paid by Sir John for what was obviously a rather special pair of boots for himself.[19]

James not only made boots and shoes for the Howards, but also galoshes (overshoes, raised on wooden platforms) and pattens (sandal-like open shoes, raised on composite leather soles, and worn directly over the hose),[20] and he also repaired footwear for them.[21] While it is not surprising that a cordwainer should have manufactured the composite leather-soled pattens, his production of the platform overshoes, which were largely made of wood rather than leather, is perhaps rather more surprising.[22] The Howard accounts show that the average cost of galoshes was 6d, and that pattens cost about 3d a pair. Neither seems to have been supplied in any great quantity. John Howard's exclusive patronage of a single Colchester cordwainer is interesting, and in this case the relationship between employer and employee appears to have been close.

The Howard household accounts also provide evidence of the ways in which Howard enjoyed himself. Payments to various musicians are often recorded. Some were professionals, directly employed by Howard himself, or by other aristocratic families. Others, such as bellringers, and the waits, were more in the nature of amateur volunteers.[23] John Howard took an interest in music that apparently went beyond merely listening and being entertained. On 28 October 1482 'my Lord made covenaunte with William Wastell, of London, harper, that he shall have the sone of John Colet of of [sic] Colchester, harper, for a yere, to teche hym to harpe and to synge, for the whiche techynge my Lord shall geve him xiij s. iiij d. and a gown; wherof my Lord toke hym in ernest vj s. viij d.'[24] Lord Howard also employed at least one other harpist on a regular basis, for there are several references in his accounts to Thomas 'the herperd', for example at Christmas 1482, when he was paid 20*d*. At the same time Lord Howard gave 'to the trompetz for a rewarde vj s. viij d.'. Thus by this period at least, he evidently had his own trumpeters.[25] He also had his own drummers ('tabaretes').[26] In addition, by the 1480s Lord Howard was maintaining his own private chapel choir of boys, resources for whom included the purchase of 'a messe [mass] of prykkyd song and an anthume for my Lordes chapell' on 2 September 1482.[27]

The not infrequent references in the household accounts to the entertainment of the Howard family by 'players' are intriguing, since 'players' in English can mean both musicians and actors.[28] Only a year or two after Howard's death, Henry VII was maintaining a company of four actors who were called *lusores regis* ('the King's Players'), and secular drama certainly existed at this period, though little has survived.[29] It is therefore quite likely that the Howards were in the habit of seeing plays performed.

Only the wealthy and educated possessed a library in the fifteenth century, but Howard was rich and unquestionably literate (his account books preserve numerous examples of his handwriting). The first Lady Howard owned books,[30] as did Sir John Howard himself.[31] It is also clear that he commissioned illuminated manuscripts on occasions. On 28 July 1467 he settled an account with Thomas Lympnour[32] of Bury St Edmunds.[33] This seems to have been for a Book of Hours intended, perhaps, as a wedding gift for his second wife.

There is evidence in the Howard papers that at least one member of the household had an interest in poetry. At the end of folio 142v, a fifteenth-century hand has written the following (possibly suggestive) verse:

A lake for low mey leyfe ys lorne, yn betture balys here mone I be, fore one of the breyteyst that ever was borne, with yowtyne speyre hat wondyd me, but but store I stoythe whane I mey love nat.[34]

Which, modernised, might run:

Alack! For lo, my life is lost.[35]
In bitter woe here must I be.
For one of the brightest that ever was born
Without a spear[36] has wounded me.
But yet I stand firm[37]
Though I may not love.

Little information is supplied in the Howard accounts relating to the playing of games. They mention, however, that on 3 September 1463 John Howard reimbursed 4s 1d to Sir William Warner of Ipswich 'for money leyd owht be hym for pleyyng at the tennys'.[38] It seems possible that this particular match was played in Ipswich, but there was undoubtedly a tennis court in Colchester at this period, for in 1481 Robert Veer and Richard Knolles were fined 6d each for playing tennis during divine service.[39] Veer was perhaps a relative of the earls of Oxford, while Knolles was regularly employed by the Howards in the 1480s, constructing the new chimneys at the Colchester house.[40]

We also find evidence for the playing of chess, dice and cards. John Howard's accounts record a payment of 20*d.* 'for peyntenge of ij chesse bordes' by Thomas Lympnour of Bury St Edmunds.[41] There is evidence that gambling with dice took place at the Cock Inn in Chelmsford – a hostelry frequented by members of Howard's retinue on the journey between Colchester and London – and that this activity was encouraged by the landlord, Robert Snell.[42] The young John Mowbray, fourth Duke of Norfolk, also seems occasionally to have gambled at cards at Sir John Howard's expense. The latter recorded in his own hand two payments of half an angel each to his cousin for this purpose in November 1463.[43]

Howard was also a devotee of hunting, his usual quarry being deer. On Wednesday 21 August 1465 he rode to Lanam (Lavenham, Suffolk) where he stayed for a week with his cousin, the Earl of Oxford, and the two men hunted. Howard was in Langam (and still hunting) on 28 August.[44] He went hunting again in September 1467,[45] evidently with some success, since he subsequently arranged to have venison sent to his second wife at Stoke-by-Nayland.[46]

During August and September 1481 Lord Howard hunted at various parks in north Essex. Parks were areas enclosed by fences or earthen banks, where deer were kept. Wivenhoe Park is mentioned,[47] as well as Elmstead Park, Greenstead Park, and also Bentley, Wix, Oakley and 'Bewre' – which the editor of the Household Books construes as Bury St Edmunds, but which is perhaps more likely to be Bures.[48] In October 1481 Howard was still hunting, this time around Woolpit and Hadleigh.[49] As Duke of Norfolk, Howard was created master forester of Desenyng (*sic*) and Hengrave by Richard III, following the execution of the Duke of Buckingham, who had previously held these posts.[50] He received similar appointments in the county of Norfolk.[51]

There is a record of Howard's purchase of a dog from Darcy on 25 July 1467.[52] On 1 September 1467 Sir John made a note in the accounts in his own handwriting, giving details of three other dogs and where two of them were kept. The note mentions a six-month-old animal called 'Kowentes', handed over to Keschen, the keeper of Lexden Park (presumably either for it to be trained, or as an aid to the keeper in combating trespassers). There is also the promise of a young hound from William Cocksal, and reference to a 'fair whelp' given to Howard by Swansey, which was being trained by the park keeper at the Hennenge, Bishop's Hatfield (Herts).[53] No indication survives of the breed of these dogs. On 11 July 1482 Lord Howard paid 16d 'to a schild of Colchester for iiij cheynes to tey dogges', and two months later, on 9 September (being then in London), he paid 20d for 'lyemes for his howndes'.[54] In August to September 1481, while Howard was hunting in the area, his dogs were fed at Manningtree, and in October, at Bildeston.[55] The intended purpose of the hunting saddle which Howard bought in London, from John Smith the saddler on 31 March 1465, is unmistakable.[56]

There was outlay also in respect of hawking, a costly sport of Middle Eastern origin, reserved for the elite by the expense involved. In December 1467, while staying in London (or more probably, at his house in Stepney), Sir John Howard purchased various paraphernalia for hawking, comprising a hawk's bag, two hawk's bells, 57 and 'a tabere [sic, tabard? = hood?] for the hawk'.[58] On 19 December 1482 20d was paid 'to Tymperleys man for brynging of a hawke'.[59] On 16 February 1483 there was a payment of 12d 'to Seyncleres man for hawkynge'.[60] Birds of prey used for this purpose were of various kinds, ranging from the large peregrine falcon, used by men, to the little merlin, a lady's hawk.[61] Hawks were highly prized,[62] and their prey was very varied, including larger birds: mallard, partridge, woodcock, heron; and small song-birds such as blackbirds, starling and larks. Hares were also hunted in this way.

Further recreational use of animals is reflected in the fact that Sir John Howard kept a stud of horses.[63] Horse riding was for pleasure, for transport, and for display. In this last connection in June 1467 Howard purchased crimson damask and black velvet, together with buckram and gold (the last being possibly in the form of gold braid), all for the manufacture of a 'traper'.[64] By the time of the 1524 inventory the stables at Framlingham Castle contained thirty-three horses, with three more stabled at Earl Soham Lodge, a few miles away.[65]

The Howard accounts also record payments in respect of bears. An angel was paid to Lord Stanley's bear-ward in November 1463.[66] Bears were extinct in England by the fifteenth century, so bears for entertainment had to be imported from mainland Europe. This was costly, and only the elite were able to provide bears, whether for baiting or as dancers.[67] Colchester's Bere Lane (modern Vineyard Street) was one site for such activities. There Colchester's Bear Hall and Bear Garden were to be found.[68]

In general John Howard seems to have been a very healthy and active man. His pursuit of hunting and his military activities would both have demanded a strong and healthy body. Only twice do we find hints of ill health. In 1464 his household accounts contain a recipe for medicine to alleviate sore eyes (though there is nothing specifically to indicate that Howard himself was in need of this remedy).[69] Much later, in 1481, Howard apparently received treatment for what may have been an anal fistula. The accounts record: 'item, *casis fistula*', listing payments for one ounce of senna and three ounces of polypody, together with the purchase of violet flowers and an unidentified herb called 'cetmal'. Senna, polypody and violet flowers all have laxative properties and were used to treat bowel disorders. The purchase of these herbs is linked with payments to a physician and his assistant.[70]

When it was not restricted by religious considerations (as most notably during Lent), the Howards' diet comprised a wide variety of foodstuffs. Damsons could be had in Colchester. Likewise sugar, sugar candy, spices (including pepper, cinnamon and saffron), almonds, nuts, raisins, figs, vinegar, mussels, oysters and shrimps could all be purchased there,[71] though spices and figs were also sometimes brought

in from London (see below).[72] Porpoise could be obtained
in the Colchester area. It was possibly sometimes bought at
St Osyth.[73] However, in 1482 Howard paid 12*d*.'to Carters son
of Colchester for bryngyng of a qrtr porpays'.[74] John Carter
was a Colchester fishmonger.[75]

Many luxury goods were obtained from Sandys, the grocer
in Cheap, who supplied Lord Howard with pepper, sugar,
almonds, raisins, currants, cloves, mace, green ginger, lemons,
'soket',[76] 'dragie',[77] rice, cinnamon (whole and powdered),
'sander powder',[78] confets[79] and apparently also gunpowder![80]
Red and white vinegar was supplied by John Swete.[81] Wine
sometimes arrived via London. On 2 September 1482, for
example, young Lalford brought a tun of wine to Colchester by
boat, from Lord Howard's cellar in London.[82] Howard himself
seems to have drunk wine for preference, though his second
wife apparently had a taste for beer. Before going to St John's
Abbey on 27 December 1482, Lord and Lady Howard were at
'Noles',[83] where Lord Howard had a 'potell of wine' while his
lady had a pint![84]

We should also note that John Howard was interested in
education. There were schools at this period at Long Melford
(1484),[85] Ipswich (1412, 1477, endowed 1483),[86] Hadleigh
(1382),[87] and Colchester.[88] In addition, a school existed at
Stokeby-by-Nayland in the 1460s, 'possibly in the household
of Sir John Howard but apparently open to others'.[89] Although
it seems probable that the school at Stoke-by-Nayland came to
a natural end in about 1465 as Howard's sons grew up, Howard
continued some expenditure on education. His probable illegitimate grandson, Richard,[90] doubtless received some sort of
education, and during the 1480s Howard was paying for two
'children' (one of whom was called Richard) to be educated
at Cambridge.[91]

9

My Lord Chamberlain

… and wel I was at London I gafe to my Lord Chamberleyn a dowbel selver desche to pote in hote water, to the valow of xij li.
Lord Howard

In the next two chapters we turn to the complex question – previously postponed – of John Howard's knowledge of and involvement in Edward IV's private life. We begin by considering the character and career of Lord Hastings, Edward IV's chamberlain, who provides one link between the topic of Howard's service to the Yorkist regime (examined earlier) and the more intimate areas which we now propose to explore. Several times already in our story we have encountered William, Lord Hastings, Edward IV's Lord Chamberlain, and at times John Howard's immediate superior. It may be helpful at this stage to discover a little more about him.

As in the case of John Howard, William Hastings' most splendid ancestry was maternal, for his mother was Alice Camoys, daughter of Elizabeth Mortimer and granddaughter of Philippa of Clarence. Thus Hastings was a descendant of Lionel, Duke of Clarence, and had a 'Yorkist' claim to the throne of his own – albeit a somewhat remote one.

Hastings' second marriage reinforced his family connection to the house of York, for his second wife was Lady Catherine Neville, sister of Warwick 'the Kingmaker', and thus a first cousin of both Edward IV and Richard III.[1] This close family relationship may be one of the reasons why later, after executing

Hastings, Richard III did not attaint his possessions, but allowed Lady Hastings and her children the rights they would have enjoyed if Hastings had simply died from natural causes.

Hastings was about eight years younger than John Howard, but he was knighted a little earlier than Howard (on the field after the battle of Mortimer's Cross) and thereafter his rise in the new Yorkist England was rapid, 'By July 1461 his closeness to the king had been recognized by his appointment as chamberlain of the royal household.'[2] During the 1460s he undertook military and diplomatic tasks for Edward IV, sometimes working with his brother-in-law, Warwick.

'Hastings has usually been portrayed as a bluff military man, loyal to Edward through thick and thin, in wartime his trusted general, in peacetime hunting, carousing and wenching at his side.'[3] Mancini (who of course knew neither of them) tells us specifically that Hastings was 'the accomplice and partner of his [Edward IV's] privy pleasure'.[4] We shall return to this alleged aspect of their relationship in the next chapter, when we explore the problematic secrets of Edward IV's bedchamber.

For the moment, suffice it to observe that as chamberlain, Hastings was a natural channel for requests to the king.[5] As such he may well have been the route by which Elizabeth Woodville first approached Edward, seeking restitution of her confiscated manors. Unquestionably Hastings knew Elizabeth Woodville prior to her secret 'marriage' with Edward IV, for on 13 April 1464 – eighteen days before the clandestine ceremony – he agreed a contract of marriage between one of Elizabeth's sons by her first husband, and one of his own daughters or nieces.[6]

Annette Carson also believes that Hastings may have had knowledge of Edward IV's earlier marriage to Eleanor Talbot.[7] Eleanor's family connections were significantly more influential in Yorkist England than those of Elizabeth Woodville, so Eleanor probably had her own means of access to the king, through her powerful relatives.[8] She would therefore have had no need to approach him via Lord Hastings. Nevertheless, it is an intriguing fact that a number of links can be substantiated between Hastings and Eleanor's family circle. We have already noted that Lady Hastings was the Earl of Warwick's sister (Warwick's wife being Eleanor's aunt). In addition, William Catesby – who is best known as the 'Cat' of the famous doggerel rhyme against Richard III – was a well-established employee of Lord Hastings long before he entered the service of Richard, Duke of Gloucester.[9] William Catesby also had a family connection with Lady Eleanor Talbot, and his father (whose second wife was one of Eleanor's cousins) had been one of her principal men of affairs, conducting business on Eleanor's behalf.[10] Moreover, in 1481 Hastings married his daughter, Anne (then aged about ten), into Eleanor's family. Her husband was Eleanor's great-nephew, George Talbot, 4th Earl of Shrewsbury.

For the moment, however, let us leave the question of Edward IV's partners to one side. Let us concentrate instead on the links between Howard and Hastings. It emerges that as early as the 1460s Howard occasionally found himself linked with Hastings in military enterprises. There must also have been unrecorded ties at a more personal level, because at the time of the Lancastrian Readeption, as we have already seen, it was with one of Lord Hastings' brothers (probably Sir Ralph Hastings) that Howard took sanctuary at St John's Abbey in Colchester.[11] While Howard remained in sanctuary, Hastings was attempting to broker an agreement between Edward IV and his brother, the Duke of Clarence. Ultimately this helped to bring about Edward IV's return to the throne. It is interesting to note that whereas John Howard seems to have been somewhat chary of close association with Clarence, Hastings may have had rather more extensive dealings with this royal duke of dubious loyalty. The surviving evidence for this is admittedly slight, but in March 1472 Clarence made Hastings his chief steward and master of game in Tutbury and steward of High Peak, with combined fees of £40.[12]

Following Edward's restoration, 'Hastings was made lieutenant [of Calais] on 17 July 1471, replacing Anthony Woodville,

Earl Rivers, and shortly afterwards crossed to Calais with his deputy, John, Lord Howard, and reduced the garrison to submission. Hastings was to hold the lieutenancy for the rest of his life, although he spent relatively little time in Calais, relying on his brother Ralph to watch his interests there'.[13] His Calais appointment as Hastings' assistant seems to have marked the start of John Howard's diplomatic career.

We saw in an earlier chapter that Howard may have fallen foul of Edward IV in the early years of his reign – though subsequently he seems to have learnt his lesson, and behaved correctly. It now emerges that Lord Hastings could likewise pursue his own line when it suited him. Despite his apparently close relationship with Edward IV, between March 1477 and January 1480 – and in response to an appeal for help from the king's sister, Margaret of York, Duchess of Burgundy – Hastings took reinforcements to Calais in defiance of the king's express orders.[14]

In the later stages of Edward IV's reign, as Mancini has already told us, Hastings is reported to have been the king's companion in various vices. What exactly this might have meant must ultimately be assessed in the light of evidence which will appear in the following chapter, but probably the two men at least partied together. Moreover, for what it is worth, Elizabeth Woodville seems to have disliked Hastings. Nor was she the only member of the Woodville clan to find herself at odds with him. In ways which are not entirely clear, faction rivalry flared up between Hastings and the queen's eldest son, the Marquess of Dorset. It has been thought that their quarrel may possibly have had something to do with Edward's last mistress, Elizabeth Lambert, whose favours Dorset is reputed to have shared with the king, or inherited from him. Annette Carson has suggested that Elizabeth Lambert also 'seems to have been suspiciously close to the old warhorse Lord Hastings, for the report in the Great Chronicle states that … [later] her goods were seized in order to return certain of them to Hastings' widow'.[15]

When Edward IV was in his last illness, he was apparently much preoccupied with the prevailing discord and disunity at his court. As we shall see later, the dying king wrote a letter summoning Lord Howard to his side. He also reportedly added codicils to his will concentrating authority in the hands of his younger brother, Gloucester, in the event of his death. At the same time he also sought to reconcile the quarrelling factions of his friend, Hastings, and his stepson, Dorset.[16]

The remainder of Lord Hastings' story – what he did, and what happened to him after the death of Edward IV – is material which may be more suitably considered in later chapters, as the events of 1483 unfold. We now return to Lord Howard, to consider possible new evidence of the links connecting him with aspects of Edward IV's private life, and what this evidence may ultimately imply in respect of the important role which Howard came to play at the very centre of the Yorkist regime when Edward IV was no more.

Secrets of the King's Bedchamber

Introduxit me rex in cellaria sua.
['The king has brought me into his chambers.']
The Song of Solomon, ch. 1, v. 34

In previous chapters evidence has been presented to suggest first, that John Howard was complicit in the sexual activity of his young Mowbray cousin, and possibly also of the teenaged Richard, Duke of Gloucester, and second, that Howard's sometime employer, Lord Hastings, is reputed to have been Edward IV's companion in vice, and possibly had knowledge of the king's secret matrimonial machinations. We are now about to consider Howard's possible knowledge of, and involvement in, the private life of King Edward IV. Before we can begin to do so, however, some preparatory groundwork is essential, because unfortunately Edward IV's private life is a minefield about which we actually know very little. We must therefore begin by digressing briefly to examine the whole question of Edward IV's reputation as a libertine.

For five centuries Edward has been universally described as a notorious womaniser. Writing a few months after Edward's demise in 1483, Mancini (who, so far as we know, never saw him) said that 'he was licentious in the extreme; ... he pursued with no discrimination the married and the unmarried'.[1] Sir Thomas More (who may perhaps have seen the king at a distance, but who was only two months past his fifth birthday when Edward died) wrote that 'no woman was there anywhere

... whom he set his eye upon ... but without any fear of God ... he would importunately pursue his appetite and have her'.[2] In the last century, Ross referred to 'Edward's numerous mistresses',[3] and a well-known novelist has described the king as 'bar Charles II – our most wench-ridden royal product'.[4] As if all this were not enough, Keith Dockray has also speculated on the possibility of a homosexual relationship between Edward and the Duke of Somerset, on the basis that they once shared a bed.[5] Let us now try to establish what solid facts underpin these allegations.

Dockray has stated that 'virtually all narrative sources allude to Edward IV's prodigious sexual appetite (with varying degrees of circumstantial details and judgement)'.[6] However, he then goes on to mention only four roughly contemporary sources on Edward IV and his sexual relationships, namely Gregory's Chronicle, the *Crowland Chronicle*, Domenico Mancini and Philippe de Commynes. When we actually examine these sources we find that Gregory's Chronicle merely says that 'men marvelled that our sovereign lord was so long without any wife ... [and] were ever feared that he had not been chaste in his living'. This brief statement indicates little more than a vague preoccupation with Edward's lack of an acknowledged consort prior to 1464, coupled with mild speculation that he might not have remained a virgin.

The *Crowland Chronicle continuation*, referring to Edward's reign, was penned more than two years after his death, so it is not strictly a contemporary source. Nonetheless, it tells us that 'although in his own day he was thought to have indulged too intemperately his own passions and desire for luxury he was nevertheless a catholic of the strongest faith'.[7] Later, at the end of his assessment of Edward's reign, the chronicler adds (mendaciously):

> I remain silent here concerning what might have been discussed earlier in a more appropriate place, namely that men of every rank, condition and degree of experience in the

kingdom marvelled that such a gross man so addicted to conviviality, vanity, drunkeness, extravagance and passion could have such a wide memory of the names and circumstances of almost all men.[8]

While we are certainly not left with the impression that the Crowland chronicler wholly approves of Edward IV's lifestyle, his comments are also vague and generalised. In this passage he makes no specific accusation of sexual intemperance and, with the two exceptions of Eleanor Talbot and Elizabeth Woodville, he nowhere names any of Edward's sexual partners.

Mancini (writing in the second half of 1483 and therefore, as we have already remarked, after Edward's demise) is likewise not strictly a contemporary source. We should also perhaps bear in mind the fact that Mancini seems to have derived his information from sources connected with the Woodvilles, so that what he wrote on the subject of Edward IV may reflect Elizabeth Woodville's feelings about her husband towards the end of his life.[9] Mancini reports that:

in food and drink he [Edward] was most immoderate; it was his habit, so I have learned, to take an emetic for the delight of gorging his stomach once more. For this reason, and for the ease which was especially dear to him after his recovery of the crown, he had grown fat in the loins, whereas, previously, he had been not only tall but rather lean and very active. He was licentious in the extreme: moreover it was said that he had been most insolent to numerous women after he had seduced them, for as soon as he grew weary of dalliance, he gave up the ladies much against their will to other courtiers. He pursued with no discrimination the married and unmarried, the noble and lowly; however he took none by force. He overcame all by money and promises and, having conquered them he dismissed them.[10]

In this case Mancini clearly does accuse the king of promiscuity. However, with the obvious exception of Elizabeth Woodville, he fails to name even one of the 'numerous women' who had succumbed to Edward's charms.

Commynes, who was certainly a contemporary in the sense that he saw Edward in the flesh at least once, in 1470, says that at that time 'he was young and more handsome than any man then alive. I say he was, because later he became very fat ... No man ever took more delight in his pleasures than he did, especially in the ladies, feasts, banquets and hunts'. Like both Mancini and the Crowland chronicler, Philippe de Commynes was aware of, and refers to, Edward's relationship with Eleanor Talbot – albeit without actually naming her. In fact he names none of Edward's partners except for Elizabeth Woodville, and his reference to 'ladies' is quite vague, and need not imply sexual dalliance.

The other writers that Dockray cites as 'roughly contemporary' are actually nothing of the sort. Polydore Vergil wrote for Henry VII, while Sir Thomas More was writing even later, in the reign of Henry VIII. Neither can be regarded as a contemporary authority on Edward IV. They do, however, supply two additional names for our very modest list. Both Vergil and More mention Elizabeth Wayte (Lucy), and we also hear from them of Mistress Shore (see below).

Thus the real contemporary evidence that Edward IV was a libertine is very slight. He may have been sexually very active, but we have to acknowledge that there is actually no specific evidence upon which to base such an assertion. As for those who might feel prompted to ask how a king could possibly have acquired a bad reputation which he did not deserve, one has only to point to the example of Edward's younger brother, Richard III. It is now generally acknowledged that Richard's reputation owes a great deal to his Tudor detractors. Might it also have suited the same people to grossly inflate Edward's reputation for promiscuity? Henry VII and his servants may possibly have felt that promoting such a reputation for Edward IV would make it easier to lose the irritating spectre of Eleanor

Talbot. Where better to conceal the highly sensitive relationship between Edward IV and a lady whose name Henry VII would much prefer that no one should recall, than amongst a welter of casual and conveniently anonymous one-night stands?

In setting out to explore the sex life of the real Edward IV, and what involvement Lord Howard might possibly have had in it, we have therefore to start by acknowledging that in reality we only have four women to deal with. Even if Edward really did have dozens of mistresses, there is no possibility of investigating unidentified individuals whose existence is unsubstantiated. Edward IV's four known sexual partners, in chronological order, were Eleanor Talbot, Elizabeth Wayte, Elizabeth Woodville and Elizabeth Lambert.[11] What evidence we have seems to show that these four enjoyed Edward's favours in sequence (albeit with short periods of overlap).[12]

Eleanor Talbot

For the past five centuries the smokescreen of verbiage about the conveniently anonymous 'numerous women' seduced by Edward IV has indeed helped to obscure one key (though hitherto much neglected) factor in the politics of the Yorkist era, namely the question of the king's alleged marriage to Eleanor Talbot, daughter of the first Earl of Shrewsbury. The allegation of such a marriage led logically to the assertion that Edward's subsequent contract with Elizabeth Woodville was bigamous, and that the children born of that union were bastards. This in turn led ultimately to the accession of Richard III. Although Henry VII made a determined effort to erase Eleanor's role in Edward IV's life from the historical record – and although many historians have happily followed this Tudor line, and entirely omitted Eleanor from their reasoning – it is the present writer's contention that actually the history of the second half of the fifteenth century makes far better sense if due account is taken of her.[13]

This brings us back to John Howard's knowledge of the women in Edward IV's life, for there is every reason to suppose that Howard was well acquainted with Eleanor Talbot.[14] Unquestionably he was closely and amicably connected with her family: a point which, as we shall shortly see, offers a marked contrast to his apparent relationship with Elizabeth Woodville and her family. Thus, when considering Howard's service to the house of York, and the choices he made in the last years of that service, we need to take account of the possibility that the nature of Eleanor's relationship with Edward IV, as Howard understood it, may well have been one of the factors which affected his decision-making.

We have already noted certain links between Lord Hastings and Eleanor's family. Since Howard worked with Hastings, this in itself constitutes a link of sorts. However, Howard was also very well acquainted with Eleanor's family in his own right. The men of her family were known to him as a result of his military service. In 1451 he apparently accompanied Eleanor's eldest full-blood brother, John Talbot, Viscount Lisle, to Guyenne. Two years later, in 1453, Howard fought at Chatillon, the battle in which both Lord Lisle and his (and Eleanor's) father, the Earl of Shrewsbury, lost their lives.[15]

There is also no doubt that Howard knew Eleanor's sister, Elizabeth Talbot, Duchess of Norfolk, who was the wife of his young cousin the last Mowbray duke. In the 1460s, when he was merely Sir John Howard of Tendring Hall, Stoke-by-Nayland, his position was essentially that of a key member of the Mowbray affinity. As a result of both this and his blood ties with them, he naturally had close dealings with the members of the ducal family. Elizabeth Talbot, Duchess of Norfolk is mentioned on a number of occasions in Howard's accounts.[16] He lent money to her, bought and sold horses and wine on her behalf, and had the loan of her minstrels. Later he was associated with her in projects such as the rebuilding of Long Melford Church in Suffolk.

Howard also knew Elizabeth's and Eleanor's only surviving brother, Sir Humphrey Talbot, and their nephew, Thomas

Talbot, Viscount Lisle (son of the Lord Lisle with whom he had campaigned in France) to both of whom, in May 1465, he delivered gifts from the Duke of Norfolk in the form of valuable crimson cloth – the livery colour of the Mowbray dukes. Given these well-established family ties it would actually have been surprising if Howard did not also have contact with Eleanor, the more so since Eleanor was resident in Norfolk during the 1460s, probably staying for part of that time with her sister at Framlingham Castle, while at other periods she resided in the duchess's dower house at Kenninghall.[17]

John Howard seems to have acted as an intermediary between the Duke of Norfolk and his sister-in-law in respect of business relating to the latter. On 23 March 1463 Howard paid Thomas Yonge, serjeant-at-law, 13s 4d 'for hys ij dayis labore att the Whyte Freyrs for my lordys matyre'.[18] This was probably in connection with the religious oblation as a *conversa* or tertiary at the Norwich Carmel which Eleanor made at about that time.[19] A few months later, in July 1463, Howard paid John Davy 16d 'to ryde on my lordys erand to Kenchale [Kenninghall]'.[20] Eleanor was almost certainly living in her sister's dower house of East Hall at Kenninghall at this time, and it is therefore probable that the Duke of Norfolk's message was addressed to his sister-in-law. On 7 January 1464, Howard again paid messengers on behalf of the Duke of Norfolk. This time he gave 20d 'to John Frawnces and Lawnesgay, to ryde to Whyte Chyrche on my lordys arende'.[21] The manor of Blakemere at Whitchurch (Shropshire) was the residence of the dowager Countess of Shrewsbury, mother both of Eleanor and the Duchess of Norfolk.

Further possible evidence of Howard's connection with Eleanor is to be found amongst the records relating to Eleanor's patronage of Corpus Christi College, Cambridge. The letter in question refers to an unnamed 'gracious Ladi ... our most bountous Lady' who was financing building work at the college. It is possible that this letter refers to Eleanor.[22] What survives is not the actual letter (which was dispatched to an unnamed recipient who might possibly have been Sir John Howard), but a draft or a duplicate 'file copy' of it in the hand-writing of its sender, Dr John Botwright.[23] Botwright was the Master of Corpus Christi College from 1443 to 1474, and the draft of his letter is now preserved bound into his *Liber Albus*. It is dated 2 August but bears no year date. However, the mention in the letter of Master Thomas Cosyn, who only became a fellow of the college in 1462, indicates that it must have been written between 1462 and 1474, while the implica-tion that Cosyn was still a young man tends to suggest a date in the 1460s.[24] The letter mentions a gentleman called Cotton who has been liaising between the college and an unnamed benefactress. The surname Cotton does not figure in the sur-viving affinity lists of the Mowbray dukes and duchesses of Norfolk.[25] This tends to suggest that, despite the application of the title 'Highness' to the unnamed lady, she was probably not Elizabeth Talbot, Duchess of Norfolk.[26] Sir John Howard did, however, have a gentleman with the surname Cotton in his entourage during the 1460s.[27] In addition, it is known that during the 1460s Eleanor Talbot was an active benefactress of Corpus Christi College, whereas the evidence for her sister's benefactions to the college is later in date.

Various indications therefore suggest that John Howard both knew, and had acted for, Eleanor Talbot. In the light of this, his subsequent response to the claim to the throne advanced on behalf of Richard III in the summer of 1483 cannot but be significant. Howard was to become one of Richard III's most loyal supporters. Despite the fact that he had previously been loyal to Edward IV, he appears to have evinced no hesi-tation in espousing Richard's cause in the summer of 1483, and accepting the evidence of the bastardy of the children of Edward IV and Elizabeth Woodville. There are undoubtedly those who will cynically maintain that it was simply in his private interests to do so. Against such assertions, nevertheless, one would need to set such evidence as we possess regard-ing Howard's character and motivation at other key junctures.

We shall later see that neither in his response to Edward IV's legislation concerning the Mowbray inheritance, nor in his conduct in August 1485, does Howard display anything but loyalty to the dynasty he served – even when this threatened to run counter to his own interests. Therefore, we should certainly take account of the fact that Howard may have been particularly well placed to comprehend the astonishing revelation of bigamy which Bishop Stillington cast before the royal council in June 1483 like the proverbial apple of discord. This is not necessarily to imply that Howard had prior knowledge of Eleanor's marriage with Edward IV (though this is a possibility). The salient point is rather that he undoubtedly had close personal knowledge of both Edward and Eleanor.

Elizabeth Wayte

We have seen that both Polydore Vergil and Sir Thomas More refer to a mistress of Edward IV called Elizabeth Lucy. Buck, writing about a century later, tells us that her maiden name was Wayte, and that she came from Hampshire. Although an unconvincing attempt was made recently to suggest that her name was really something quite different,[28] the fact is that Edward IV unquestionably did have a mistress who belonged to the Wayte family of Hampshire. We can be quite certain of this because the king recognised the son she bore him. This boy was initially known as Arthur Wayte,[29] and some of Arthur's correspondence to both his Hampshire relatives and to his royal cousins survives. It is true that we cannot be absolutely certain that Arthur's mother was called Elizabeth, but three sources combine to indicate that she was, and there is also further circumstantial evidence.[30]

As the present writer has shown previously, there was a connection between the Wayte family of Hampshire and Lady Eleanor Talbot.[31] Subsequently Arthur Wayte (Plantagenet) reinforced this connection by marrying Eleanor's great-niece

and ultimate heiress, Elizabeth Grey.[32] There is a strong probability that Eleanor Talbot knew Elizabeth Wayte. However, no
direct connection between John Howard and Elizabeth Wayte
is known.

Elizabeth Woodville

We have already encountered evidence of links between
Elizabeth Woodville and Lord Hastings before the former contracted her clandestine 'marriage' with Edward IV. As for John
Howard, obviously he knew her, as queen, as queen mother,
and finally as the person without status that she became when
Parliament legislated that her marriage to Edward IV had
been a pretence and sham.

Judging from one record of the exchange of New Year's
Day presents preserved in the Howard accounts, Howard's
relationship with Elizabeth Woodville as Edward IV's official
consort was neither particularly warm nor particularly close.
Despite the fact that in England the calendar year began on
25 March (Lady Day), it was always (and somewhat confus-
ingly) traditional to refer to 1 January as 'New Year's Day', and
to exchange presents on that occasion. On 1 January 1464/5
Sir John Howard gave gifts of horses to both Edward IV and
Elizabeth Woodville.[33] Edward IV's gift was a courser called
'Lyard Duras', valued at £40, while Elizabeth Woodville's
horse, 'Lyard Lewes', was worth a mere £8. This gift to the
queen was almost certainly Sir John Howard's 'grey hobby,
Lyard Lowas', recorded in the list of his stud in 1463–64 when
he was at Holt Castle with the Duke of Norfolk.[34] 'Lyard'
means 'grey'. In return, Howard received gifts from the king,
from the Duke of Clarence, and from Elizabeth Talbot, the
Duchess of Norfolk.[35]

Probably this record of gifts as it now stands is not complete, since we have no mention of what Howard had sent
to Clarence or to the Duchess of Norfolk. Their gifts had

doubtless been dispatched in advance, and no record of them has been preserved. However, the record of incoming presents does appear to be complete, and Howard evidently received nothing from Elizabeth Woodville.

In fact, she is very rarely mentioned in the surviving Howard accounts, though a passing reference to a payment of ten marks to Howard from the lawyer James Hobart 'at the coronacyon of the Quene' does imply that Howard was probably present at that event.[36] Moreover, Elizabeth Woodville was almost certainly the moving force behind attempts to ensure that Howard would never acquire any significant part of the Mowbray inheritance. In 1478, at the time of her youngest son's marriage to Lady Anne Mowbray, Edward IV, probably at Elizabeth's prompting, and with very doubtful legality, had Parliament enact that should Anne die without heirs of her body, her young husband should retain her entire inheritance. This was in flagrant breach of the normal laws of inheritance in such a case, whereby the inheritance should have reverted to the collateral heirs (in this case Howard and his cousin, Lord Berkeley).[37] In fact, so dubious was the legality of this legislation that in 1483, *after* Anne's death, the king went to the extraordinary length of having Parliament re-enact it. Howard 'had never been involved with the Woodville faction and can hardly have failed to blame the Queen for his exclusion from his inheritance in favour of her younger son'.[38]

We shall see further evidence in a later chapter which implies that after Edward IV's death, Elizabeth Woodville continued to treat Lord Howard with casual indifference and disregard.

Elizabeth Lambert

For the sake of clarity we had perhaps better establish that Edward IV's last known mistress, Elizabeth Lambert, is the person who still frequently masquerades under the pseudonym of 'Jane Shore'. This confusing alias was completely unknown during her lifetime, but was invented for her many years after her death by two seventeenth-century playwrights.[39] No records appear to survive specifically linking Howard's name with hers. However, we can be certain that he must have known her because very concrete evidence does exist to show that Howard was very well acquainted with her sometime husband William Shore.

Elizabeth Lambert had been married to William Shore by her father's arrangement at a relatively early age. The marriage was evidently not a success, and Elizabeth claimed that Shore was impotent and incapable of consummating their union. Following her seduction by Edward IV she petitioned the Bishop of London for an annulment on the grounds of non-consummation. Her case was referred to the pope (1476). No doubt a commission of suitably experienced women was then appointed locally to carry out the usual physical examination, on behalf of the church, of William Shore's capacity to consummate his marriage.[40] After this somewhat embarrassing procedure Shore's marriage with Elizabeth was, in due course, annulled. Having thus been formally declared impotent, William was subsequently unable to remarry.

He had been born in Derby in about 1436. In 1451–52 he was apprenticed to John Rankyn, citizen and mercer of London, and his apprenticeship may have included a period in Ghent.[41] His sister married John Agard of Foston in the early 1470s. John Agard had been married before and had a son, Ralph, by his first wife.[42] This step-nephew was later associated with William Shore. Shore was by this time both a mercer of London and a merchant adventurer, and was developing business connections in East Anglia.[43] During the 1470s Lord Howard apparently became his patron.[44] This must have been at about the same time as William's wife (as Elizabeth Lambert then was) became Edward IV's mistress, and the validity of the Shore marriage was first called into question.

Shore's business links with John Howard can be discerned not only through Howard's accounts, but also via the

Colchester borough records. Shore, described as a merchant (*mercator*), first figures in the Colchester Court Rolls towards the end of 1476, when he appeared in person at Colchester's Moot Hall to prosecute John Williamson in respect of a debt of 26s 8d[45] Conducting the case for Shore was a Colchester lawyer, Richard Hervy, who was probably a relative of John Hervy, Colchester's town clerk in the 1480s, and a lawyer known to have acted for Lord Howard.[46] The alleged debt owed by a Colchester man to William Shore implies that this was not Shore's first connection with the town. The following spring (on Thursday 19 March 1476/7) William appears again in the court rolls. Described this time as 'citizen and mercer of London', he is associated with Ralph Agard, gentleman, in the prosecution of Roger More of Colchester for debt.[47]

On 11 May 1477 the Colchester attorney, John Algood senior, and his wife Alianora, issued a quitclaim to Lord Howard, Sir William Pyrton, William Shore, citizen and mercer of London, Ralph Agard, gentleman, John Daubeney and Richard Hervy, and granted 'to the use of William Shore … all those lands and tenements [… &c] called Algoods, formerly Bulbekkes in West Donyland', just south of Colchester.[48] Pyrton was a well-known member of Lord Howard's circle. Agard was Shore's step-nephew, and John Daubeney was one of Shore's apprentices.[49] Hervy, as we have seen, was a Colchester lawyer with Howard links. It seems that Shore was acquiring a pied-à-terre in the vicinity of the town. There were later difficulties over this transfer, however, and Shore took the case to Chancery.[50] The Lord Chancellor referred the case to the Abbot of Colchester and to John Sulyard, the noted lawyer who, as we saw earlier, also had strong Howard connections, and who was the Colchester legisperitus at this time. The final outcome is unknown. No land in Essex is mentioned in Shore's will of 21 November 1494 but he may have obtained possession of the estate and then later disposed of it.

There are various other mentions of William Shore in the Colchester records,[51] and in April 1481, Dalamar, Lord

Howard's steward, recorded a payment of £3 13s 4d to 'Master Shore' for a tun of wine.[52] William Shore is known to have had other commercial dealings with Lord Howard which involved wine. On 19 September 1481 Shore and others chartered two of Howard's ships, the Barbara and the Paker, for a wine run to Bordeaux. The two vessels sailed from Harwich, and brought back a total of 64 tuns of wine.[53] Shore also imported wine and exported English woollen cloth through the port of Ipswich.[54]

Shore's influence in East Anglia survived the Yorkist collapse and the death of John Howard. In November 1485 he was appointed a searcher of ships in the ports of Ipswich and Yarmouth, and in 1490 he helped to obtain settlement of outstanding debts in Colchester which had probably been incurred during Henry VII's visit to the town in 1487.[55] The precise date of Shore's death is not known, but he was buried by his sister's family in their parish church at Scropton, where his tomb, with its incised alabaster effigy of him, survives.[56]

What has emerged from this survey of John Howard's relationship with Edward IV's known sexual partners? First, Howard seems not to have been at all close to Elizabeth Woodville. Second, he was close to Eleanor Talbot and her family, and apparently undertook commissions for Eleanor. There is no surviving evidence of his relationship (if any) with Elizabeth Wayte, while the extant evidence of his connection with the Shores links him principally with the estranged husband, William, rather than with Elizabeth Lambert herself. The logical conclusion is that, despite his apparent complicity in the extramarital sexual activity of the Duke of Norfolk and possibly also of the Duke of Gloucester, Howard probably had no particular involvement in the sexual activities of Edward IV, and was not, for example, in the habit of procuring women for the royal bed.

As for the comparison between his relationship with Eleanor Talbot and his relationship with Elizabeth Woodville, this is both interesting and potentially illuminating. Human nature being what it is, the very different nature of his relationships with these two partners of Edward IV may well have exerted some influence over Howard's later choices and decision-making. It is also not impossible that his closeness to Eleanor and her family meant that he had heard hints, at least, of the marriage between Eleanor and Edward IV, in advance of Bishop Stillington's formal revelation of this information to the royal council in 1483.

11

The Death of Edward IV

Iam sol recedit igneus.
['Now the blazing sun is setting.']
Office hymn for first Vespers of Sunday

…forasmyche as we and our right dier said entierly welbeloved son of
Gloucester ar fully agried …
Cecily, Duchess of York

In September 1482 King Edward IV made his last pilgrimage to the miracle-working shrine of Our Lady of Walsingham, in Norfolk. The forty-year-old king had grown obese and may already have been feeling unwell. His old ally, Lord Howard, had set off from Tendring Hall[1] to meet his sovereign on 18 September,[2] and subsequently accompanied the king on his trip through the eastern counties.[3] It was almost the last time they saw one another. When they parted, in October, they were to meet on only two more occasions, and during the second of these the king may well have been unconscious.

Howard returned home to Stoke-by-Nayland. During the late autumn and winter he paid visits to Colchester and Ipswich, as usual. Due to the fact that building work had then been in progress at Tendring Hall, he had spent the previous Christmas of 1481 at his house in Colchester's High Street, attending mass of the Nativity at St John's Abbey Church. But this Christmas of 1482 was spent at Stoke-by-Nayland. There was a 'Dysgysing', perhaps accompanied by fireworks;[4] the minstrels Thomas Stokes of Hadleigh and Thomas Gardener of Hersted (Halsted?) entertained the company,[5] and three players borrowed from the Duke of Gloucester performed on Christmas Day.[6]

Meanwhile, Howard's young friend, Richard, Duke of Gloucester, spent the Christmas of 1482 at court with his brother, Edward IV.[7] If the Crowland chronicler is to be believed, it was a splendid occasion,[8] despite the fact that there was faction rivalry at court between the king's old friend, Lord Hastings, and the queen's eldest son, the Marquess of Dorset.[9]

Soon after Christmas Edward IV received news that the peace which he had been trying to avert had at last been concluded between Louis XI of France and Maximilian of Austria.[10] Under the terms of this treaty the heir to the French throne was now betrothed to Maximilian's daughter, Archduchess Margaret. This meant that Edward IV's own eldest daughter, Elizabeth of York, for whom a French royal marriage had been intended, had been jilted.[11] Philippe de Commynes later imagined that the chagrin of this diplomatic *contretemps* might have been the cause of Edward's death, but in reality this seems rather unlikely. Edward lived on for another three months or more after receiving the news, and the treaty, although a setback, was scarcely a disaster. Edward seemed inclined to adopt a bellicose stance in response. Perhaps a greater threat to the king's health was the dreadful weather which afflicted England during the winter of 1482–83. The West Country was battered by high seas and gale force winds,[12] and judging from Mancini's later account it seems that even at the end of March and during the first week of April the weather continued to be very damp and chilly.[13]

Parliament had been summoned for 20 January.[14] John Wode was the chosen speaker of the Commons, a protégé of the king's brother, the Duke of Gloucester.[15] At this Parliament, Gloucester was made hereditary warden of the West Marches, strengthening his authority in the north of England. Lord Howard (who otherwise remained at home in Suffolk and north Essex during the early months of 1483) naturally attended Parliament. He left Stoke-by-Nayland for London on Monday 20 January, travelling as usual via Colchester, Easthorpe, Chelmsford and Romford.[16] Ten days later, while in London, he gave 2*s* 6*d* to a man called Poynes, a servant of Edward IV's younger son, Richard of Shrewsbury, Duke of York. The money was for the purchase of a bow.[17]

In February came the Feast of Candlemas, followed just over a week later by carnival celebrations: two days of fun and frivolity before the austerities of Lent. Monday 10 February was Collop Monday, when every scrap of meat was used up. On Tuesday 11 February the remaining 'white meats' (eggs and dairy produce) were consumed, and people went to confession to be shriven of their sins. Wednesday 12 February was Ash Wednesday, the first day of Lenten abstinence. Before the celebration of mass, in churches throughout the land, priests consecrated penitential ashes. These were then sprinkled on the heads of king and queen, lords and commons, with the solemn adjuration: *memento, homo, quia pulvis est, et in pulverem reverteris.*[18] The solemn words are traditional, but with hindsight in February 1483 they might almost have seemed to have a prophetic ring, for the doomed king Edward IV now had less than two months to live. People of all social stations now embarked on the Lenten diet of fish.

Parliament concluded its business on Thursday 20 February,[19] and Richard, Duke of Gloucester, who had attended the session, presumably took leave of his brother, the king, and departed for Middleham shortly after this date.[20] He was never to see Edward again. On Saturday 22 February Lord Howard's servants noted in their accounts that 'my Lordes beinge at London at the Parlement draweth to',[21] and by Sunday 23 February Howard had arrived back in Colchester.[22]

On Tuesday 4 March, King Edward IV, then in residence at Windsor, embarked upon his twenty-third regnal year. It was to be his last. The king was still building his new chapel at Windsor Castle, and on Friday 14 March instructions were issued to John Sommer to provide men, horses and barges for the transportation of stone to the castle for the work in progress.[23] The king appears to have celebrated Palm Sunday at Windsor, but shortly afterwards he returned to Westminster, probably on the Tuesday of Holy Week.[24]

27 March was Maundy Thursday. The mass of the Last Supper was celebrated, and, in accordance with tradition, the king (whose forty-first birthday was still a month off) knelt down and washed the feet of forty poor men – the number corresponding to the years of his age. Afterwards he gave to each and every one of them the apron he had worn to wash that man's feet and the towel with which he had dried them. In addition he gave each man a gown, a hood, a pair of shoes, gifts of bread, fish and wine, and a purse containing forty silver pennies.[25]

On Good Friday (28 March) the king and court presumably took part in the solemn liturgy of the Passion, approaching the altar on their knees to venerate the cross, while choristers intoned in a mixture of Greek and Latin the improperia (Divine Reproaches):

'Popule meus, quid feci tibi: aut in quo contristavi te? Responde mihi.'
Αγιος ο Θεος. Αγιος ισχυρος. Αγιος αθανατος, ελεισον ημας.

['Oh my people, what have I done to you? How have I offended you? Answer me.' Holy is God. Holy and strong. Holy and immortal, have mercy on us.]

It was very soon after Easter, perhaps on Monday 31 March, that the king was taken ill. He was 'a tall man and very fat though not to the point of deformity, [and he] allowed the damp cold to strike his vitals, when one day he was taken in a small boat with those whom he had bidden to go fishing and watched their sport too eagerly. He there contracted the illness from which he never recovered'.[26]

It was probably on 2 April that Edward IV, who was already seriously ill, wrote a letter to Lord Howard (then at home at Tendring Hall, Stoke-by-Nayland) summoning him to the royal bedside. It is not surprising that Edward IV should have sought Howard's support at this time. What is perhaps curious, however, is the fact that, so far as is known, similar messages were apparently not dispatched to the king's brother in the north of England, nor to Edward IV's brother-in-law and eldest son at Ludlow Castle. At about the same time as writing his letter to Lord Howard, Edward is said to have added codicils to his will, and to have attempted to reconcile the quarrelling factions of his friend, Lord Hastings, and his stepson, the Marquess of Dorset.[27]

Rumours of the king's sudden illness ran through London like wildfire during the first week of April, giving rise to premature speculations of a fatal outcome. It is to this period that a surviving, nervous-sounding and ill-founded note written by a middle-class Londoner called George Cely should properly be dated.[28] This note, which speculates upon Edward IV's death and which contains other, quite wild rumours, runs as follows (the original spelling, which makes the note even harder to interpret, has in this instance been modernised):

> There is great rumour in the realm. The Scots has done great [sic] in England. Chamberlain is deceased in trouble. The chancellor[29] is disproved [? dyssprowett] and not content. The Bishop of Ely is dead.[30]
>
> If the king, God save his life, were deceased, the Duke of Gloucester[31] were in any peril, if my lord prince[32] which God defend were troubled, if my lord of Northumberland were dead or greatly troubled, if my lord Howard were slain.[33] De Monsieur Saint John.

Others in London were also retailing premature tidings of Edward IV's demise at this time, and this false news of the

king's death reached York on Sunday 6 April where a sacri-
legious and inappropriate requiem mass was offered for the
repose of his soul on the following day (7 April).[34] A degree
of confusion over the date of Edward IV's death subsequently
persisted, for Domenico Mancini reported, later in the year,
that he had died on 7 April.[35]

On Friday 4 April, at his home in Suffolk, Lord Howard
received Edward IV's letter.[36] Although the text of this missive has not been preserved, it seems evident that it must have
contained a summons from the dying monarch. It must also
have conveyed a sense of urgency without actually inspiring
panic, for Howard did not leave immediately, although when
he did depart he journeyed speedily. 'On vij day of Aprill my
Lord set off for London',[37] spending that night just south of
Colchester, at Easthorpe, and hastening on the next day, with
only a brief stop at Romford for refreshments. In terms of
mileage the two legs of Howard's journey were very unequal.
The first stage, from Stoke-by-Nayland to Easthorpe, was con-
siderably shorter than the second, from Easthorpe to London.
Presumably this unequal division was due to the fact that the
roads from Stoke-by-Nayland to Colchester were far inferior
to the main road from Colchester to London – and in the
damp spring weather of 1483 those minor roads were probably also quite muddy – so the comparatively short trip from
Stoke to Easthorpe was rather slow going. Nevertheless, Lord
Howard reached London the day after he set out: on Tuesday
8 April,[38] probably towards evening. He may have arrived just
in time to find his sovereign still conscious. The king died in
the early hours of the following morning.[39]

Although the surviving evidence is patchy, making it difficult to follow the evolution of his policy precisely, Howard
played a significant role in the complex events which followed. In the immediate aftermath of the king's death, he
remained in London, making frequent visits to the royal palace
at Westminster. On 9 April, the day of Edward IV's death, he

expended 12*d* on boat hire.[40] Given that the usual cost for
a boat from his London home to the palace at Westminster
seems to have been 3*d*,[41] this sum would have financed two
return trips to Westminster. On 10 April a further 1*s* 6*d* was
paid for hiring boats, suggesting three more possible return
visits to the palace, where arrangements for the royal funeral,
the coronation of the new king, and the interim government
of the realm were no doubt being avidly discussed.

Some peers advanced the view that the Duke of Gloucester
should govern for the young king during his minority, this
being in accordance both with established English precedent
and also (reputedly) with the codicils added to the last will of
Edward IV. This notion found scant favour with the queen's
supporters, however. They opposed this suggestion, preferring
instead governance by a large council, 'among whom the duke
... should be accounted the chief ', as Mancini tells us. The
latter view carried the day.[42]

At some point, someone made the decision to inter Edward
IV at St George's Chapel, Windsor (as he had himself requested)
on Friday 19 April.[43] It can hardly have been an accident that
the gap of only ten days between the death and the interment
offered insufficient time to allow the news of the king's demise
to be transmitted to the senior adult Prince of the Blood, the
Duke of Gloucester (then at Middleham Castle), and for him to
travel south, properly escorted, to attend his brother's exequies
as chief mourner. Since the burial could very easily have been
delayed, as Henry VIII's was later,[44] it is apparent that the person
or persons in charge of the funeral arrangements had decided
that Gloucester's presence was not required.

On Thursday morning 10 April Edward IV's body, which had
spent the last twenty-four hours in the hands of the embalmers,
was borne to St Stephen's Chapel in the Palace of Westminster,
where it would lie in state for a week. There, requiem mass was
celebrated by the Bishop of Chichester. Lord Dacre, Elizabeth
Woodville's chamberlain, made an offering at the mass on her
behalf.[45] On Friday 11 April Lord Howard dispatched a letter to

Stoke-by-Nayland, presumably giving his family and his household the news of Edward IV's demise, and probably detailing
the funeral arrangements.[46] He may also by this time have been
in a position to inform his wife of the proposal regarding the
new king's coronation. Apparently at the queen's behest this,
like the funeral, had been fixed for a very early date: the first
Sunday in May.[47] Further Howard correspondence and a good
deal more hiring of boats followed.

On Monday 14 April, tidings of the king's death reached
Ludlow Castle, where Edward IV's elder son was in residence, in the care of his maternal uncle, Earl Rivers. The latter
received a message on the subject from his sister, the queen
– no doubt accompanied by instructions as to how he should
proceed. Two days later, on 16 April, Rivers had his nephew,
the new king, Edward V, write to the burgesses of Bishop's
(now King's) Lynn in Norfolk, and this letter contains the
boy's first recorded use of the royal title.[48]

On Wednesday 16 April, exactly one week after Edward IV's
death, Lord Howard commissioned a mass from Sir John
Mason. Doubtless this was for the repose of the deceased
monarch's soul.[49] On that same day the king's body was
transferred from St Stephen's Chapel to Westminster Abbey,
suitably attended in solemn procession, with Lord Howard
immediately preceding the coffin, bearing the king's personal
banner.[50] The body was placed on a great hearse before the
high altar, surrounded by candles. The Archbishop of York celebrated the funeral mass, at which the chief mourner (in the
absence of the Duke of Gloucester) was the dead sovereign's
next nearest living adult male relative, his nephew, the Earl of
Lincoln.[51] The appropriate Hours of the Office for the Dead
were probably also celebrated, and the solemnities continued
into the night.

In the early hours of the morning of Thursday 17 April[52]
the funeral procession reformed and, leaving the abbey
church, began the journey to Windsor, with Lord Howard,
still bearing the king's banner, riding immediately in front

of the 'chariot' which bore the royal body. The procession
made its way slowly as far as Syon Abbey, where it halted for
the night. The next morning, Friday 18 April, the procession
continued to Windsor, where the body was received into
St George's Chapel. It probably arrived during the afternoon,
for subsequently the Office of Matins for the Dead (Dirige)
was celebrated there. Meanwhile in London, a convocation
of the clergy had been summoned for that same Friday. At
this assembly prayers were offered for the new king, Edward V,
and for Queen Elizabeth, the queen mother. The Duke of
Gloucester was not mentioned in these prayers, still less was he
called 'protector'.[53]

On Saturday 19 April Edward IV's body was buried in
St George's Chapel, Windsor Castle. Lord Howard was present, and both his close friendship with the dead king and his
personal status and importance had been underlined throughout by the role which he had played during the funeral. He
had spent 25s 8d on black fabric on 17 April,[54] and his accounts
contain brief records of expenditure in connection with his
trip to Windsor for the funeral.[55] After the burial more money
spent on boat-hire presumably reflects further trips to and
from Westminster. During this period arrangements were
being made by the court to bring the late king's eldest son
from Ludlow Castle to Westminster, and to crown him early
in May.

Meanwhile, the late king's only surviving brother, Richard,
Duke of Gloucester, was still in the north of England.
Gloucester appears to have received no official notification of
his brother's death from the queen, nor any other member of
the royal family in London. By about 20 April, however, the
news of Edward IV's demise had finally reached Middleham
Castle. Gloucester's informant was the late king's chamberlain,
Lord Hastings. Disturbed by the course of events in London,
Hastings had taken it upon himself to acquaint Gloucester – the
most senior surviving adult Prince of the Blood Royal – with
what was taking place.[56] The Crowland chronicler attributes

this decision on Hastings' part to the fact that 'he was afraid that if supreme power fell into the hands of the queen's relatives they would then sharply avenge the alleged injuries done to them by that lord [for] much ill-will ... had long existed between Lord Hastings and them'.[57] The Crowland chronicler implies (though he does not explicitly state) that Hastings also sent news of events to the Duke of Buckingham.

Leaving his wife at Middleham, the Duke of Gloucester set off for York, where he exacted oaths of fealty to Edward V from the city magistrates.[58] Gloucester remained in York until St George's Day (Wednesday 23 April), though he probably left the city that same day, heading south.[59] According to the Crowland chronicler, despite having apparently received no message from Elizabeth Woodville or the government in London, 'Gloucester wrote the most pleasant letters to console the queen', offering fealty to his nephew the new sovereign.[60] Meanwhile, that nephew remained at Ludlow to celebrate the Feast of St George. However, the following day (Thursday 24 April), accompanied by his maternal uncle, Lord Rivers, he too set out for London.[61]

In the capital, on Monday 21 April, a number of legal appointments had been made (or confirmed) for the new reign: Sir William Huse was named as chief justice of the king's bench, while Sir Richard Neel, Sir Richard Chokke, Sir John Catesby, Sir Guy Fairfax and William Jenny were all named as justices of the king's bench.[62] At this time Thomas Rotherham, Archbishop of York, held the office of chancellor, to which he had been appointed by the late king. He would retain this until after the arrival in London of Edward V and the Dukes of Gloucester and Buckingham (at which point Bishop John Russell of Lincoln succeeded to the chancellorship).[63]

As the Duke of Gloucester travelled to Nottingham some authorities state that he received a message from Rivers informing him that Edward V would be leaving Ludlow on 24 April, and suggesting that Gloucester should meet them at Northampton on 29 April.[64] If so, this was his first official correspondence from any member of the court. Gloucester may subsequently have timed his journey to fit in with Lord Rivers' programme, for he stopped briefly at Pontefract, reached Nottingham on 26 April, and duly arrived at Northampton on Tuesday 29 April.[65] Gloucester also seems to have timed his arrival at Northampton to meet his cousin Henry Stafford, Duke of Buckingham, from whom he is said to have received word (although once again no documentary evidence survives).[66]

In London, meanwhile, Sunday 27 April saw the issue of a number of commissions. Prominent among those named in them were Elizabeth Woodville's son by her first marriage, Thomas, Marquess of Dorset, and her eldest brother, Anthony, Earl Rivers, 'uterine uncle to the king'. Lord Howard's son, Sir Thomas Howard, was named in respect of Norfolk. Curiously, Howard himself was named in respect of the county of Kent. However, he was addressed not by the baronial title which he had now held for more than twelve years, but simply as 'Sir John Howard, knight'.[67] This was not perhaps the most tactful of approaches on the part of the new administration towards one who had enjoyed the favour and trust of the late king, and it may have been quite a serious error on the part of Elizabeth Woodville or those acting for her. No one in government circles can possibly have been in any doubt about Lord Howard's peerage. Coming on top of the harm that Elizabeth Woodville had already done to Howard's prospects by attempting to ensure that almost none of the Mowbray inheritance should ever come his way (see above), it seems virtually certain that this manner of addressing him was fully intended on her part as a deliberate insult. If not, it was an example of inordinate carelessness. Certainly it was destined to contrast markedly with the very generous – even deferential – treatment which Howard was subsequently to receive at the hands of the deceased king's brother, Richard of Gloucester.

Just as Lord Howard was slighted by having his peerage ignored, and just as the Duke of Gloucester's unquestionable right to be chief mourner at his brother's funeral had been

insultingly passed over, so now Gloucester was about to be
offered yet another insult at the hands of the Woodvilles. He
held the high office of Lord Admiral of England, Ireland and
Aquitaine, and thus commanded the English navy. Yet on
Tuesday 29 April the queen's brother, Edward Woodville, put
to sea in command of a fleet of twenty vessels, and carrying
part of the royal treasure.[68] 'For no sooner had the death of
King Edward [IV] become known, than the French not only
made the seas unsafe, but even bore off prizes from the English
shores.[69] ... Therefore in the face of threatened hostilities a
council, held in the absence of the Duke of Gloucester, had
appointed Edward [Woodville]: and it was commonly believed
that the late king's treasure, which had taken such years and
pains to gather together, was divided between the queen, the
marquess [of Dorset] and Edward [Woodville]'.[70] On the same
day as Edward Woodville set sail, Lady Howard arrived in
London.[71] Doubtless she was expecting to attend the coronation of Edward V, which was then still set for Sunday 4 May.[72]

Although the fact has not been generally noticed, the
Crowland chronicler gives two slightly different versions
of what took place at Northampton on Tuesday 29 April.[73]
According to his initial account, when the Duke of Gloucester
reached Northampton 'the Duke of Buckingham joined him,
[and] there arrived to pay their respects, Anthony, Earl Rivers,
the king's maternal uncle, Richard Grey ... uterine brother
to the king and others'.[74] This version of events assumes that
Buckingham joined Gloucester before the arrival of Rivers.
Later, however, the Crowland chronicler directly contradicts
this, stating that Rivers and his companions arrived first, and
dined with Gloucester. 'They passed the whole time in very
pleasant conversation. Eventually Henry, Duke of Buckingham
also arrived, and because it was very late, they went off to their
various lodgings.'[75]

The difference between these two accounts is by no means
immaterial. If Gloucester and Buckingham met before Rivers
arrived then Gloucester's friendly reception of Lord Rivers

must have been duplicitous. On the other hand, if Rivers arrived first, Gloucester's friendly greeting may have been quite genuine. It may have been only that night, after Lord Rivers had departed and returned to his lodgings, that Buckingham persuaded Gloucester to take a different view. According to this version of events, Gloucester may have greeted Rivers in good faith, but Buckingham, the *eminence grise* of the meeting, was out to destroy Rivers and subsequently persuaded Gloucester that this was necessary. Indeed, the Crowland chronicler gives implicit support to this view, for he says that what happened the following morning was in accordance with 'a plan [which] had been made during the night'.[76]

What followed next morning (Wednesday 30 April) was the arrest of Lord Rivers, his nephew Richard Grey, and Sir Thomas Vaughan. They were dispatched northwards. Gloucester and Buckingham then rode on to overtake Edward V at Stony Stratford.[77] There Rivers had left the boy king overnight, ostensibly because there was not enough accommodation for all of them at Northampton, but possibly, in fact, with the intention of speeding him on to London and keeping him out of Gloucester's hands. No action appears to have been taken against other members of the Rivers party, and it is obvious that at least one member of Earl Rivers' suite must have been free to dash off at top speed towards London. Only thus could the news of the arrest of her brother and her son, Richard Grey, have reached Elizabeth Woodville that same night.[78]

During the night of Wednesday 30 April to Thursday 1 May, while London slept, Queen Elizabeth Woodville, her brother Lionel, Bishop of Salisbury, her son the Marquess of Dorset, her daughters by Edward IV and her youngest surviving son, Richard of Shrewsbury, all took sanctuary at Westminster Abbey.[79] The Crowland chronicler reports that factions now began to emerge. 'Some collected their associates and stood by at Westminster in the name of the queen, others at London, under the protection of Lord Hastings.'[80]

On Saturday 3 May Lord Howard, still in London, commissioned a second mass from the priest John Mason, and we may
suppose that this too was a mass offered for the soul of the late
king.[81] Although it would have been a little early, it may have
been intended as his 'month-mind'.[82] On that same day the
young king, Edward V, together with his new escort, reached
St Albans, spending the night at the abbey.[83]

On the morning of Sunday 4 May — the day which had
originally, and somewhat optimistically, been fixed for his
coronation — Edward V and the Dukes of Gloucester and
Buckingham set out from St Albans Abbey on the last stage
of their journey to London.[84] They were welcomed into the
capital that afternoon by the city dignitaries.[85] Edward V was
taken directly to the Bishop of London's palace.[86] He was still
staying there on Friday 9 May — the day after Ascension Day.
On that same day, thirteen Howard retainers from Hadleigh,
thirteen from Stoke-by-Nayland, and four from Nayland,
were sent home, and they were followed the next day by a
further four men from Chelmsford.[87] The exact significance
of these moves on Howard's part is unclear. Possibly the men
had attended their lord in the late king's funeral procession
and were no longer required. However, Gloucester was about
to be formally named as Protector, and Howard was almost
certainly aware of that. His decision to send home thirty of his
men is therefore a very interesting one, since it implies that no
trouble or opposition was anticipated at this juncture.

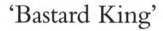

12

'Bastard King'

Spuria vitulamina non dabunt radices altas, nec stabile firmamen-
tum collocabunt. [Bastard slips shall not strike deep root, nor take
firm hold.]
Wisdom, ch. 4, v. 3

Anno regni Regis Edwardi Regis spurii quinti ... primo.
[In the first year of the reign of King Edward V, the bastard king.]
Colchester Oath Book, 1483

Soon after Edward V's arrival in the capital a council meeting
was held which lasted for several days. We must assume that
Lord Howard attended this meeting, which included discussion about removing the king from the Bishop of London's
palace to some other, less restricted residence. The Hospital
of St John at Clerkenwell and Westminster Palace were both
considered, but the Duke of Buckingham proposed the Tower
of London. Since this was a normal royal residence in the capital, nothing sinister need be read into this, and Buckingham's
proposal was finally accepted. It is fascinating, in the light of
the comments of some later writers, to note that according to
contemporary sources, part of the motivation for selecting the
Tower of London as the new king's abode was that it was seen
as being a place where he would enjoy greater freedom!

The council meeting also officially appointed the Duke of
Gloucester as Protector of the Kingdom.[1] Gloucester now
formally assumed the reins of government, and 'exercised this

authority with the consent and good-will of all the lords'.[2] On Saturday 10 May he appointed Bishop John Russell of Lincoln to the chancellorship in place of Archbishop Rotherham.[3] On the same day Sir Thomas Fulford was ordered to try to wrest control of the fleet from Edward Woodville.[4] On Sunday 11 May the Protector dispatched an envoy to propose a truce with the French, with whom a kind of unofficial naval conflict was in progress.[5]

On Tuesday 13 May writs were issued summoning Parliament to meet on 25 June, and it was probably at the same time that Edward V's coronation – which had originally been intended by his mother to take place on 4 May – was rescheduled for the Feast of the Nativity of St John the Baptist (Tuesday 24 June).[6] On the same day John Howard was granted the office of chief steward of the duchy of Lancaster south of the Trent – in the name of Edward V, of course, but no doubt at the Duke of Gloucester's instigation.[7]

On Wednesday 14 May Sir Edward Brampton and others were ordered to follow Thomas Fulford to sea in pursuit of Edward Woodville.[8] That same day William Catesby esquire, servant of Lord Hastings and connection of Lady Eleanor Talbot and the Duchess of Norfolk, was appointed chancellor of the earldom of March.[9]

On Thursday 15 May 'my Lord [Howard] gave unto my Lord Protectour a coppe of golde and a cure [cover], weying lxv unces of goolld'.[10] Doubtless it was new, so its hallmark will have borne the date letter 'E'.[11] The entry recording this gift is the first in the Howard accounts specifically dated to the first year of the reign of the new king, Edward V. Significantly, however, the word 'first' referring to the regnal year has subsequently been crossed out, and the number 'xxiij' substituted, as though the present had been given in the twenty-third year of the defunct Edward IV. This later modification clearly reflects the subsequent setting aside of Edward V, and also the difficulty of then knowing how to date events which had occurred during the brief period while he had been

acknowledged as king.[12] It was also on 15 May that the Duke
of Gloucester acknowledged his debt to his cousin, the Duke
of Buckingham, by 'two vast grants of concentrated authority
and patronage'.[13]

On Friday 16 May there were further grants to the Duke of
Buckingham,[14] and Edward V sent a diplomatic letter to the
Archduke of Austria, expressing his 'thanks for continuation of
peace'. In another official document the same day the young
king explained that he was acting on 'thadvise of our derrest
uncle the Duc of Gloucester, protector of this our royalme
during our yong age'.[15]

On Saturday 17 May William, Earl of Arundel, was appointed
master of game of all the king's forests and hunting parks south
of the Trent.[16] That same day Lord Howard received the writ
summoning him to attend the new Parliament, which was to be
opened on 25 June, immediately after Edward V's coronation.[17]
At the same time Howard himself dispatched further letters,
and paid for the hiring of more boats. Doubtless these were still
conveying him to and from the Palace of Westminster.[18] At this
stage preparations for Edward V's coronation to take place on
Tuesday 24 June were still going forward.[19]

On Monday 19 May Francis, Viscount Lovell, was appointed
chief butler of England in succession to the late Lord Rivers.[20]
Lovell had trained at Middleham with the Duke of Gloucester
in their youth, and was a connection by marriage of Lady
Eleanor Talbot. In a letter from the Duke of Gloucester, written
on that same day, the Protector describes himself grandilo-
quently as 'Richard Duc of Gloucester, brother and uncle of
kinges, protector and defensor, gret Chamberleyn, Constable
and Admirall of England'.[21] On or just before Monday 19 May
the boy king moved into residence at the Tower of London,
where his uncle, Gloucester, joined him at the latest by the
following day.[22] The royal apartments at the Tower constituted
the usual accommodation for medieval kings awaiting their
coronations, and this move was no doubt seen by contemporaries as a perfectly normal part of the coronation preparations.

On Tuesday 20 May William, Lord Hastings, 'who seemed to serve these two dukes [Gloucester and Buckingham] in every way and to have deserved favour of them',[23] was appointed master of the mint, while Sir Robert St Laurence was given the office of chancellor of Ireland.[24] We have already seen that at this stage Lord Hastings – who, like Gloucester and Buckingham, was descended from Edward III – was perhaps still inclined to think of the three of them as representing the extended royal family, which now had the person of the young Edward V safe in its care. That same day letters were dispatched to all the sheriffs, advising them that those eligible for knighthood should present themselves in London by 18 June, so that they might be knighted before the forthcoming coronation.[25] Clearly no one had yet contemplated the possibility that Edward V would not be crowned. Further (but undated) grants to the Duke of Buckingham were issued about this time; perhaps on 20 or 21 May.[26]

On Friday 23 May the Protector, the Cardinal Archbishop of Canterbury, the Duke of Buckingham and others issued an appeal to Elizabeth Woodville to leave her sanctuary at Westminster Abbey.[27] Their appeal was unsuccessful.

Yet more grants were made in favour of the Duke of Buckingham on Monday 26 May.[28] On Tuesday 27 May, 'by the advice of the king's uncle, Richard, Duke of Gloucester, protector and defender of the realm during the king's minority', the king's clerk, William Felde, received a grant.[29] On Friday 30 May John Kendale esquire, 'servant of the king's uncle, Richard, Duke of Gloucester', was appointed chief clerk of the common bench.[30]

As May passed into June, Elizabeth Woodville and her immediate family continued in sanctuary at Westminster Abbey. Meanwhile Anne Neville, the Protector's wife, had been slowly journeying southwards, and on Thursday 5 June she arrived in London.[31] On this same day the Howard accounts were still referring to the Duke of Gloucester as 'the Lord Protectour'.[32] Nevertheless, in all probability by this date the issue of Edward

IV's marriage to Eleanor Talbot, and the consequent bastardy of his children by Elizabeth Woodville, had already been mooted. The news was presented to the royal council only four days later, and it seems probable that Bishop Stillington would have first laid his information privately before the Protector, who is then likely to have discussed it with his most trusted advisers. The Crowland chronicler later recalled that at this time 'the protector did not show sufficient consideration for the dignity and peace of mind of the queen'.[33] If Gloucester did indeed begin to treat Elizabeth Woodville differently, this may well be because the question of the validity of her marriage had now been brought to his attention. Further evidence which suggests that the validity of Edward IV's marriage to Elizabeth Woodville had been raised is the fact that apparently moves were already afoot to reassign the Mowbray inheritance, and to raise Lord Howard to the dukedom of Norfolk. On 5 June 'my Lord [Howard] paied be his own handes to John Feeld, for to have owt sertayn wrytenges of lyvelode from my Lord Berkeley'.[34] Lord Berkeley and Lord Howard were the Mowbray co-heirs, and a mutual agreement would obviously be desirable if the Mowbray estates and titles were to be divided amicably between them. As for Lord Berkeley, he was not only Lord Howard's cousin, but also a cousin of Eleanor Talbot.

We have already seen that Lord Howard had almost certainly been acquainted with Eleanor Talbot and unquestionably knew her sister, Elizabeth, Duchess of Norfolk, and other members of her family very well. It is therefore entirely plausible that when talk of Eleanor's marriage with Edward IV began to be heard, this came as no surprise to Howard. Even if he had heard no previous mention of such a union, evidently the notion did not cause him great astonishment. The fact that negotiations took place between Howard and his cousin, Lord Berkeley, as early as 5 June is extremely interesting.

Some authorities have suggested that Howard's elevation to ducal rank was contingent upon the death of Richard of Shrewsbury (who had been created Duke of Norfolk by his father, Edward IV).The issues involved are fully explored in the next chapter. For the moment, however, we shall merely observe that on 5 June, far from being dead, Richard of Shrewsbury was still in sanctuary at Westminster Abbey with his mother and sisters. The evidence from the Howard accounts of discussions between Lords Howard and Berkeley therefore tends to imply that the partition of the Mowbray inheritance and Howard's subsequent ducal elevation were consequent not upon Richard of Shrewsbury's death, but upon the recognition of his bastard status, and the consequent setting aside of his royal rank. We have already seen with what dubious legality Edward IV had deprived Lords Howard and Berkeley of their legitimate shares of the Mowbray patrimony in favour of his younger son. Lord Berkeley, at least, seems to have been quick to realise that the now doubtful status of that younger son gave grounds for renewed hope.[35]

On Friday 6 June a grant was issued by Edward V in favour of Thomas Fowler esquire and the widowed Alice Hulcote, the latter being the servant 'of our mother, Elizabeth, Queen of England and France and Lady of Ireland'.[36] Although this grant was a confirmation of a previous grant by Edward IV to Alice's deceased husband, John Hulcote, and may therefore have derived its wording from an earlier text, it provides documentary evidence that as late as 6 June Elizabeth Woodville was still being officially acknowledged as queen.

On Monday 9 June Simon Stallworthe wrote a letter to Sir William Stonor. In this he noted that:

the Quene [Elizabeth Woodville] kepys stylle Westminstre my lorde of Yorke [Richard of Shrewsbury] my lorde of Salysbury [Bishop Lionel Woodville] with othyr mo wyche wyll nott departe as yytte [yet]. Wher so evyr kanne be founde any godyse of my lorde Markues [the Marquess of Dorset] it is tayne. The Priore of Wesyminstre wasse and yytt is in agret trobyll for certeyne godys delyverd to hyme by my lorde Markues. My lorde Protector, my lorde of Bukyngham, with all othyr lordys as wele temporale as spiritual wer at Westminstre in the councelchamber from 10 to 2 butt there wass none that spake with the Qwene. There is gret besyness ageyns the Coronacione wyche schalbe this day fortnight as we sey.[37]

It is evident from the various sequels (below) that the important 'council' meeting to which Simon Stallworthe refers must have been the occasion on which the allegation of Edward IV's marriage with Eleanor Talbot was finally brought out into the open, and the consequent bastardy of Edward's Woodville offspring discussed. Stallworthe reports that the meeting was attended by all the lay peers who were then in the vicinity of the capital, with the exception of those who had taken sanctuary with Elizabeth Woodville. We can thus be confident that Lord Howard was there. Since the spiritual lords were also present, we can also confidently assert the presence of Bishop Stillington of Bath and Wells. In fact, this 'council' meeting was actually virtually a meeting of the upper house of Parliament. This was so extraordinary that the business before the assembly must have been quite exceptional. One cannot doubt, therefore, that Stillington had by this time told Gloucester of Edward IV's Talbot marriage, and that Gloucester had summoned this extraordinary assembly in order that Stillington's evidence might be presented to all the available peers. Clearly this 'council' meeting of 9 June was of vital, even earth-shattering importance, for shortly afterwards Gloucester dispatched a series of letters asserting that the Woodvilles were plotting to destroy him and all the old royal bloodline and appealing for aid against them.38 Some of these letters have survived. The Protector's letter to Lord Neville was dated 11 June, and requested Neville to 'come to me with that ye may make, defensibly arrayed, in all then hast that ys pssyble'.[39] Unfortunately Gloucester left his messenger, Richard Ratcliff, to elaborate the circumstances to Lord Neville, so no further details were actually written down in his letter.

Next, two further council meetings were held simultane-
ously: at Westminster and at the Tower of London.[40] There
can be no possible doubt that by this time the question of
setting aside the young King Edward V had been raised, and
that the ensuing debate had clearly shown the assembled lords
to be divided into two parties: those in favour of this move,
and those who opposed it. It is equally evident that Lord
Hastings, who had hitherto been well-disposed to the Duke
of Gloucester, had broken with him absolutely over this issue,
vigorously opposing any move against the young son of his old
friend Edward IV, perhaps even to the extent of threatening
Gloucester's life. The split 'council meeting', in two separate
venues, was the Protector's response to this division. It deliberately segregated those peers who favoured retaining Edward V
as king, from the other (and presumably larger) group of lords
who had accepted the evidence of the Talbot marriage, and
who now believed that in consequence Edward V had to be
set aside as illegitimate.

An account by a London citizen reports that 'in the mene
tyme ther was dyvers imagenyd the deyth of the Duke of
Gloceter, and hit was asspiyd and the Lord Hastinges was
takyn in the Towur and byhedyd forthwith, the xiij day of
June Anno 1483'.[41] Although this London citizen cannot
possibly have been privy to the intimate detail of this affair,
his account is valuable because of its probable contemporary nature. However, the *Crowland Abbey Chronicle*, written
up a little later, also records the event, albeit bereft of back-
ground details. 'On 13 June, the sixth day of the week [Friday],
when he came to the Council in the Tower, on the authority of the protector, Lord Hastings was beheaded.'[42] At the
same time Archbishop Rotherham and Bishop Morton were
sent to prison in Welsh castles. Mancini's account, written
later that same year, and basically hostile to Gloucester, nevertheless reveals that Hastings, Rotherham and Morton were
known to have held secret meetings in one another's houses.[43]
Presumably they had been planning action of some kind in

defence of Edward V, and therefore against the Protector. It is interesting to note that Gloucester's response was very mild. He would perhaps have been better advised had he arranged for Morton and Rotherham to exit this world in the wake of their co-plotter, Hastings, but he was too gentle a man, or had too much respect for their cloth. On 15 June Gloucester wrote to the mayor of York:

> Right trusty and welbelovyd, we grete you well, and as ye love the wele of us, and the wele and sortie of your oun self, we hertely pray you to come unto us in London in all the diligence ye can possible, aftir the sight herof, with as mony as ye can make defensibly arrayed, their to eide and assiste us ayanst the Quiene, hir blode adherents and affinitie, which have entended and daly doith intend, to murder and utterly destroy us and our cousin, the duc of Bukkyngham, and the old royall blode of this realme.[44]

There are variant versions of the course of events on Monday 16 June. The Crowland chronicler states that Cardinal Bourchier, acting under compulsion, visited the former queen in sanctuary at Westminster Abbey and 'asked her to allow her son Richard, Duke of York, to leave and come to the Tower for the comfort of his brother, the king'. Perversely, according to this account, Elizabeth Woodville surrendered her son voluntarily. 'She willingly agreed to the proposal and sent out the boy who was taken by the Lord Cardinal to the king in the Tower of London.'[45] Mancini, on the other hand, suggests that she was swayed by the fact that an armed force was sent to surround her sanctuary (though he also says that she trusted the word of the cardinal archbishop).[46]

Either way, at first glance Elizabeth Woodville's decision to give up her younger son at this specific juncture seems extraordinary. Nevertheless, it becomes intelligible if we assume that Cardinal Bourchier explained to her that her marriage was now held to be invalid and her children by the king

John Howard Duke of Norfolk.

From a Drawing by Vertue, in the Collection of Rich^d. Bull Esqr. taken from the original Painting on Glass, now preserved in the Royal Society.

His Autograph from the Original in the Possession of John Thane.

John Howard. An engraving from around 1790, after the painted copy by George Vertue (1684–1756) of a lost fifteenth-century stained-glass portrait at Stoke-by-Nayland. Beneath the portrait is Howard's signature as Duke of Norfolk.

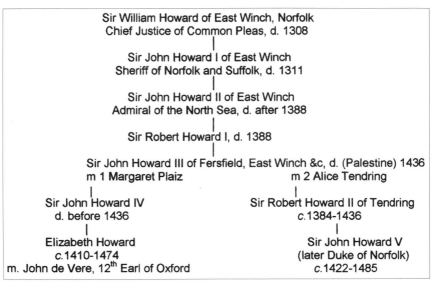

Simplified Howard family tree (male line).

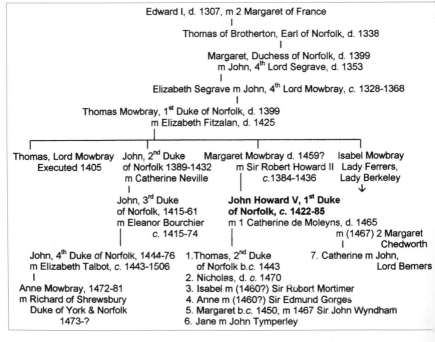

Howard family tree – Norfolk Descent.

Left: Stoke-by-Nayland Church tower, rebuilt by John Howard V.

Below, left: Rose-en-soleil on the base of the font, Stoke-by-Nayland Church. This representation of the well-known Yorkist badge was commissioned by John Howard.

Below: Late fifteenth-century shoe buckle in the form of a rose (possibly representing the 'white rose of York'), excavated from the vicinity of Sir John Howard's house in Colchester. It is made from copper alloy and has a maximum diameter of 42mm. (© Colchester and Ipswich Museums (COLEM 1986.65.1480))

Above, left: Upper room in John Howard's Colchester House (now the 'Red Lion' Hotel), *c.* 1482.

Above: The Church of St Mary-at-the-Quay was probably John Howard's parish church in Ipswich.

Left: The fourteenth-century nave of St Nicholas Church, looking west. This was John Howard's parish church in Colchester. Sadly the building was demolished in 1955. (© Colchester and Ipswich Museums)

Cecily Neville, Duchess of York, redrawn by Geoffrey Wheeler from an illumination in the Neville Book of Hours, Bibliothèque Nationale, Paris, MS Latin 1158, f 34v.

Right: A reproduction of the Clare Cross (front and back), commissioned by the author as part of the rosary to be buried with the remains of Richard III.

Below: St John's Abbey Church, Colchester (south side). Redrawn by the author from BL, Cotton MS Nero D viii, f. 345.

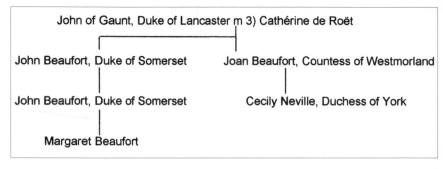

The Relationship of Cecily Neville and Margaret Beaufort.

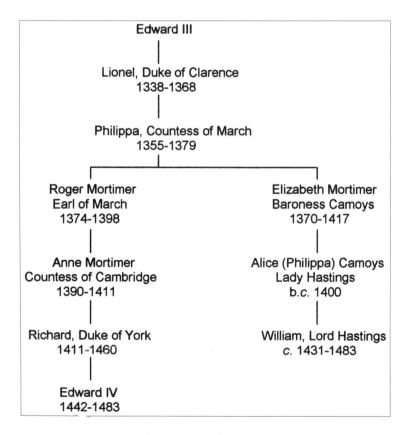

Lord Hastings' blood relationship to the house of York.

The room above the fifteenth-century gatehouse of St John's Abbey, Colchester. Here the Office of Vespers for the Dead was celebrated for John Howard and his men in August 2007.

A fifteenth-century carvel. Illustration by C.H.B. Quennell (1872–1935) originally published in *A History of Everyday Things in England*, vol. 1 (1918).

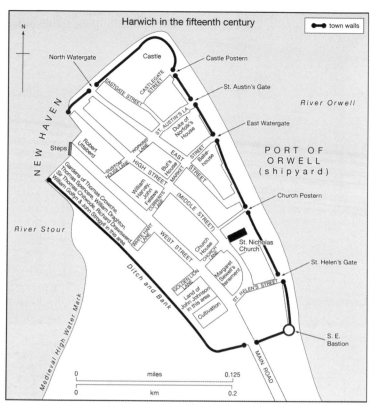

Above: Plan of fifteenth-century Harwich.

Left: Edward IV in about 1475.

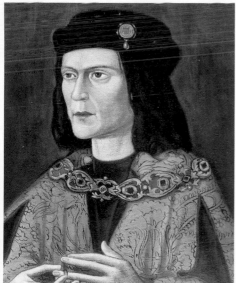

Above, left: Incised alabaster tomb slab with the effigy of William Shore. Scopton Church, Derbyshire. (Courtesy of Geoffrey Wheeler)

Above: The great hall of Crosby's Place. It was perhaps in this room that a *sege* was set up for John Howard to sit in judgement in August 1483. (© Geoffrey Wheeler)

Left: Richard III, a copy of the earliest surviving portrait. (Private collection)

Above: Framlingham Castle from the site of the Duchess of Norfolk's private garden. The stone piers in the foreground supported the footbridge by which she and her ladies crossed the moat.

Left: Map showing John Howard's tour of the eastern counties, August 1483.

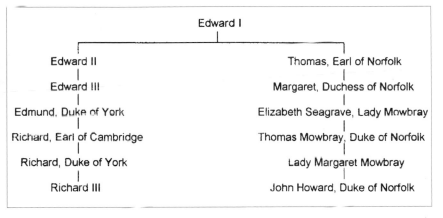

The relationship of Richard III and John Howard.

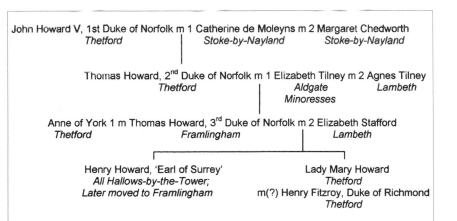

Howard family tree showing locations of burial.

Above: A modern reconstruction displayed at the 'Slipper Chapel' of Walsingham Priory in about 1470. The newly built, fifteenth-century shrine chapel, enclosing the eleventh-century 'Holy House' and thirteenth-century image of Our Lady of Walsingham, lies to the north (left) of the main church.

Left: The restored shrine of Our Lady of Walsingham in the fourteenth-century 'Slipper Chapel' houses a reproduction of the lost medieval cult image, based on depictions from pilgrim badges and from the thirteenth-century priory seal.

Left: Our Lady of Ipswich? This rescued late medieval English cult image of Our Lady of Grace is now enshrined at Nettuno, Italy. (Photograph courtesy of the *Confraternita Nostra Signora delle Grazie di Nettuno*)

Right: Copy (with colours restored) of the sixteenth-century brass of Catherine, Lady Howard, Sir John's first wife, Stoke-by-Nayland.

Below: The gold and bejewelled shrine of St Edmund, King and Martyr in the Abbey Church at Bury St Edmunds.

The ruined shrine chapel of Our Lady of Thetford, Thetford Priory.

The annual procession for the 'Homecoming' of Our Lady of Sudbury leaves the site of the medieval shrine in St Gregory's Church, August 2008.

The east end of All Saints
Church, Dovercourt, with
superimposed photographic
reconstruction of the rood
loft and miraculous Holy
Rood.

The site of the
medieval shrine
of Our Lady of
Woolpit.

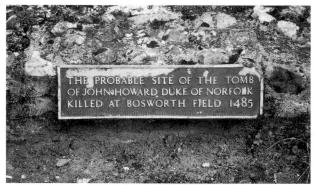

The probable site of the former tomb of John Howard, Duke of Norfolk in the ruins of a small chapel on the north side of the aisle at Thetford Priory. Here Howard lay buried from about 1486 until the mid sixteenth century.

The tomb of Henry Fitzroy, Duke of Richmond at Framlingham Church. Evidence from the investigation of 1841 suggests that the vault beneath this monument may also contain the body of John Howard, first Duke of Norfolk.

Coat of Arms of Sir John Howard, 1st Duke of Norfolk, KG. (Rs-nourse, licensed under CC BY-SA 3.0 via Wikimedia Commons)

had been adjudged illegitimate and without any rights to the throne. Probably she had hitherto seen Richard of Shrewsbury as an alternative heir, and hence, some kind of guarantee for her dynasty. Elizabeth Woodville had reportedly been aware since at least 1477 that she was balanced on a knife-edge: that her marriage was susceptible to a grave challenge, and that if that challenge were ever voiced, her sons had little chance of succeeding to the throne.[47] The worst had now happened. Therefore, provided the cardinal was able to offer her reasonable guarantees for her younger son's safety, there was no longer any reason to keep him shut up with her in Westminster Abbey.

A contemporary entry in the *Colchester Oath Book*[48] dates the end of the reign of Edward V, the 'illegitimate king', to Friday 20 June. Assuming that this is not a mistake, it suggests that by that date, at the latest, news of his bastardy had reached Colchester.[49] It was probably around the same date that men-at-arms were summoned from the north and from Wales by the Dukes of Gloucester and Buckingham.[50]

On Sunday 22 June Friar Ralph Shaw (Shaa) preached a sermon at Paul's Cross against 'bastard slips', taking his text from chapter 4, verse 3 of the Book of Wisdom. On Thursday 26 June a formal petition was presented to the Duke of Gloucester at his mother's London home, Baynard's Castle, inviting him to take the throne as the legitimate heir, given that all the issue of Edward IV by Elizabeth Woodville was illegitimate, and the only son of the Duke of Clarence was excluded by his father's attainder.[51] The chosen venue for this event strongly suggests that the dowager Duchess of York and other living members of the royal family fully accepted the bastardy of Edward IV's children and supported the invitation to Gloucester to accede to the throne. This view is further supported by the argument *ex silentio* – namely that no member of the house of York ever spoke against Gloucester's accession, even after his death, when it would have been safe to do so.

The reign of Richard III officially began on Thursday 26 June.[52] On that date the Patent rolls record the reappointment (in the name of the new sovereign) of those judges who had been appointed to the king's bench in the name of Edward V on 21 April.[53] This move was presumably thought to be necessary in view of the dubious legality of appointments made in the name of a child who had now been proclaimed illegitimate, and whose reign, therefore, had never legally taken place. In fact, this was only the first of a number of re-enactments of grants and appointments which had been made earlier in the name of Edward V. The situation was unprecedented, and no doubt all those who had received such grants and appointments were extremely anxious to ensure the legality of their tenure.

On Friday 27 June the new king, Richard III, was still operating from his mother's home, Baynard's Castle, which seems to have remained his base until the start of July.[54] Once again, this fact strongly reinforces the notion that Cecily Neville backed Richard's accession up to the hilt, and we shall see evidence in due course that Richard's relationship with her remained extremely cordial after his accession.[55]

On the following day (Saturday 28 June) John Howard was created Duke of Norfolk and Earl Marshal of England. His eldest son, Thomas, became Earl of Surrey, while their cousin, Lord Berkeley, received another of the Mowbray titles, being created Earl of Nottingham.[56] At the same time, or very soon afterward, Howard's appointment as chief steward of the duchy of Lancaster south of the Trent, previously made in the name of Edward V, was confirmed by Richard III.[57] Howard was also created Admiral of England, Ireland and Aquitaine in succession to Richard himself,[58] and he was granted the castle and lordship of Farley, powers of supervision and array in Norfolk, Suffolk and Essex, various lordships and manors, and a license to import 100 tuns of wine.[59] In addition, on Monday 30 June, the new Duke of Norfolk was appointed to execute the office of Steward of England at the forthcoming coronation of Richard III. At the same time William Catesby esquire, former servant of Lord Hastings, and stepson of Eleanor Talbot's cousin, was appointed Chancellor of the Exchequer, chancellor of the earldom of March and Chamberlain of the Exchequer (the latter being a position previously held by the executed Lord Hastings).[60]

On Monday 30 June Edward Plumpton was in London, and wrote to his kinsman and master, Sir Robert Plumpton (whom he served as a legal adviser), at home in Yorkshire. The Plumpton estates were near Knaresborough, but they were embroiled in an inheritance dispute at this time. What is absolutely fascinating about Edward Plumpton's letter is its complete (and to the modern reader, quite astonishing) lack of interest in the politics of the day. Not a single word is said about bastard heirs, bigamous marriages, or even the change of monarch.[61] The first reference to John Howard's ducal elevation in his surviving accounts comes on Tuesday 1 July, when his wife is called 'my ladys grace' when she pays the East Anglian lawyer, Thomas Appleton, for 'my Lordes letteres patent of the dukedom'.[62]

On Wednesday 2 July Richard III seems to have been in residence at the Palace of Westminster.[63] The following day (Thursday 3 July) the General Court of the Mercers' Company reported as follows:

Forasmuch as therle of Northumberlande & therle of Westmorland with many other knyghtes, esquyers, gentilles & comens now comen oute of the North, to the nomber x M men or mo, unto the Coronacion of Kyng Richard the iijth &c. And that the said Kyng pourposyng to ryde oute into the Felde betwene London and Halywell, where as the forsaid ij Erles with their compeny according to the Kynges commaundment there doth hove & abide for that the Kynges desire is to se all the said Compeny holle in theire arrey &c. And so to com yn alle together at Besshopgate thoroue the Citie to Poules &c.

For the whiche the Mayre commaunded that the Wardens of euery felishipp with all the clenly besene men in hernes, that every man can make withyn his said felishipp

shuld be redy & at Leden Hall with the Mayre & Aldremen
at ferthist by xi of the Clok at none. And so to be sett in a
raye from Besshopgate to Leden Hall & so to Poules &c.[64]

On Saturday 5 July the Howard accounts record 18*d* paid for
boat-hire, no doubt to allow the Howard contingent to join
Richard III's pre-coronation procession.[65] More boats were
hired the following day for the coronation itself, including 'ij
botes that awayted a pon my Ladys grace, whan sche come
downe fro the Crownacion'.[66]

The coronation of King Richard III and Queen Anne
Neville took place on Sunday 6 July at Westminster Abbey.[67]
The new Duchess of Norfolk was granted a gown for the
occasion, and attended on the queen.[68] On that same day
Richard repeated in his own name Edward V's grant of restoration of the temporalities of the see of St David's to the
bishop-elect, Thomas Langton.[69] On 12 July another repeat
grant was made by the new king, this time of the office of
chancellor of Ireland to Robert St Laurence.[70] From 13 to
19 July the royal couple stayed at Greenwich Palace.[71] During
this period, on Tuesday 15 July, Henry, Duke of Buckingham,
was granted the offices of steward and constable of a number
of castles. He also received various offices and powers in Wales,
and was appointed constable of England.[72] On Wednesday
16 July a wide range of supervisory powers was granted to
John Howard, Duke of Norfolk.[73]

On Saturday 19 July the king and queen moved to
Windsor,[74] and the king's son, Edward of Middleham, was
appointed lieutenant of Ireland for the next three years.[75] 'In
the meantime … the two sons of King Edward remained in
the Tower of London with a specially appointed guard.'[76] The
Crowland chronicler does not precisely date the establishment
of this special guard, which was set up at some point between
6 July and 29 August 1483. However, it was presumably not so
much a safety precaution as a response to a real threat which
had arisen, for as we shall see shortly, at least one attempt had

been made to extract the two boys from the royal residence and use them as a focus for trouble-making.

Richard III now embarked on a royal tour of parts of his kingdom. On Monday 21 July he rode from Windsor to Reading, where he remained until Wednesday 23 July.[77] From 24 to 26 July the new king and queen were at Oxford.[78] The Duke of Norfolk, who had 'departed to Wyndysor with the Kyng',[79] initially set out on the journey with him, but in the event accompanied the royal party only as far as Caversham before turning back to London,[80] where he seems to have been deputed to carry out certain uniquely important functions at Crosby's Place during the king's absence.[81] Howard's probable motive for travelling with the king as far as Caversham is discussed below (see Chapter 15).

Work was in progress at some of the royal residences, and on Friday 25 July Robert Mannyng was appointed to provide workmen for the Palace of Westminster and for the Tower of London.[82] At the same time £350 was granted to (Sir) Edward Brampton,[83] while numerous additional manors and lordships were granted to John Howard, Duke of Norfolk.[84] That same day Howard's accounts record a payment of 4d by his trusted servant, Giles St Clare, on the duke's behalf 'for Seynt Anne, when he went to Crossbys place'.[85] The feast day of St Anne was 26 July, and this was the name-day of the new queen, Anne Neville. Nevertheless, the precise significance of this payment is obscure, although the Duke of Norfolk's visit to Bishopsgate may have been connected with the detention of certain prisoners at Crosby's Place, which until recently had been Richard III's London home as Duke of Gloucester.

From 26 to 28 July the king and queen were at the Palace of Woodstock.[86] On Tuesday 29 July they visited Minster Lovell,[87] and it was from there, and on that date, that Richard III issued a warrant as follows:

> To the Right Reverend fader in god, our Right trusti and welbiloved the Bishop of Lincoln', our Chauncellr' of England.

By the King RR

Right Reverend fader in god right trusti and welbeloved
We grete you wele And where as we undrestand that cer-
taine personnes (of such as of late had taken upon thaym
the fact of an entreprise, as we doubte nat ye have herd) bee
attached and in warde, we desir' and wol you that ye doo
make our letters of commission to such personnes as by you
and our counsaill shalbee advised forto sitte upon thaym,
and to procede to the due execucion of our lawes in that
behalve. Faille ye nat herof as our perfect trust is in you.
Yeven undre our signet at this Manoir of Mynster lovel the
xxixth day Juyll.
Herbert.[88]

The letter is vague about what exactly the 'enterprise' might
have been, but modern speculation inclines to the view that
unauthorised attempts had been made to extract Edward IV's
daughters from sanctuary at Westminster and/or to remove his
sons from the Tower of London.[89] The Crowland chronicler
states specifically that there were both open and covert plots
to achieve these two objectives at about this time, and that
'when this became known the sacred church of the monks
of Westminster and the whole neighbourhood took on the
appearance of a castle and a fortress, and men of the greatest
strictness were appointed as keepers there by King Richard.
Over these men, as captain and chief was a certain John
Nesfield esquire; he watched all entrances and exits of the
monastery so that no one from outside could get in without
his permission'.[90]

John Nesfield, who outlived Richard III and died in 1488,
was probably one of Richard's own servants from the north of
England. The manor of Nesfield (which, however, John did not
hold) is in Yorkshire. A month earlier, on 28 June 1483, Richard
III had appointed him a squire of the body, and granted him
the office of constable of Hertford Castle, together with the
manor of Heytredesbury (Haytesbury) in Wiltshire.[91] Although

the Crowland chronicler makes Nesfield sound rather like a gaoler, Elizabeth Woodville may not have so perceived him. At all events, the following spring he was appointed to care for her and ensure the payment of her pension.[92]

It seems probable that upon receipt of the king's instructions from Minster Lovell, Bishop Russell and the council deputed the Duke of Norfolk to 'sit upon' those who had been detained in connection with attempts to gain unauthorised possession of some or all of Edward IV's children, and that the trial of at least some of these individuals took place at Crosby's Place during the following month. References to Crosby's Place continue in Howard's accounts at the beginning of August. There are further references to Howard's presence at Crosby's Place on 1 and 5 August. On Friday 1 August Giles St Clare paid 'for bere and alle, whan my Lord was as Crossbyes Place'.[93] On 5 August there was a small payment of 1d to provide drink for someone called Burgesse 'at Crossbyes Place'.[94] On 10 August St Clare paid 2d 'for nayles for makyng of the sege at Crosbyes Place'.[95] This may be a reference to making a throne or chair – possibly the formal seat from which the Duke of Norfolk could preside over a court hearing. On Monday 11 August the Duke of Norfolk left London for Stoke-by-Nayland, but St Clare remained behind and paid out 3s to Thorpe 'for straw leyde in Crosbys Place'.[96]

That something significant had been happening in Bishopsgate is obvious, but precisely what it was remains a mystery. Curiously, this point seems to have passed hitherto entirely unnoticed. The most likely explanation, however, seems to be that Howard, as the new Earl Marshal, had been deputed to preside at an important treason trial which was conducted privately at the new king's former London home.

Evidence of treasonable activities at about this time does certainly exist, though it is frustratingly incomplete. A plot by a number of Londoners in favour of the sons of Edward IV, which apparently failed to gain any popular support, was reported by the Frenchman, Thomas Basin, who probably wrote down his account early in 1484.[97] Much later, the six-teenth-century chronicler John Stow recounts a foiled plot to abduct Edward V and his brother from the Tower after setting off diversionary fires.[98] According to Stow the chief culprits were apprehended, and he names four of them as Robert Russe, sergeant of London, William Davy, pardoner of Hounslow, John Smith, groom of King Edward IV's stir-rup, and Stephen Ireland, wardrober of the Tower. 'They were tried at Westminster, condemned to death, drawn to Tower Hill and beheaded, and their heads were exhibited on London Bridge.'[99] It is possible but not certain that Basin's plot is actu-ally identical with the one reported by Stow.

It has also been argued that Richard III's letter of 29 July, addressed to Chancellor Russell from Minster Lovell (see above) which comprises a warrant to try persons unknown, may have been the king's formal instruction to proceed against the culprits of the Basin plot and/or the Stow plot. However, it could equally well have referred to the case which was tried by John Howard at Crosby's Place, which may or may not have been related to the Stow plot, the Basin plot, or both. On the face of things, Howard's trial could not have concerned the four men named by Stow, since the latter were reportedly tried not in Bishopsgate but at Westminster.

Nevertheless, the fact that plotting, possibly by more than one group, did take place in London in the summer of 1483, and that this plotting was focused upon the children of Edward IV, lends support to the notion that Howard's task at Crosby's Place was to preside over an important trial. Certainly some-thing significant happened at Crosby's Place. What became of Edward IV's sons by Elizabeth Woodville is, of course, the great and abiding mystery of this period. We shall explore this mystery further, insofar as it concerns John Howard, in our next chapter, but meanwhile it is very tempting to believe that the newly revealed, but equally unexplained activity which took place secretly at Richard III's former London home in late July and early August 1483 – presided over by Richard's newly appointed Earl Marshal and Duke of Norfolk – might somehow have been connected with their disappearance.

Frustratingly, no further details seem to remain on record. Nonetheless, if Howard's activities at Crosby's Place did indeed include presiding over a secret treason trial, particularly one involving putative claimants to the throne, nothing could more completely underline the key role which he was now playing at the very highest levels of the Yorkist hierarchy.

13

Ducal Progress

*I become yowre liege man of lyf and lyme and trouthe and erthely
honoure schall bere to yow ayens all men that lyve mowe or die.*
Peer's Oath of Homage at the Coronation

*In viam pacis et prosperitatis dirigat nos omnipotens et misericors
Dominus: et
Angelus Raphael comitetur nobiscum in via.
[May the almighty and merciful Lord lead us into the way of peace and
prosperity and may the Angel Raphael be with us along the way.]*
Prayer from the Itinerarium[1]

As we have seen, it has been suggested by some previous writers that Richard III's creation of John Howard as Duke of
Norfolk proves that by 28 June 1483 Richard of Shrewsbury
(who had previously held the Norfolk title) was dead.
Moreover, thanks to the prevalence of that pesky and inaccurate portmanteau term 'Princes in the Tower', which makes
it so difficult to separate the possibly different individual fates
of the two sons of Edward IV, the same evidence has also been
extended to supposedly 'prove' the death of Edward V. In fact,
the case is far from being so simple, as a careful examination of
the enactments of Edward IV and Richard III in respect of the
various aspects of the Mowbray inheritance will reveal.

The legal position was that under normal circumstances, and
in default of a direct Mowbray male heir, the last Mowbray
duke's only daughter, Anne Mowbray (and by extension,

iure uxoris, Anne's husband), would have a right to inherit Mowbray *lands* (including reversionary rights to those held in dower by Anne's widowed mother and great-grandmother, the dowager duchesses of Norfolk) and to pass them on to their eventual offspring. Failing future offspring, all such lands should subsequently have reverted, on Anne Mowbray's death, to the Mowbray collateral heirs (who in this case were Lords Howard and Berkeley).

In respect of the Mowbray *titles*, the position was different. All titles above the rank of baron automatically reverted to the crown on the death (without a direct male heir) of the fourth Mowbray Duke of Norfolk. In this particular case the reversion to the crown may have been briefly delayed, because Elizabeth Talbot, the Duchess of Norfolk, was pregnant at the time of her husband's death, raising the prospect that she might give birth to a posthumous heir.[2] In the event, she seems to have miscarried. At any rate, no living son was born, and the major Mowbray titles thereupon reverted to the crown, which then had the right to bestow them at will.

However, Edward IV enacted legislation in respect of the Mowbray *lands*, whereby the collateral heirs by blood were deprived of their right to inherit, in favour of his own younger son, who was to retain the Mowbray lands even if Anne died without producing children (as in fact she did). This legislation, which anticipated Richard of Shrewsbury's marriage to the Mowbray heiress (but actually preceded that marriage) was of such dubious legality that the king thought it as well to have Parliament enact it twice: first in 1478 (when Anne Mowbray was still alive), and again in 1483 (when she was dead). Moreover, the king sought to augment the immediate holdings thus accruing to his younger son by trying to 'persuade' the junior dowager duchess, Elizabeth Talbot, to surrender her jointure. In addition to these moves in respect of land holdings, Edward IV also bestowed on Richard of Shrewsbury the major Mowbray *titles*. Thus Richard became the first Duke of Norfolk of the second creation.

It seems clear that Edward IV's legislation in respect of the Mowbray lands was widely perceived at the time as unjust. There is no doubt whatever that Lord Berkeley took exception to it, and one can hardly doubt that Lord Howard was also very unhappy about it (though in his case no record of any protest survives). More or less immediately upon his accession to the throne, Richard III simply set Edward IV's questionable legislation aside, to allow Howard and Berkeley to divide the Mowbray estates between them. Strictly speaking he should probably have taken the matter back to Parliament, and maybe he intended to do so in due course, when Parliament assembled. However, no such formal action to legalise the new position seems ever to have ensued. Since the two co-heirs, Lords Berkeley and Howard, were evidently in full agreement, both with one another and with Richard, it was perhaps thought unnecessary to do anything further.

At the same time, Richard III seems also to have simply set aside the grant of the major Mowbray titles to Richard of Shrewsbury. Although Edward IV's grant of these titles (unlike his disposition of the Mowbray lands) was not of obviously questionable legality, there are several factors which might have motivated the new king. First, as Edward IV had done in the case of the inheritance of John Neville, Lord Montague, and as the Tudor monarchs would do later in the case of the dukedom of Suffolk and the earldom of Essex, Richard III may have simply assumed that once deprived of the Mowbray lands, his nephew would no longer have the means to support such titles, which were therefore forfeit to the crown for that reason. Second, the bastardisation of Richard of Shrewsbury may have been seen as an important factor. Although both earldoms and dukedoms have (subsequently) been granted openly to acknowledged royal bastards,[3] in this particular case the titles had ostensibly been granted to a royal prince. We shall return to this point in a moment. In third place one has Richard's possible wish to see natural justice prevail. Fourth, there was no doubt also of a desire on his part to encourage both Howard and Berkeley to continue to favour his cause.

It is difficult to ascertain what difference, if any, the change in Richard of Shrewsbury's status from prince to bastard might have made to the legality of Edward IV's grant of titles. The closest parallel seems to be offered by the case of Henry VIII's children. Like Edward IV's children by Elizabeth Woodville, Henry VIII's daughters, Mary and her half-sister, Elizabeth, were both assumed to be legitimate at the time of their birth, but were later declared bastards. Both daughters were accorded the title 'princess' from birth. However, both of them subsequently forfeited this title when they were adjudged illegitimate. Some might wish to argue that the title 'princess' is different from a title of nobility, since it is not granted, but belongs automatically to the legitimate children of the sovereign. In later periods (and down to the present day) it would probably be correct to make such a distinction, but the application of princely title to children of the king was something of an innovation in Tudor England and it is difficult to be certain whether it was perceived at that time as an automatically inherited dignity or as a granted title.

Possible further elucidation may be provided by the dispute which erupted in the Fitzgerald family in the late 1460s.[4] The marriage between Thomas fitz James Fitzgerald, Earl of Desmond, and Ellis Barry had been publicly acknowledged for many years. However, this did not stop the earl's younger brother, Gerald, from claiming, after Thomas's execution in 1468, that the marriage had been invalid, and that all the children born of it were bastards. Although in this instance Gerald's action failed (because he could produce no evidence to prove his case), there is no doubt that, had he been able to demonstrate a legal impediment, the children would all have been bastardised, despite having long been held legitimate. The Desmond title would then have been forfeit to their uncle. Indeed, that was the object of the exercise. The difference, of course, in the case of the Desmond inheritance, is that it concerned not the granting of a new title but the inheritance of an established one.

At all events, one must conclude in the final analysis that Richard III's grant of the dukedom of Norfolk to Lord Howard, and of the earldom of Nottingham to Lord Berkeley, certainly cannot be adduced as proof that Richard of Shrewsbury was dead by 28 June 1483, nor that Lord Howard's ducal elevation was in any way dependent upon the boy's demise. It follows that Lord Howard would have had no motive whatever to murder Richard of Shrewsbury for the dukedom of Norfolk, as some writers have sought to allege.

Comparing Howard's career with those of other 'new magnates' such as Anthony Woodville, Richard, Duke of Gloucester, and Charles Brandon, Duke of Suffolk, Howard's experience can be seen as constituting part of a wider pattern. The general 'rule' seems to have been that if a rising lord possessed the right family connections, a suitably homogeneous landed base and royal support, and if there was a power vacuum which he could fill, he might well succeed. If the outcome in Howard's case was not entirely typical for a would-be 'new magnate' in the second half of the fifteenth century, neither was it without parallel. His close family ties with his Mowbray predecessors, his intimate knowledge of the Mowbray client network, and the unique role which he had enjoyed as mentor and banker of the last Mowbray duke during the latter's brief minority and beyond,[5] all combined to place him in a uniquely advantageous position to succeed his Mowbray cousins. Had Richard III assigned the Norfolk dukedom to Lord Berkeley instead of to Lord Howard, Berkeley, as Duke of Norfolk, would have found himself in a position akin to that of Anthony Woodville – or, early in the following century, Charles Brandon – who had no geographical region which owed them traditional loyalty, and who therefore failed to become established.[6] Although William Lord Berkeley was as closely linked to the Mowbrays by blood as his cousin, John Howard, Berkeley had none of the latter's advantages in terms of personal friendship within the Mowbray network. Nor did he have the established position in the eastern counties which John Howard had by that time built up for himself. Indeed, it is probable that Lord Berkeley himself was conscious of his disadvantages, and was therefore content to see the dukedom of Norfolk pass to John Howard. As we have seen, there are indications that discussions took place in London early in June 1483, between these two cousins, in respect of the Mowbray inheritance.[7]

All John Howard's local connections amongst gentry and tradesmen paid off with a vengeance in the summer of 1483, and this point is amply demonstrated by the local response to his triumphal tour of the eastern counties as the new Duke of Norfolk. We have already observed that the mysterious events at Crosby's Place continued into the month of August 1483. It was therefore probably during the first full week of August that the Duke of Norfolk, Earl Marshal of England and sometime Lord High Steward, sat in judgement upon the king's detainees at Crosby's Place. The affair must have been concluded by the end of that week, for on Monday 11 August Norfolk left London for Stoke-by-Nayland. His steward, St Clare, remained behind and, as we have noted, made one further payment in respect of the 'straw leyde in Crosbys Place'.[8]

Meanwhile, the king and queen were continuing their royal progress. On 2 August they stayed at Gloucester Abbey,[9] where the Duke of Buckingham took his leave of the king.[10] On Monday 4 August the royal couple visited Tewkesbury, where they may perhaps have paid their respects in the abbey at the grave of the Duke and Duchess of Clarence (respectively Richard III's brother and Anne Neville's sister).[11] On Tuesday 5 August the royal pair stayed at Worcester Priory.[12] From 8 to 13 August they were in residence at Warwick Castle.[13] On Thursday 14 August various grants were made to Sir Francis Lovell, Viscount Lovell, whose appointment as chief butler of England, made earlier in the name of Edward V, was now reiterated by Richard III.[14]

As for the Duke of Norfolk, his mysterious work in London completed, he set off for Tendring Hall on 11 August 1483. He thereupon embarked on a formal progress of his own through his new ducal territory. In part, of course, this was to 'show his face' in north Suffolk and Norfolk – those parts of the eastern counties which had newly come into his hands – and to receive the allegiance of the gentry there. However, the ducal progress also had an important spiritual dimension, which is probably to be interpreted as John Howard's thanksgiving for the very great gifts in terms of both land and status which he had recently received at the hands of Richard III.

His tour began with a pilgrimage to the shrine of Our Lady of Grace at nearby Ipswich, and went on, as we shall see, to encompass every significant Marian shrine in the region. Also, while the dates of this progress had obviously been in part determined by external factors (such as his attendance on the king, and the completion of his task at Crosby's Place) the greater part of the tour was completed during the octave of the Feast of the Assumption of the Blessed Virgin Mary.[15] By the octave day (eighth day) of the feast every Marian shrine in the area had been visited with the exception of Sudbury (to which the duke made pilgrimage two days after the octave) and Woolpit – which he was unable to visit in person on this occasion, but for which he commissioned a silver gilt statuette of himself, which was delivered to the shrine, together with money as an offering and for votive candles, a month later.[16]

The new Duke of Norfolk arrived in Ipswich on Saturday 16 August (the morrow of the Feast of the Assumption).[17] From there he proceeded to Framlingham to take possession of the castle: his prestigious new home. He paid a visit to his son, the new Earl of Surrey, at Ashwell Thorpe on 18 August, and then journeyed on via Long Stratton, reaching Norwich on 19 August. On 20 August he travelled on to Bawdeswell, and thence to Walsingham, where he made suitably grateful offerings at the Virgin's 'Holy House'. On 22 August he passed through East Dereham and spent the night at Thetford, where the miracle-working image of Our Lady of Thetford, in the priory church which had become the Mowbray mausoleum, also received his homage. The night of 24 August was spent at Bury St Edmunds Abbey, where offerings were made at St Edmund's shrine, and on 25 August he was in Lavenham. He seems finally to have made offerings to Our Lady of Sudbury,[18] before returning at last to Stoke-by-Nayland.

The local gentry clearly responded positively to his presence. This impression emerges incontrovertibly from the figures, preserved in his accounts, relating to the provision made during this tour for the stabling of horses – his own, and those of the men who flocked to wait upon him. At the outset, in Ipswich, stabling had to be found for seventy horses (twenty-four of which belonged to the duke and his personal retinue). By the time he reached Framlingham – where he was, of course, very well known – the number had more than doubled, and room was required for 143 horses. Seventy horses were stabled at Long Stratton (though Howard only passed through it on his way to Norwich). In Norwich 124 horses had to be stabled. In Bawdeswell there were 130 horses; in Walsingham 122. Thereafter the numbers gradually fall: 107 horses in East Dereham, 117 in Thetford, 113 in Bury St Edmunds. By the time the duke reached Lavenham 108 horses (and their riders) were in attendance, and Howard regained Stoke-by-Nayland with twenty-nine horses, just five more than when he set out on his progress.[19]

Meanwhile, the king and queen had spent the Feast of the Assumption and the following day (15 and 16 August) at Coventry.[20] Thence they journeyed to Leicester, where they spent the nights of 17, 18 and 19 August.[21] From 20 to 23 August they resided at Nottingham Castle,[22] and by Wednesday 27 August (possibly earlier) the royal couple had reached Pontefract Castle.[23] On 27 August Richard III issued a signed warrant, conferring on Buckingham his share of the Bohun inheritance.[24] On Thursday 28 August Richard appointed Buckingham to preside at commissions of oyer and

terminer which were to range all over the southern counties.[25] On 23 August the Duke of Buckingham, who had taken
leave of the king three weeks earlier in Gloucester, signed a
document at his Brecon home.[26] The two cousins were never
to meet again. However, the fact that Richard III continued
to show favour to the absent Buckingham until at least mid-
September 1483,[27] suggests either that if Howard's activities
on Richard's behalf at Crosby's Place between 25 July and
10 August were indeed concerned with plots concerning the
sons of Edward IV, Buckingham cannot have been implicated,
or at least – if he had been involved in such plots – that the
king must have remained ignorant of the fact.

On Friday 29 August the king and queen arrived in York
where they stayed until Saturday 20 September.[28] On the
Feast of the Nativity of the Blessed Virgin Mary (Monday
8 September) their son was invested as Prince of Wales.[29]
On 21 September the king rode back to Pontefract, residing at the castle there until 8 October.[30] At about this time
news reached Richard that there were risings against him in
the south.[31] These comprised the opening stages of what is
generally (if somewhat misleadingly) known as 'Buckingham's
rebellion', and they were initially undertaken with the aim
of restoring Edward V to the throne. As we shall shortly see,
soon after receiving the news of the uprisings, Richard must
have sent instructions to his trusted Earl Marshal, the Duke of
Norfolk, to take action against the rebels.

Meanwhile in Colchester, on or about 29 September
(Michaelmas day), John Hervy, the town clerk, penned his
end-of-year entry in the Colchester Oath Book. In this he
described Edward V as an illegitimate king, and as the late son
of Edward IV.[32] This record suggests that by 29 September
1483 at the latest, reports of Edward V's death had reached
the Colchester authorities. The Crowland chronicler (writing, of course, with hindsight) goes even further and refers
the rumour not just to Edward V, but to 'King Edward's sons',
thus implying that Richard of Shrewsbury was dead too.[33] It is

also the case that Robert Ricart, Recorder of Bristol, noted in his Kalendar for the civic year September 1483 to September 1484 that 'in this year the two sons of King Edward were put to silence in the Tower of London'.[34] However, it is not clear at which precise date this Bristol record was written down. Whether at the time both boys were mentioned, and indeed, whether the news was genuine, or merely a ploy to divert the southern rebellion from its support for Edward in the interests of other possible contenders (the Duke of Buckingham and/ or Henry Tudor), cannot be ascertained.

In point of fact, reports of Edward V's demise had probably begun circulating a week or two earlier.[35] By the end of September the news (or rumour) seems to have been known as far away as Rome. As a result, on 23 September 1483, in the presence of Pope Sixtus IV, requiem mass for 'Edward, King of England' was celebrated with full solemnity in the new Sistine Chapel.[36] Such pontifical requiems for deceased monarchs were normally celebrated as early as possible after news of the demise reached the papal court.[37]

By early October the Duke of Norfolk had received his instructions from Richard III to proceed against the rebels. On Friday 10 October a clerk in Norfolk's service wrote the following letter to John Paston III, and the duke personally signed it:

> Right welbeloved frynde, I commaunde me to you. It is soo that the Kentysshmen be up in the Weld, and sey that they wol com and robbe the cité, which I shall lett [prevent] yf I may.
>
> Therfore I pray you that with alle dillegence ye make you redy and com hidder, and bring with you six talle felawes in harnesse; and ye shall not lyse [lose] your labour, that knaweth God, whoo have you in his keping,
> Written at London the xth day of Octobre.
> 3ower frend J. Norffolk.[38]

It was probably at about the same time that Sir George Browne, who was later executed by Richard III for his involvement in the rebellion, wrote the following mysterious and intriguing missive to John Paston III:

> To my trusty and welbelowyd cosyn Jhon Paston, esquyere, in haste. Loyawlté Aymé.
> Be 3owre howne G. Browne, K.
> Hyt schal newyr cum howte for me.[39]

It is possible that this also refers in some way to the uprising, but its meaning is obscure. Whatever it was that Browne vowed should 'never come out' has remained his secret.

The Duke of Norfolk was meanwhile sending forces into Kent, and Sir John Norbery (cousin by marriage of Eleanor Talbot) occupied Gravesend to ensure that the rebels should not cross the Thames. 'The duke was also busy advising the council at Westminster and doubtless helping the citizens prepare the defences of London.'[40] Norfolk's prompt and vigorous action cut off the rebels in Kent and Surrey and left them powerless to act. Nothing could have demonstrated more clearly than the events of 'Buckingham's Rebellion' and its sequel, Richard's absolute trust and confidence in John Howard. The new Duke of Norfolk was now established as the king's right-hand man in time of need. Those same events also clearly demonstrated the fact that this time the king's trust had not been misplaced. Howard's loyalty on this occasion made plain once and for all the absolute opposition between his character and that of Richard's other erstwhile ally, the fickle and inconstant Duke of Buckingham – now the great traitor. The Duke of Norfolk rose magnificently to the occasion. It was he who, in the king's absence, was responsible for successfully nipping in the bud the whole rebellion around London and in the south-eastern counties. Thus he fully repaid Richard's trust in him; a trust which the king had already epitomised by the ducal rank and high offices bestowed upon him.

On Friday 10 October Richard III left Pontefract for Gainsborough, and the following day he rode on to Lincoln, where he stayed until 17 October.[41] On Saturday 18 October the king stayed at Nottingham.[42] That day Edward Plumpton wrote to Sir Robert Plumpton as follows:

> To the ryght honourable & worshipfull Sir Robt Plompton knight these be delivered.
>
> The most humble & due recomendations premysed, pleaseth your mastership to recomend me unto my singuler good lady your moder, & my lady your wyfe, humble praying your good mastership to take no displeasure with me that I sent not to you afore this, as my duty was. People in this country be so trobled, in such comandment as they have in the kyngs name & otherwyse, marvellously, that they know not what to doe. My Lord Strayng goeth forth from Lathan upon Munday next with x ml men, whether, we cannot say. The Duke of Buck: has so many men, as yt is sayd here, that he is able to go where he wyll, but I trust he shalbe right withstanded & all his mallice, & else were great pytty. Messingers comyth dayly both from the kings grace & the duke into this country. In short space I trust to se your mastership. Such men as I have to do with be as yet occupied with my sayd lord. Sir, I find my kynsmen all well dysposed to me. If your mastership wyll command me any service, I am redy & ever wilbe to my lifes end, with th[e] grace of Jhesu, who ever preserve you. Wrytten at Aldclife vppon St Luke Day
>
> Your servant   Ed: Plompton.[43]

On Wednesday 22 October the king arrived in Leicester,[44] where various forces from the north of England were awaiting him. The following day (Thursday 23 October) he granted a general commission of array to Francis, Lord Lovell, Chamberlain, 'for the resistance of the rebel, Henry, Duke of Buckingham'.[45] At the same time he issued orders to 'the sheriff of Devon to issue a proclamation, denouncing Thomas Dorset, late Marquess of Dorset, who holds the unshameful and mischevious woman called Shore's wife in adultery', and also various other named individuals 'who have assembled the people by the comfort of the great rebel, the late Duke of Buckingham, and [the] bishops of Ely and Salisbury [John Morton and Lionel Woodville]'.[46] Rewards were to be offered for the capture of the individuals named in this proclamation.

On 24 October Richard III arrived back in Coventry.[47] On this date, and in view of the fact that the constable of England (Buckingham) was leading the rebellion against him, by word of mouth the king personally appointed Sir Ralph Assheton vice-constable of England 'for the time, to proceed against certain persons guilty of lèse majesté'.[48] The king then marched south to engage the rebels, but in the event military action proved unnecessary, for the rebellion simply collapsed before the royal advance. The king's cousin and sometime trusted ally, the traitor Buckingham, was captured, tried and executed in Salisbury.

14

'The King's Kinsman'

… for the good & laudable service done to us by oure said Cousyn,
the duc of Norffolk …
Richard III

The Duke of Norffolke that day thé slowe.
Ballad of Bosworth Field

Two days before Christmas, on 23 December 1483, Richard III granted to John Howard, Duke of Norfolk, a house known as 'La Toure' in London (parish of St Thomas the Apostle). This house had previously belonged to the late Henry, Duke of Somerset.[1] It is possible that this grant was retrospective, as grants sometimes were, and that John Howard had actually held this property for several months already, for on 12 May Howard had paid a workman called Bassley for various woodwork and plastering at 'the Tower'.[2] Norfolk also received manors in Essex and Suffolk which had been held before his rebellion by the Duke of Buckingham.[3] In February 1483/4 Howard was granted the greater part of a reversionary inheritance which he shared with the Earl of Nottingham and others.[4] The following month he was named to serve on a commission,[5] and a debt which had been owing to the late Anne Mowbray was ordered to be paid over to him.[6] This confirms that although John Howard had received the dukedom of Norfolk as a new creation and not by inheritance, he was also clearly acknowledged as the heir of his Mowbray cousins and predecessors. The king also granted him the post of Master of Game and Forests, a post formerly held by the Duke of Buckingham.[7] Month by month grants continued to come Howard's way. In about April 1484 he received a one-off payment of 2,000 marks[8] and in May he was named to a commission of array for the counties of Norfolk, Suffolk and Essex.[9] As initially with Buckingham, Richard III felt he had found a servant whom he could trust. On this occasion, however, his trust was to prove well-placed.

On 1 March 1483/4 Richard III achieved a major diplomatic success when the ex-queen Elizabeth Woodville finally agreed to leave the sanctuary of Westminster Abbey (where she had been for almost a year) bringing her daughters with her.[10] From the king's perspective, at that point things must have seemed to be settling down and returning to normal. Sadly, only a month later disaster struck the new royal couple when Richard's only legitimate child, Edward of Middleham, Prince of Wales, died, apparently quite suddenly. Richard was now a king without a clear heir. His nephews, John de la Pole, Earl of Lincoln, and Edward of Clarence, Earl of Warwick, both seem to have been considered at the time as possible alternatives to the dead prince, but no immediate decision appears to have been taken. Warwick had the advantage of being a legitimate heir in the male line of descent, but he was a minor, and was also disabled by the attainder of his father, the Duke of Clarence (though if necessary this could have been reversed).[11] Lincoln, the son of Richard III's sister Elizabeth, Duchess of Suffolk, was a young adult, and he was certainly given prominent roles to play. However, he was never formally recognised as heir presumptive.

It was probably not long after the death of the Prince of Wales that Queen Anne Neville began to exhibit symptoms of the illness (perhaps tuberculosis) which would claim her life less than a year later. A letter surviving from this period serves to illustrate that at least Richard III's relationship with his mother, Cecily Neville, continued to be close. Evidently he found her very supportive. On 3 June 1484 Richard wrote to her from Pontefract Castle:[12]

> Madam, I recommaunde me to you as hertely as is to me possible, beseching you in my most humble and effectuouse wise of youre daly blessing to my synguler comfort & defence in my need. And madam I hertely beseche you that I may often here from you to my comfort. And suche newes as bene here my servaunt Thomas Bryane, this berere, shall shew you, to whome please it you yeve credence unto. And madam I beseche you to be good & gracious lady to my lord, my chambreleyn, to be your officer in Wilshire in such as Colingbourne had. I trust he shall therein do you good service, and that it please you that by this berere I may understande youre pleasure in this behalve. And I pray God sende you th'accomplishemnent of youre noble desires. Written at Pountfreit the iijde day of Juyne, with the hand of
> Youre most humble son
> Ricardus Rex

As 1484 continued, there are further records of grants from the king to the Duke of Norfolk. On 16 August Howard received the reversion of the manor of Vaus together with an annuity from lordship of Dovercourt.[13] About the same time there were also further, undated grants of land and revenue.[14] On 7 December Richard again displayed his trust in John Howard by assigning to him the wardship and marriage of the young Henry Bourchier, Earl of Essex.[15] As the grandson of Richard III's aunt, Isabel of York, Henry was one of the king's closest relatives, and possessed quite a strong claim to the throne. In fact, after the immediate descendants of Richard III's own father, Henry Bourchier was the next heir by right of blood. Given the recent death of the Prince of Wales, Essex was an important child. His guardian therefore needed to be a man whom the king could trust completely. The following day,

Norfolk was named in a commission of array for the counties of Essex and Norfolk.[16] On 12 September 1484, when ambassadors from the King of Scots were received by Richard III at Nottingham Castle, the Duke of Norfolk was prominent amongst the courtiers attending the king.[17]

It is also clear that the Duke of Norfolk was very much in Richard III's confidence when it came to the sad matter of his queen's decline and death. On the one hand, this was, of course, a deeply personal matter for the king, who had been married to Anne Neville, apparently happily, for a number of years, and who had known her even longer, having lived in the household of her father the Earl of Warwick for a time in his youth. But it was also an affair of state, and a matter of grave dynastic importance, for the king had no direct heir and was young enough to remarry. As we shall see shortly, his councillors apparently urged Richard to give consideration to this question even before Anne Neville passed away. It must have been quite evident for some time to those close to the royal couple that Anne was dying, and the formal approaches in quest of a new queen seem to have been inaugurated very quickly after her death. Heads of state do not always have the luxury to indulge in prolonged mourning.

Queen Anne lingered, perhaps in pain, to the apparent distress of members of her family.[18] She finally slipped quietly out of the world at the Palace of Westminster, on Wednesday 16 March 1484/5. It was the fourth week of Lent and, for the superstitious majority, the day probably seemed ill-omened because of the dark sign that appeared in the heavens. Just after 9 o'clock that morning, as the monks in their choirstalls at nearby Westminster Abbey were singing the Office of Terce, the sky darkened as the shadow of the moon crept across the face of the sun, obscuring it almost completely for some five minutes.[19] As the queen lay dying in this unwonted darkness, the voices of the monks, standing in their choirstalls or perched on their misericords, arose, chanting the almost prophetic-sounding words of the second Psalm of their Office for that morning:

Cor meum conturbatum est in me:
et formido mortis cecedit super me.
[My heart is in anguish within me,
the terrors of death have fallen upon me].[20]

Almost as soon as the queen was dead, it seems, Richard dispatched envoys to both Spain and Portugal in quest of a new partner. In Toledo, the 'Catholic Kings', Ferdinand V of Aragon and Isabel of Castile, were sounded regarding a marriage between Richard and their eldest daughter, the infanta Isabel of Aragon. In Lisbon, John II of Portugal was approached for the hand of his sister, the infanta Joana.[21] Both infantas were direct descendants of Henry IV's sisters. Evidently Richard III was planning to use his second marriage to reconcile the long divided houses of York and Lancaster.

The Portuguese infanta seems to have been the preferred candidate, for two reasons: first, the Portuguese royal family represented the senior living line of descent from John of Gaunt and his first wife, Blanche of Lancaster – they were thus the Lancastrian heirs to the English throne; the second point was that in Portugal Richard's envoys were negotiating a double marriage: Richard to Joana, and his illegitimate niece, Elizabeth of York, eldest child of Edward IV and Elizabeth Woodville, to King John II's cousin, Manuel, Duke of Beja.

It was almost certainly in connection with this mooted Portuguese marriage that Elizabeth of York penned a letter to the Duke of Norfolk, cited by George Buck, but now lost. Elizabeth thanked Howard for his many courtesies to her, and asked him to act as her mediator to the king to urge him to hasten her proposed marriage.[22] However, the salient point in the present context was that Norfolk was so deeply trusted by the king, and so much a part of his inner circle, that even before Anne Neville was dead he was evidently aware of possible plans for Richard's remarriage to a Portuguese/Lancastrian princess. It is also interesting to see that the daughter of his former friend, Edward IV, clearly still trusted John Howard implicitly.

Howard's record of trustworthy service to Richard III continues up to the last month of Richard's reign. In February
1484/5 he received confirmation of his post as constable of
Norwich Castle, and of his manorial holdings.[23] Additional
grants of manors, revenues and an annuity followed.[24] Almost
our last direct record of John Howard's loyalty to Richard survives in the form of his letter, written probably on or about
12 August 1485, and summoning John Paston III to his array in
Bury St Edmunds in preparation for the campaign which was
to end ten days later in the battle of Bosworth.[25]

John Howard was probably about sixty-three years old
when he met a courageous death commanding the vanguard
of Richard III's royal army at Bosworth. The circumstances
of the battle, like its location, are the subject of much debate.
They have been reconstructed very imaginatively and in great
detail by various writers, based, however, on quite slender
contemporary evidence. Of the Duke of Norfolk's role in the
battle, little is said in contemporary sources, so we can only do
our best with what we have.

Even the earliest accounts of Norfolk's death actually tell us
very little, and they also contain manifest inaccuracies. Thus
Henry VII's immediate post-battle proclamation lists Norfolk
amongst the dead. Yet it goes on to state, incorrectly, that his
son, Surrey, together with Richard III's nephew, Lincoln, and
Lord Lovel, had also been killed. The next closest source to the
battle in terms of date is the reference in the York city records,
which reports the death of Richard III in moving and often-
quoted words. However, this account goes on to falsely accuse
Norfolk of having betrayed Richard, so its evidential value has
to be somewhat questionable.

According to Hall (1548), on the night before the battle
someone pinned the following verse to John Howard's tent flap:

> Jack of Norfolk be not too bold
> For Dickon, thy master, is bought and sold.[26]

This same warning is also recorded in slightly variant versions by subsequent writers, but they could have been merely copying Hall, and the story may or may not be true. Nevertheless, it is certain that the Duke of Norfolk did keep faith with his king, and with the royal house of York. As Grafton reported in 1569, the duke regarding 'more his oath, his honour, and promise made to king Richard, like a gentleman, and a faithful subject to his prince, absented not himself from his master; but as he faithfully lived under him, so he manfully died with him, to his great fame and laud'.[37]

The *Crowland Chronicle,* one of our earliest sources, has Norfolk confronting the Earl of Oxford in the battle, and goes on to say that Norfolk was killed in the battle, though without supplying any details. Buck (who here, as elsewhere, quotes his own, slightly variant version of the *Crowland Chronicle*) interprets this reference to mean that 'the Duke of Norfolk was slaine in the Battaile by the Earl of Oxford'. The latter was the Duke of Norfolk's forty-two-year-old cousin, John de Vere, who was fighting on Henry Tudor's side. Buck's contemporary, the poet Sir John Beaumont (1629), as we shall shortly see, also had Norfolk killed by Oxford.[28]

On the other hand the Burgundian chronicler, Jean Molinet, writing in about 1490, claimed that Norfolk was captured in the battle and that Henry Tudor then sent him to the Earl of Oxford, who had him put to death.[29] 'The Song of Lady Bessy' (*c.* 1600) produces yet another version. This would have us believe that Norfolk and his men took refuge on a hill, where the duke was killed by Sir John Savage. More recent writers have tried bravely to reconcile these essentially conflicting accounts by having Norfolk captured by Savage and then killed by Oxford.[30]

Let us, however, leave the last word to Sir John Beaumont who, in his poem of 1629, *Battle of Bosworth Field*, tells the story of John Howard's death as follows:

Here valiant Oxford and fierce Norfolke meete,
And with their speares each other rudely greete;
About the ayre the shiver'd pieces play,
Then on their swords their noble hands they lay,
And Norfolke first a blow directly guides
To Oxford's head, which from his helmet slides
Upon his arme, and, biting through the steele,
Inflicts a wound, which Vere disdaines to feele:
He lifts his fauchion with a threat'ning grace,
And hewes the bever off from Howard's face.
This being done, he, with compassion charm'd,
Retires, asham'd to strike a man disarm'd:
But straight a deadly shaft sent from a bow
(Whose master, though farre off, the Duke could know)
Untimely brought this combat to an end,
And pierc'd the braine of Richard's constant friend.
When Oxford saw him sinke, his noble soule
Was full of griefe, which made him thus condole:
'Farewell, true Knight, to whom no costly grave
Can give due honour. Would my tears might save
Those streams of blood, deserving to be spilt
In better service'.[31]

Thus, according to Beaumont, John Howard was not killed directly by his cousin, but having lost his helmet in hand-to-hand combat with Oxford, was struck down by an arrow aimed at him from a distance. No earlier source is now known for this detailed account of his last moments, but it could, nevertheless, have been a well-established oral tradition. At all events, the curious fact remains that, as we shall see in our last chapter, what may be the skull of John Howard V, first Duke of Norfolk, does indeed exhibit a wound consistent with Beaumont's account of his death.

15

John Howard's Religious Life

O engelonde great cause thou hast glad for to be
…To be called in every realme and regyon
The holy lande oure laydes dowre.
Fifteeth-century Walsingham Ballad[1]

In the final analysis, what sort of man had John Howard been?
Was he a man of principle, or a cynical and calculating self-
seeker? Is it likely that – as some have suggested – he would
have killed (or connived at the killing of) Edward IV's sons?
At the most fundamental level was he a man who acted out of
sincere belief and conviction or was he chiefly motivated by
self-interest? The material does not survive to allow a complete reconstruction of Howard's character, but in the course
of this book we have discovered various clues. Also, *faute de
mieux*, other historians in quest of a fifteenth-century individual's motivation have sought to formulate deductions based
upon their subject's religious beliefs. In this penultimate chapter, we shall therefore seek to summarise the information we
have regarding Howard's character and motivation, adding to
it the evidence of his spiritual life.

Later generations of Howards are noted for their devotion
to Catholicism. The cynical might choose to see this as proof
of a remarkably stubborn trait in the family – and we have
already noticed that at times John Howard V could be perceived as a stubborn man with a temper. However, there is no
possible room to doubt that the recusancy of later Howards

cost them dear, nor that they have remained to this day very notable benefactors of the Catholic Church.[2]

As for John Howard V's immediate descendants, they comprised an interesting mixture. Amongst them links with the sea and the navy continued, of course, but we also encounter the second Duke of Norfolk: hero of Flodden; the third duke: a wife-beater; and two queens: Catherine Howard – a silly girl, and Anne Boleyn – a rather ruthless and unattractive figure who was quite prepared to sacrifice everyone and everything else if necessary for the sake of her own ambition. Which, if any, of these descendants most closely reflect the character of the founder of the Howard dynasty of dukes of Norfolk?

One problem when we try to assess evidence of religious faith at this period is the fact that, considered at one level, the practice of religion by a lord was simply one of the many forms of patronage. Like secular patronage it afforded opportunities for display, whereby his status and importance were manifested. 'The religion of the fifteenth-century nobility and gentry … was therefore as much a matter of custom, honour, and "worship" as other, secular, aspects of their lives.'[3] Thus involvement in religious appointments; public ceremonial observances such as funerals and anniversaries; religious endowments of various kinds; the rebuilding and redecorating of churches; the embellishment of religious buildings with the patron's coats of arms and portrait; the membership of religious guilds, may all serve to indicate nothing more than a desire for self-aggrandisement within the context of a religious framework which, in the second half of the fifteenth century, was both customary and generalised throughout Western Europe.

However, 'the vicarious mediation of the Church remained the main route to salvation, alongside which lay the meditative and devotional road. Personal devotion, in other words, was a supplement to, not a substitute for, external religious observation'.[4] The fact that public and even ostentatious religious display was *expected for religious reasons* makes it difficult for the modern historian to penetrate the private motivation

underlying the public religious acts of fifteenth-century individuals. Such motivation may well have comprised a mixture
of secular and religious considerations. Public religious display may have been rooted in personal piety, but evidence of
the former does not, in itself, guarantee the latter.

Evidence of private religious observances, where this can
be found, doubtless offers a better chance of evaluating the
underlying personal views and intentions of an individual.
Clearly there were those who sought a personal relationship with God, and who 'developed a more sophisticated
knowledge of liturgy'.[5] In most cases, however, there is some
difficulty in isolating evidence of private religious observance.
The maintenance of private chapels and oratories, and of
household chaplains, may constitute such evidence, but these
were also undoubtedly an expected concomitant of high social
status. 'Household chaplains had other, administrative and
secretarial functions; but nevertheless the numbers retained
in household service suggests that their religious duties were
considered important.'[6] The commissioning of personal books
of devotion, such as primers and books of Hours, may also
be evidence of personal faith, although such items were certainly also potential occasions for display. Professor Colin
Richmond's contention that private pews 'are a manifesta-
tion of the interiorization of religion' is perhaps questionable,[7]
while the endowment of votive lights or chantry masses might
be viewed either as private acts of devotion or as public religious statements. As for wills, while these regularly contain
religious statements, Pollard contends that they may give a dis-
torted view of the testator's lifetime religious beliefs, written,
as they generally were, at a time when death was looming.

Certain aspects of John Howard's religious practice are
certainly known. He cultivated a special connection with
St Nicholas' Church in Colchester (which was his parish
church in that town) by maintaining a perpetual votive light
burning there. Since we know of this only from a record of
payments in his household accounts, the funding of this votive

light might be interpreted as a private act of devotion rather than as an opportunity for display. It is also known that Howard commissioned masses for the dead on several occasions. Thus he ordered two masses for Edward IV in the summer of 1483.[8] Earlier he commissioned a trental of masses at the Franciscan Priory in Colchester immediately following the death of his first wife. The latter could perhaps be dismissed as merely something that would have been expected of a man in his position, but the masses for Edward IV were privately celebrated, and the world at large would have known nothing of them. This appears to suggest that they (and perhaps all the masses for the dead which Howard commissioned) did have a genuinely religious motivation.

In Ipswich Howard is recorded as having visited the prior of Woodbridge, but the motives for that visit could have been commercial rather than religious. Howard also maintained a relationship with St John's Abbey in Colchester where, as he himself noted in his accounts in June 1464, 'I made … him that is Abbot of Saint John's now, abbot'.[9] This kind of activity certainly looks more like local politics than religion. No doubt John Howard visited Colchester Abbey on numerous occasions, and we have seen that he took sanctuary there during the Lancastrian Readeption.[10] Lord Howard was at the Hythe on Christmas day 1481 and attended mass at St Leonard's Church, where he made an offering of 10*d*.[11] He also participated regularly in the Hocktide festivities at Easter. Again, all this evidence is difficult to evaluate. While personal faith may have underpinned his attendance at the Christmas mass, such attendance was also certainly an expected public religious act. As for the Hocktide celebrations, these were charitable in inspiration, but they were essentially secular festivities. It is difficult to say, then, to what extent this selection of activities represents genuine personal piety. It is certainly arguable that some of John Howard's religious observances were merely those customarily expected of a man in his position and in his period. When Lord Howard gave 2*d* to a poor man at the Hythe, on 19 March 1483,[12] was this piety or *noblesse oblige*?

It is nevertheless the case that Howard's accounts regularly record expenditure in connection with public religious celebrations. On Easter Sunday (1 April) 1464, when he seems to have been at home in Stoke-by-Nayland, he offered 20*d* at the Cross.[13] Two months later he paid 2*d* to the holy water clerk, once again, probably at Stoke-by-Nayland.[14] The second of these payments, to the man who carried the holy water bucket and aspergillum in processions for the performance of the rite of aspersion, was probably connected in this instance with the celebration of the Feast of Corpus Christi two days previously, when the fields had been blessed.[15] Later entries in the accounts include Howard's offering and almsgiving on Palm Sunday (15 April) 1481. On this occasion he also paid for bread and wine, which may indicate that he took communion at the Palm Sunday mass.[16] In addition to feasting at Christmas in 1465, the surviving accounts show that Howard and his family also regularly observed the Friday abstinence from meat enjoined upon the faithful by the church. They also prove that the family abstained on Ash Wednesday.[17] Further evidence for the observance of Lent can be found later in Howard's career. During the period 20–24 March 1480/1, records survive of purchases of food which include shellfish (whelks and oysters), salted fish (including eels) and a variety of fresh fish, comprising salmon, herring, plaice, eels, cod, and 'stokfish' (dried fish). Nuts, spices and dried fruit were also purchased during this period, but no meat.[18] There are also records of the purchase of wax candles for the processions of the Feast of the Purification of the Blessed Virgin Mary (Candlemas) on 2 February. In February 1465/6 the candles were made and supplied by Roger of Nayland, at a cost of 12*d*.[19]

At the same time, private payments to priests, together with certain other indications, suggest a degree of personal piety on John Howard's part. In October 1463, while he was staying in Lincoln, he paid 4*d* to a priest for saying vespers before him.[20]

On 2 June 1464 he gave 4*d* to a friar. On 26 June 1464, two days after the summer Feast of St John the Baptist, and probably in Ipswich, he paid an angel (6*s* 8*d*) to Richard Fellow's priest. On the same day he paid 10 marks to the prior of Prittlewell.[21] On 18 October, while at his house in Stepney, Sir John arranged for 4*d* to be paid to a priest for saying mass for him.[22] Later, on 12 December, he himself recorded payments totalling one and a half angels to 'Thomas my preste'.[23] None of this expenditure is likely to have been widely known during Howard's lifetime, so its propaganda value would have been non-existent.

Account book entries in Sir John's own handwriting tend to be dated by religious feast days more frequently than the entries made by his employees. There are examples of this practice in September 1467, when Sir John dates several events in relation to 'Holy Rood Day'.[24] It is possible that a personal devotion to the Holy Cross was one feature of Sir John Howard's religious life, since he patronised the Holy Rood of Dovercourt.[25] Some weeks later Sir John was dating payment of wages in relation to 'Soulmas Day'.[26]

The activities which took place in his private chapel may also give some indication of his personal religious commitment. Howard may have had such a private chapel at Tendring Hall in the 1460s, for in 1463 he borrowed 'a pair of organs' from the Greyfriars at Christmas.[27] We have also noted the reference in 1464 to 'Thomas my preste'. However, the one-off payments to various priests when he was away from home suggest that at this period he had no large-scale establishment of private religious staff. By 1482 Lord Howard certainly maintained his own chapel, for the choir of which he purchased 'a messe of prykkyd song and an anthume'.[28] On 21 March 1482 Howard paid 7*s* to Robard Borton of Stowmarket, organ maker, 'for mendyng of orgenys'.[29] There are a number of references to Howard's chapel choir at this period. Later his eldest son, the second Howard Duke of Norfolk, seems to have maintained a choir of eight boys for the private chapel at Framlingham Castle, and a similar choir probably existed there in John Howard's own lifetime.[30] Sir John Howard commissioned what was perhaps a Book of Hours from an illuminator in Bury St Edmunds about the time of his second marriage. It was possibly also for the chapel or oratory in one of his houses that, in 1482, Howard commissioned leaded windows of coloured glass.[31] The gold chalice which he had 'dressed'[32] by Hew the goldsmith in April 1481, and then 'hallowed' or blessed by a priest, may have been either for use in his own chapel, or intended as a votive offering.[33] Doubtless other chapel furnishings existed which are not recorded. Margaret Chedworth, former Duchess of Norfolk, and John Howard's widow, referred, in her will dated 13 May 1490, to what belonged to her chapel, and specifically mentioned a chalice.[34] It is also helpful to refer to the Framlingham Castle inventory of 1524, since this castle was held by Howard at the end of his life, and some of the items recorded there may well have belonged to him. The castle chapel had a pair of organs, and its plate comprised a hanging sanctuary lamp, a pax, a holy water bucket and aspergillum, two boxes for Hosts, two pairs of cruets, two basins, an incense boat, two sanctus bells, a set of four candlesticks for the high altar, together with a further three pairs of candlesticks,[35] four thuribles, three chalices, two pyxes, two pattens, two crucifixes, one image each of Our Lady and of St John the Evangelist, and one processional cross (or at least, the staff for one).[36]

The devotions and liturgy of the Catholic Church to which John Howard of course belonged have never been immutably fixed. There has always been evolution. One example of this is the present cycle of liturgical colours for vestments, altar frontals and lectern palls.[37] This cycle was only formally instituted in the mid-sixteenth century, and we have no direct evidence of the practice in the Howard family chapel in John Howard's lifetime. The Framlingham Castle inventory of 1524[38] lists chasubles (mass vestments) of black, red, green and white, but it seems there was no purple chasuble at the castle. There were purple, black, green and white copes, but no red copes were provided.[39] The antependia for the altar were red, green or white. There was also one of mixed gold, black and white, but there was no purple antependium. On the other hand there was a blue one. Blue is associated with feasts of the Virgin Mary, but is not formally recognised as a liturgical colour. Nevertheless, the only lectern palls at the castle were either blue or red. It is difficult to escape the conclusion that at Framlingham Castle chapel in the fifteenth century the use of mixed colours was considered perfectly acceptable.[40]

Modern Catholic liturgical practice focuses attention strongly on the mass. In consequence a modern sacristy would contain far more chasubles than copes. Yet at Framlingham in 1524 there were twelve copes and only nine chasubles. This clearly reflects a somewhat different liturgical focus, in which solemn celebrations of offices such as vespers played a much greater role than they do today. Various levels of solemnity are possible in liturgical celebrations. The evidence from the Framlingham inventory suggests, however, that solemn high mass was rarely celebrated at the castle chapel. Such a celebration would have required the presence of assistants (deacon and sub-deacon) in addition to the presiding priest, yet the vestments for such assistants (dalmatics and tunicles) were lacking.[41] Nevertheless, the inclusion of four thuribles amongst the chapel plate, and the provision for liturgical music, both argue a degree of solemnity.

The ecclesiastical calendar was not static, and new religious observances continued to evolve. Following the trauma of the Black Death in the fourteenth century there had been a growing cult of the dead, with a mushrooming of chantry and anniversary foundations.[42] In the early fourteenth century the new Feast of Corpus Christi was introduced into England.[43] Late in the fifteenth century the Feasts of the Ascension and of the Holy Name of Jesus were also to be instituted. These three new feasts indicate a Christocentric trend in late medieval Catholicism.[44] This was accompanied by an important secondary focus on the person of the Virgin Mary at the expense of lesser saints. The intercession of the saints was not neglected, but there was a change of emphasis in the later Middle Ages. Hitherto, saintly cults had tended to focus on relic shrines. By the fifteenth century, however, relic-cults were decreasing in popularity; replaced by cults of the saints (and in particular, of the Virgin and of Christ himself) based on particular images.

The religious devotion of John Howard, as attested by his practice as a pilgrim, possibly reflects this ongoing evolution. He certainly visited Canterbury, but nothing in his accounts attests any particular devotion paid to the shrine of St Thomas Becket while he was there,[45] although he sent an offering of £3 19s 3d to St Thomas's shrine in the spring of 1481.[46] There is also a record of his eldest son, Thomas, offering 2s 6d at the shrine of St Edmund at Bury, and paying a further 8d for a candle to burn before the shrine.[47] John Howard also visited the shrine of St John at Beverley. Beyond this, there is little evidence of any great devotion to relic shrines to be found in the surviving Howard accounts. On the other hand, these testify that he frequented a number of cult centres of the Virgin Mary. At some of them specific devotional payments are recorded. He and his family also supported at least one Christocentric cult of the Holy Rood.

Howard certainly seems to have taken an active part in pilgrimages. A number of well-known fifteenth-century pilgr image centres are mentioned in his accounts, although as has been noted in the case of Canterbury, a visit to the shrine in question is not invariably specified. He naturally made pilgrimage to the shrine of Our Lady of Walsingham in Norfolk, which was then one of the chief centres of pilgrimage devotion in England.[48] Howard attended King Edward IV on pilgrimages to Walsingham in 1469, 1482, and perhaps on other occasions not recorded.[49] As we have seen, Walsingham was also the focal destination of his own triumphal tour of the eastern counties in 1483 as the new Duke of Norfolk.[50] In fact, it is notable that Howard's progress in 1483 took in all the known Marian shrines in the eastern counties, except that at Woolpit – which he was unable to include on his tour, but to which he

sent a surrogate figurine of himself in silver gilt to make up for
the omission.[51] This suggests that Marian devotion may have
been a significant feature of Howard's religious life.

Walsingham is a shrine focused on an apparition of the
Virgin Mary, traditionally dated to 1061.[52] Although it had
been a major shrine since at least the reign of Henry III (who
patronised it lavishly), the reputation of Walsingham seems
to have enjoyed something of an explosion in the fifteenth
century, and much of the surviving documentation regarding popular devotion at Walsingham dates from that period.
Howard's accounts record an offering of 4*d* sent to Our Lady
of Walsingham in April 1481, together with oil (for a votive
light) and 1lb of wax (for candles).[53]

Howard likewise visited the shrine of Our Lady of
Doncaster, where he made an offering of 4*d*,[54] and in 1483,
as the newly created Duke of Norfolk, we have seen that he
accompanied King Richard III to Caversham. Thereafter,
however, he didn't continue with the royal party, but returned
to London. Although a devotional visit to the shrine of Our
Lady of Caversham is not specifically mentioned in Howard's
accounts,[55] there is the distinct possibility that he travelled
with the king and queen only as far as Caversham because he
particularly wished to give thanks for his new ducal title at the
Blessed Virgin's shrine there.

One notable feature of Howard's piety seems to have been
his devotion to a number of local cult centres. On several
occasions he visited the shrine of Our Lady of Ipswich (Our
Lady of Grace).[56] He was there, for example, in August 1463,
making an offering of 2*d*. The shrine of Our Lady of Grace
stood just outside the West Gate of medieval Ipswich,[57] in what
is still called Lady Lane.[58] John Howard had his own house in
Ipswich, but it seems that, at least on some occasions, he made
the journey to the Ipswich shrine specifically for the purpose
of religious devotions. Thus on 5 May 1481 (by which time
Edward IV had elevated him to the peerage as Lord Howard)
he expended 10*s* on a pilgrimage to Our Lady of Ipswich.[59]

This sum represents, presumably, his own costs on the journey rather than his donation at the shrine (though it may well include the latter). On 22 January 1482 he went to Our Lady of Ipswich once again. On this occasion he made an offering of 10*d*. On 16 August 1483, setting out on his first formal progress as Duke of Norfolk, he again visited the shrine, and gave 20*d*.'for his offering at Our Lady of Grace', a further 4*d* 'to bow on Our Lady's foot' and 11*d* 'in alms at Our Lady of Grace'.[60] Both when he was on pilgrimage and at other times, there is ample evidence of Howard's almsgiving.[61]

The shrine of Our Lady of Woolpit also received patronage from John Howard. Indeed, he seems to have regarded it with particular favour. He offered the quite considerable sum of £7 9*s* there in 1481,[62] and in September 1483, following his elevation to the dukedom, Howard again sent a notable offering, comprising five groats in cash, a silver gilt image, and 5*d* for votive candles.[63] The Woolpit cult is first attested in a mandate issued by the Bishop of Norwich in about 1211.[64] The devotion is reported to have centred in part upon a holy well, 'the Lady's Well', which still exists, sited some distance to the north-east of the church. There is no evidence, however, that there was ever a building near the well, and the focal location at the shrine of Our Lady of Woolpit was undoubtedly the parish church, where an image of the Virgin was venerated, probably in a now vanished chapel on the north side of the choir.[65]

It is likely that Howard also patronised Our Lady of Sudbury, for his accounts record 'your offering at Sudbury 4*d*' in March 1482.[66] Mention of 'my lord's offering at Our Lady' in 1483, when John Howard was in the vicinity of Lavenham, is also almost certainly a reference to Our Lady of Sudbury, the only significant Marian shrine in the eastern counties not specifically named in connection with Howard's tour of 1483.[67] The shrine of Our Lady of Sudbury was formerly in St Anne's chapel, which comprises the eastern half of the large south porch of St Gregory's Church, a former collegiate foundation endowed by Simon of Sudbury, Archbishop of Canterbury. No clear evidence on the point survives, but by a process of argument ex silentio it is thought that the devotion to Our Lady of Sudbury (which, like the Walsingham and Ipswich cults, has been revived in modern times) may have been a comparatively late development, dating, like the college foundation, from the reign of Richard II. The former shrine chapel survives, complete with statue niches in its east wall, one of which probably once held the cult image.

The Marian shrines of Ipswich, Woolpit and Sudbury were all in Suffolk, but John Howard also patronised two cult centres in Essex, both of which were dedicated to the cult of the Holy Cross. Howard went to Waltham Abbey (home of the Holy Cross of Waltham) in February 1463/4,[68] and on 27 August 1463 his accounts record his offering of 8d at Dovercourt, a small shrine which pilgrims frequented to honour the Holy Rood of Dovercourt. Eighteen years later, on 5 May 1481, Howard's second wife, Margaret Chedworth, made an offering of 4d at the same place.[69] Eighteen years may seem a long gap, but there are no surviving Howard records for the years 1469–80. It is probable that there were other offerings for which no evidence now survives. The focus of attention was the Holy Rood of Dovercourt, atop the rood screen in All Saints' Church. Pilgrims had resorted to this crucifix for many years, and they were estimated to generate an annual income for the parish of £10.[70]

Although the principal focus for Dovercourt pilgrims was the great crucifix above the rood beam, an important secondary focus was the small chapel on the south side of the nave, directly in front of the rood screen.[71] Indeed, the impracticability of allowing a stream of pilgrims to mount and descend the rood stair (which is very narrow) means that most Dovercourt pilgrims must have prayed and offered their votives in this chapel. Pilgrims from afar were probably accommodated in the nearby 'Cross House'.[72]

At the Dovercourt rood's destruction in 1533,[73] before incinerating the effigy, its destroyers removed the clothing with

which it was adorned, and sent this to Thomas Rose, curate of
Hadleigh, who burned it. It was and is a custom for an image
which constitutes the focus of a significant pilgrimage cult
sometimes to be dressed with rich clothing, specially made to
fit the figure. This was clearly the pre-Reformation practice at
Dovercourt, and it was endorsed and funded by Lord Howard,
for on 25 February 1482 Thomas Dalamar recorded that 'I took
Hew Wryte, for dressing of the rood at Dovercourt 21s, with
xxx sterys of gold, prise viijd. a piece'.[74] Twenty-one shillings
would have purchased about two yards of velvet. The stars were
presumably to be sewn on like spangles. Since no subsequent
records of the purchase of clothing for the Rood of Dovercourt
survive, it is possible that it was the robe supplied by Howard
which was destroyed in 1533. A fifteenth-century pilgrim
badge at Bodiam Castle, Sussex, depicts a rood whose *corpus* is
apparently robed in a dalmatic with two orphreys, suggesting
the probable appearance of the Holy Rood of Dovercourt.

It seems that Howard's ships may also have enjoyed the ben-
efits of religion. On 22 April 1466 he paid for two yards of
ash for 'a lantern and a stock for an image of Our Lady, 3d'.
Since this purchase is included with a list of supplies bought
in connection with the fitting out of the caravel which he was
building, the implication is that this post, intended to support
an image of the Virgin, together with a votive light, was to
constitute part of the ship's furnishings.[75]

Howard's participation in the social life surrounding the
practice of religion, while it may not reveal much about his
faith, does add to our knowledge of his character. The festivities
associated with major religious festivals were an important and
colourful part of medieval life, and John Howard's accounts
take special note of the now defunct custom of the Hockday
(Hokeday), which was kept on or about the quindene of Easter
(the second Sunday after Easter).[76] At Hocktide money was
extracted from passers-by. This was particularly done to members of the opposite sex, so that, for example, women took
men prisoner and held them to ransom. The money collected

went to parish funds. There were also games which centred on the hockerope and involved a tug-of-war with rival teams.

Easter Day in 1464 fell on 1 April. Two weeks later, on Sunday 18 April 1464, Sir John Howard kept Hocktide at his home in Stoke-by-Nayland, followed by a visit to nearby Sudbury. His accounts record 'to the Hokkepot at Stoke, 12*d*. ...[and] the same day in Hokkynge at Sudbury, 16*d*.'[77] Presumably Sir John had been captured by the women in both places and had to ransom himself. On Tuesday 22 April 1466, when he seems to have been staying in Harwich or Dovercourt, Howard was evidently caught again, and gave the women 'for hokkenge' 20*d*.[78] The picture that emerges from these brief accounts is of a good-natured man, who entered cheerfully into the boisterous but charitable festivities of the local populace.

Another social aspect of religious observance was the membership of religious guilds. This was popular in the fifteenth century, and John Howard seems to have belonged to at least one of these. On 1 July 1464 his accounts record a payment 'for my dinner for the brotherhood of the guild of St John'. The date is probably significant, for 24 June was the Feast of the Nativity of St John the Baptist, in whose honour this particular guild was presumably named. Membership of a guild of St John – who was his name-saint – was particularly apposite in Howard's case. No location is given for the guild in question. However, there were guilds of St John in both Colchester and Stoke-by-Nayland. Alternatively, it may perhaps have been the guild of St John the Baptist in Clare, a town with which John Howard is known to have had connections through his employment as steward of the honour of Clare by the dowager Duchess of York.[79] The Stoke-by-Nayland guild of St John seems the most likely candidate in this case, for it was later mentioned in the will of Howard's widow, Margaret Chedworth. She left 20*s* to this guild with the proviso that it should keep her obit and pray for her.[80]

Howard's one well-documented bereavement provides an interesting mixture of evidence in respect of his and his family's

religious belief and practice. Not unnaturally we find the standard ceremonies which surrounded a fifteenth-century death.
We should also note Howard's curious failure to take advantage
of one potential opportunity for a public display of wealth and
family pride, for he neglected to commission a tomb monument for his wife.[81] On Monday 30 September 1465, the first
Lady Howard (Catherine de Moleyns) had herself given the not
inconsiderable sum of 5s. to the Greyfriars in Colchester.[82] She
was clearly already seriously ill at this time. Another entry for the
same date records the purchase of medicine for her in Colchester,
together with sugar candy, water of honeysuckles and wine (also,
no doubt, intended as remedies). Catherine had bought medicine previously from John Clerke, a London apothecary (with
whom she had settled an account in the sum of 16s 8d at the
end of March 1464/5).[83] More medicine was bought for her the
following month in Ipswich.[84] All was ineffectual, however, and
she died, probably on Tuesday 12 November 1465. The following
day her widower sent 40s to the Colchester Greyfriars in payment for a trental of masses for the repose of her soul.

The death of the first Lady Howard gave rise to inevitable
expenditure related to her funeral costs and the well-being
of her soul. A further entry in the accounts on 13 November
recorded the expenditure of 1d on a pound of wax,[85] an essential ingredient for the candles which would burn about her
hearse. Agnes Baynard, Lady Howard's servant, was reimbursed
for the purchase of another pound of wax, and for commissioning a man called Frere to make candles.[86] On 14 November
a rather mangled entry records that 5s 8d was spent in Ipswich
on 'wax and therede [*sic*, thread, for making wicks?] for a hay
[*sic*, hearse?] against my lady's [in]terment'.[87] Two months after
Catherine's death, Sir John Howard established a chantry mass
for her soul in Cambridge. A priest called Benet Albry was to
'synge for my lady' annually for four years. The endowment
cost 40s.[88] There are records of further subsequent payments to
Benet Albry 'that syngethe at Caunbrege'. Twenty shillings, for
example, was paid to him on 23 July 1467.[89]

Catherine was buried in the parish church at Stoke-by-Nayland. As we have seen, no tomb was erected there for her during her husband's lifetime. The brass which now covers her grave was installed much later, by her son. This lack of a tomb is an interesting omission on John Howard's part if religious ostentation was one of his objectives. He is known to have spent money on improvements at the church at Stoke, and a grandiose tomb to his first wife would have offered an ideal opportunity for glorification of himself and his dynasty. The fact that Howard did not take this opportunity, and preferred to spend money on prayers for Catherine's soul, suggests that his religious priorities may have been more concerned with spirituality than with public display.

After Bosworth, Howard's body was eventually interred with his Mowbray cousins and predecessors at Thetford Priory. We have no idea what additional mortuary provisions he himself may have envisaged, but a clue may be provided by those ordained by his widow in her own will of 1490.[90] The ex-duchess requested burial at Stoke-by-Nayland, before the image and altar of Our Lady. Three hundred priests were to offer three hundred masses and diriges, and two priests were to maintain chantry masses for her soul and for those of her three husbands at Stoke-by-Nayland Church for three years. She also left the following sums to endow prayers for her soul:

20*s* to the Guild of St John at Stoke-by-Nayland
26*s* 8*d* to St John's Abbey, Colchester
26*s* 8*d* to the Benedictine nuns of Bruisyard, Suffolk
26*s* 8*d* to Clare Priory
20*s* to St Botolph's Priory, Colchester
20*s* to the Franciscan Friary at Sudbury
20*s* to the [*Dominican?*] Friary at Sudbury.

She made no provision for the erection of any permanent memorial, and none was ever commissioned.

16

Post-Mortem Moves

Proficiscere, anima christiana, de hoc mundo, in nomine Dei Patris omnipotentis, qui te creavit: in nomine Iesu Christi, Filii Dei vivi, qui pro te passus est: in nomine Spiritus Sancti, qui in te effusus est …

[Go forth, Christian soul, out of this world, in the name of God the Father Almighty who created you; in the name of Jesus Christ, Son of the living God, who suffered for you; in the name of the Holy Spirit who was poured out upon you …]
Extract from the Prayers for the Dying

After the battle of Bosworth the Duke of Norfolk's body was first transported to Leicester, where it was temporarily interred.[1] At some later stage his family made arrangements for his remains to be moved to Thetford Priory, where they seem to have been entombed in a small chapel on the north side of the nave. Although no will survives for John Howard, it seems likely that he must have expressed a wish to be buried at Thetford Priory – a building which the later Mowbray dukes of Norfolk had made their dynastic mausoleum. This presumption is based upon the fact that otherwise the parish church at Stoke-by-Nayland might have seemed a more obvious choice. In that church other immediate family members, including his first wife Catherine, were already buried, and in due course his second wife, Margaret, Duchess of Norfolk, would also be laid to rest there.

In the 1530s, however, a problem arose with the Thetford burial, when Henry VIII embarked on the Dissolution of the Monasteries. In most cases, as the monastic churches were secularised, the tombs and burials which they contained were simply abandoned in the ruins to decay. Occasionally, close family members intervened to salvage and rehouse the burials. This happened in the case of the Earl and Countess of Essex (uncle and aunt of Richard III), and also in the case of Henry VIII's sister, Mary Tudor, Queen of France and Duchess of Suffolk. These, nevertheless, were rather rare exceptions.

John Howard's grandson, Thomas, third Duke of Norfolk, found himself faced with a dilemma. A significant number of important family burials was housed in the priory church at Thetford. These included the last two Mowbray dukes of Norfolk, and the first two Howard dukes (his own father and grandfather). At first, the third Duke of Norfolk tried to persuade the king not to dissolve Thetford Priory on the gounds that members of the king's own family (his aunt, Anne of York, Thomas's own first wife, and his illegitimate son, the Duke of Richmond, who had married, or at least been betrothed to, Thomas's daughter) were among the persons buried there. When this ploy failed, Thomas petitioned for the secularised priory to be granted to him; a request to which the king acceded. Originally the third Duke of Norfolk seems to have intended to preserve the church building as his family mausoleum. However, his own long imprisonment, together with the temporary confiscation of the Thetford property, probably allowed the building to deteriorate excessively.

The third Duke of Norfolk seems to have commenced the construction of his own tomb at Thetford during his lifetime. But after his demise his heirs decided to abandon both this project and the former priory church. They moved the third duke's unfinished tomb, together with that of the Duke of Richmond, to the parish church neighbouring Framlingham Castle, where a large new sanctuary was constructed to house them. Another Howard monument had already by this time been removed from Thetford to the Howard Chapel at Lambeth. This removal to Lambeth of parts, at least of the second Howard duke's tomb, had apparently been undertaken on the orders of his widow, Agnes Tilney, who was herself buried at Lambeth in 1545.[2] However, she seems to have had only the decorative brasswork brought from Thetford. This was then affixed to a new stone base at Lambeth in order to constitute both a memorial to her late husband and also her own tomb. It seems that the old stone base of the second Howard duke's tomb was left at Thetford, with, presumably, his body still lying beneath it.

Yet no human remains were found in the former Howard vault at Thetford when this was cleared by the Office of Works in 1935.[3] It has therefore generally been assumed that the bodies of the first three Howard dukes of Norfolk, the remains of an unspecified selection of Howard consorts, and the bodies of the Duke of Richmond and his bride, were transported from Thetford to Framlingham along with the Duke of Richmond's tomb superstructure, and the incomplete tomb superstructure of the third Howard Duke of Norfolk. These two tombs now stand to the north and south respectively of the high altar at Framlingham. The vaults beneath these two monuments were opened in 1841. A contemporary manuscript account exists of what was discovered, and a transcript of this was published for the first time by the present writer in 2008. It was written by Revd J.W. Darby, the Framlingham Church reader, who was present at the opening of the vaults.[4] Darby's account of the Framlingham investigations was in the form of a letter, addressed to an unknown recipient. It states that the tombs were explored two days after Easter Sunday in 1841. The vaults beneath the monuments were opened, and the human remains interred there were subject to a somewhat rudimentary examination. Darby's manuscript makes frustrating reading. There is much that one would like to know, which he does not tell us. It is, however, the only extant description of the contents of these two vaults.

Six bodies were discovered: two in the northern vault and four in the southern. It seems clear that these were the remains of:

John Howard, first Duke of Norfolk;
Thomas Howard, second Duke of Norfolk;
Thomas Howard, third Duke of Norfolk;
Anne of York, daughter of Edward IV and first wife of the
    third Howard duke;
Lady Mary Howard, daughter of the third duke;
Henry Fitzroy, Duke of Richmond, illegitimate son of
    Henry VIII and betrothed to Lady Mary Howard.

All of these bodies, with the exception of that of the third duke, had originally been buried at Thetford Priory, and they had presumably been transported to Framlingham from Thetford together with the two tomb superstructures.

Darby's account describes how, on Tuesday 13 April 1841, the vault beneath the tomb of the Duke of Richmond was opened first. The complete body of a young man was discovered, wrapped in cere cloth, and originally enclosed in a wooden coffin which had decayed. This was identified as the remains of the seventeen-year-old Henry Fitzroy, Duke of Richmond, illegitimate son of Henry VIII and Elizabeth Blount.

Beside this, in the same vault, lay a second body, 'wrapped in sheet lead. On cutting through the lead near the place where there were three folds of lead, the skull of an older person presented itself – if we may judge from the state of the teeth. There was a large hole in the front of this skull, as if the head must have had some severe blow at some time or other. The hair was in a good state of preservation, and was of a fair or sandy colour'. It seems that only the head area of the lead sheeting was cut open, and that no further examination of the body took place. Darby specifically stated that the gender of these bones was not established. Nevertheless, he went on to speculate that they might be 'the body of the Duke of Norfolk slain at Bosworth, when an arrow pierced his brain'. Darby's evidence for this identification seems to have comprised the age of the individual and the apparent cause of death. However, the fact that the remains were not apparently embalmed (since he speaks of a skull) and were enclosed in lead may constitute additional supporting evidence. If the first duke's body was initially interred unembalmed at Leicester, then dug up some weeks or months later for removal to Thetford, enclosing it in lead would probably have been a good idea. It is also likely that its soft tissue would have disappeared, leaving only bones and hair. An alternative possibility is that a body with a damaged skull (the crown being detached), which was found in the southern vault, might have been that of the Bosworth duke.

Sadly, there seems to be little immediate prospect of clarifying the situation by opening the vaults again and subjecting the remains to a more thorough and careful examination. There is currently no obvious entrance within the chancel to either of the vaults opened in 1841. An extensive restoration of the church was carried out during the period 1888–1909.[5] Among other changes this work completely replaced the flooring around the tombs, and the new flooring allows no visible means of access to the vaults. Nevertheless, should an occasion for reopening either or both of these vaults ever present itself, further examination of the remains would be highly desirable. It might then be possible to confirm the last resting place of John Howard, first Duke of Norfolk, and to finally determine how he met his death at the battle of Bosworth.

Appendix 1

The 'Gregory's' Dispute: Cecily Neville's Draft Letters

Letter 1

Cecilie, mother &c, to the justices of peas, sheriffs, constables, bailiffs and all others the Kenges ministers in the c[ounty] of E[ssex], gretyng:

Where now late, that is to sey the Sonday [*blank*] day of Fevers the xiij yere[1] of our most dere and biloved son E[dward] the iiijth, by the grace of God Kyng of Yngland and of Fraunce and Lord of Irlond, oon Thomas Wethiale[2] by a feyned pretence with others entered in to the londe of our welbiloved servant J[ohn] P[rince], called 'Gregoryes', contrarie to the lawes and peas of our said son, and incontinent, therof enfeoffed our right dere biloved son, R[ichard], Duc of G[loucester], with others, souly for maintenance of the said feyned title, as we be credibly enfor med. Wherof pitefull compleynt aswell unto us as to our seid son the duc of G[loucester] on the bihalf of our seid servant Joh[n] P[rince] hath be made. And we both therunto takyng respect and tendre consideracion, have comuned togiders, and for paccificcie of bothe partiers, be concluded that aswell two of our lerned counseill to be elect by our said servant, as two of the lerned counseill of our seid son the duc of G[loucester] to be elect by the seid Th[omas], shall have the title and enteresse of both

the same partiers in the seid londe in examynacion, accordyng
unto conscience and to the Kynges lawes, the same our son
permittyng us nothyng to doo or maintene them,[3] whether
our both counseill juge fynally the seid title or not, but suffre
the Kynges lawes for to have there verry cource after the due
ordre of the same. Yeven &c.[4]

Letter 2

Trusty and welbeloved we grete you well. And forasmy-
che as we and our right dier said entierly welbeloved son of
Gloucester ar fully agried that the mater betwex our welbeloved servant, John Prince, and our Thomas Withiale, be put in
the determynacion of John Catesby and Roger Towneshend
(elect and named be us) and of Guy Fawefox[5] and Sulyard
or elles Pigot[6] (named and ellect be our said son) we be fully
acertayned ye will confourme you to the said appoyntement,
and when we wrot unto you but late for the said mater, we
be credibly enformed ye be well disposed theron, and the
bothe[?] at the contemplacion of us, wherfor we thank you.
And for the contynuaunce of the same, if ther be any thing
we may doo for you herafter, ye shall fynd us right agreable to
your desir. Yeven, &c, the xxij day of March.[7]

Appendix 2

Parliamentary Representatives for Ipswich and Colchester during the Yorkist Period.[1]

Ipswich

1460–61	Richard Fellow, merchant, of Ipswich, ex-bailiff, Mowbray client, and William Baldry, merchant, of Ipswich, ex-bailiff.
1463–65	William Worsop Esq., of Ipswich, lawyer, and John Loppam of Ipswich.
1467–68	John Wymondham senior, Esq., of Felbridge and Norwich (father of John Howard's son-in-law), and James Hobart, gentleman, of Hales, Loddon, Norfolk, lawyer, and Mowbray and Howard client.
1470–71	Thomas Sampson, gentleman, of Playford, servant of the Duke of Norfolk.
1472–75	William Worsop Esq., of Ipswich, lawyer, and John Walworth junior of Ipswich, ?lawyer.
1478	James Hobart, gentleman, of Hales, Loddon, Norfolk, lawyer, and Mowbray client, and John Tymperley junior, Esq., of Hintlesham, son-in-law of Sir John Howard.
1483 (Jan.)	James Hobart, gentleman, of Hales, Loddon, Norfolk, lawyer, and former Mowbray client and Howard client, and John Tymperley senior,

Esq., of Hintlesham, former Mowbray client and
father-in-law of Jane Howard.

1483 (June)   John Tymperley junior, Esq., of Hintlesham, son-
in-law of John Howard, Duke of Norfolk, and
Roger Wentworth of Codham, Essex, cousin of
John Howard, Duke of Norfolk.

1484   Benet Caldwell of Ipswich and Southwark,
lawyer, and Thomas Baldry of Ipswich.

Colchester

1460–61   John Bishop of Colchester and Springfield,
lawyer.[2]

1467–68   William Ford of Colchester and Hadleigh
(Suffolk), clothmaker and ex-bailiff,[3] and John
Butler of Colchester.[4]

1470–71   John Butler of Colchester, ex-bailiff (see above).

1472–75   John Wright, of Colchester, ex-bailiff and
lawyer,[5] and John Butler of Colchester, ex bailiff
(see above).

1478   Richard Marks of Colchester, ex-bailiff,[6] and
Thomas Smith of Colchester, ex-bailiff.[7]

1484   John Ellis of Colchester (born Witham, lived
Mile End) and John Virtue of Colchester.

Appendix 3

1483: The Calendar of the Year of the Three Kings

JANUARY

S	M	T	W	Th	F	S
			1	2	3	4
5	6	7	8	9	10	11
12	13	14	15	16	17	18
19	20	21	22	23	24	25
26	27	28	29	30	31	

FEBRUARY

S	M	T	W	Th	F	S
						1
2[1]	3	4	5	6	7	8
9	10	11	12[2]	13	14	15
16	17	18	19	20	21	22
23	24	25	26	27	28	

MARCH

S	M	T	W	Th	F	S
						1
2	3	4[3]	5	6	7	8
9	10	11	12	13	14	15
16	17	18[4]	19	20	21	22
23[5]	24	25[6]	26	27	287	29
30[8]	31					

APRIL

S	M	T	W	Th	F	S
		1	2	3	4	5
6	7	8	9	10	11	12
13	14	15	16	17	18	19
20	21	22	23[10]	24	25	26
27	28	29	30			

MAY

S	M	T	W	Th	F	S
				1	2	3
4	5	6	7	8[11]	9	10
11	12	13	14	15	16	17
18[12]	19	20	21	22	23	24
25[13]	26	27	28	29[14]	30	31

JUNE

S	M	T	W	Th	F	S
1	2	3	4	5	6	7
8	9	10	11	12	13	14
15	16	17	18	19	20	21
22	23	24[15]	25	26[16]	27	28
29	30					

JULY

S	M	T	W	Th	F	S
		1	2	3	4	5
6	7	8	9	10	11	12
13	14	15	16	17	18	19
20	21	22	23	24	25	26[17]
27	28	29	30	31		

AUGUST

S	M	T	W	Th	F	S
					1	2
3	4	5	6	7	8	9
10	11	12	13	14	15[18]	16
17	18	19	20	21	22	23
24	25	26	27	28	29	30
31						

SEPTEMBER

S	M	T	W	Th	F	S
	1	2	3	4	5	6
7	8	9	10	11	12	13
14	15	16	17	18	19	20
21	22	23	24	25	26	27
28	29[19]	30				

OCTOBER

S	M	T	W	Th	F	S
			1	2	3	4
5	6	7	8	9	10	11
12	13	14	15	16	17	18
19	20	21	22	23	24	25
26	27	28	29	30	31	

NOVEMBER

S	M	T	W	Th	F	S
						1
2	3	4	5	6	7	8
9	10	11	12	13	14	15
16	17	18	19	20	21	22
23	24	25	26	27	28	29
30[20]						

DECEMBER

S	M	T	W	Th	F	S
	1	2	3	4	5	6
7	8	9	10	11	12	13
14	15	16	17	18	19	20
21	22	23	24	25[21]	26	27
28	29	30	31			

Appendix 4

Men-at-Arms of Known Origin in North Essex
and South Suffolk, Contracted to Serve John
Howard in the 1480s

John Asche junior of Nayland
Nicholas Asche of Nayland
… Baker of Bentley (brother of John)
John Baker of Bentley
John Baker of Colchester
John Baker of Harwich
John Bale of Woodbridge
William Balle of Stoke-by-Nayland
… Bando of Harwich
John Barker, the butcher, of Nayland
Richard Barker of Stoke-by-Nayland
Thomas Barker of Stoke-by-Nayland
William Baske of Hadleigh
William Bateman of Hadleigh
… Beaucham of Hadleigh
Thomas Benet of Woodbridge
John Benyngfelde of Ipswich
Thomas Bett of Stoke-by-Nayland
John Beyrde of Nayland
Richard Blomfele of Woodbridge

John Bodyvale of Stoke-by-Nayland
Alysander Boche of Ipswich
John Bosche junior of Hadleigh
Robert Bockase of Nayland
Richard Boner of Woodbridge
William Braby of Hadleigh
John Braham of Woodbridge
Thomas Brewer of Hadleigh
Ralph Broke of Nayland
Richard Bromster of Stoke-by-Nayland
John Bronde of Stoke-by-Nayland
Geoffrey Brown of Nayland
Thomas Brown of Bentley
Andrew Brownsmyth of Hadleigh
John Brownsmyth of Hadleigh
John Bryan of Nayland
William Bryan of Woodbridge
John Burgess of Harwich
Thomas Cane of Ipswich
William Clerke of Witham
... Cok of Colchester
John Cole of Woodbridge
Robert Colvyle of Woodbridge
John Companon of Woodbridge
Thomas Companon of Woodbridge
John Cooke of Harwich
John Crawe of Nayland
John Davy of Nayland
John Davy of Shelley
John Davy of Thorington Street
John Debnam of Nayland
Richard Debnam of Stoke-by-Nayland
John Edon of Stoke-by-Nayland
John Elys of Woodbridge
John Emrygalbe of Hadleigh
... Finch of Dedham

Robert Freeman of Ipswich
John Fydrygge of Woodbridge
Wiliam Fytt of Nayland
William Gam of Ipswich
John Gant of Stoke-by-Nayland
Steven Gardner of Hadleigh
Thomas Garland of Woodbridge
John Gelderscleff of Stoke-by-Nayland
Richard George of Manningtree
John Graunt of Stoke-by-Nayland
Thomas Grymstyd of Sudbury
John Hammond of Woodbridge
Robert Hardyng of Ipswich
John Harrys of Bentley
Thomas Hervy of Nayland
Robert Heyrde of Nayland
Geoffrey Hille of Hadleigh
William Isabell of Nayland
John Jacob of Woodbridge, mason
John Kenflegge of Woodbridge
Thomas Kobe of Nayland
Robert Kurtesse of Woodbridge
John Kuttyng of Stoke-by-Nayland
John Kyngam of Woodbridge
John Lalleford of Sudbury and Colchester (St John's Green?
Richard Lalleford of Colchester
Thomas Lalleford of Colchester
William Lanam of Sudbury
William Landdey of Hadleigh
Richard Langley of Stoke-by-Nayland
John Lawsell of Nayland
William Lewe of Stoke-by-Nayland
Robert Loppam of Woodbridge
Richard Lullay, trumpeter, of High Street and West Street,
     Harwich
Henry Lyghtskyrt of Nayland

Robert Lynt of Woodbridge
Thomas Mannyng of Hadleigh
John Meddowe of Hadleigh
John Myldnall of Stoke-by-Nayland
Robert Myllys of Hadleigh
William Neyte of Stoke-by-Nayland
Richard Omfrey of Stoke-by-Nayland
Robert Osburne of Woodbridge
Robert Page of Woodbridge
... Parker of Harwich
Robert Parker of Woodbridge
John Parson of Manningtree
John Partryge of Woodbridge
Robert Pashle of Hadleigh
Thomas Paskell of Hadleigh
John Payne of Stoke-by-Nayland
John Piper of Brightlingsea
Robert Porter of Stoke-by-Nayland
John Posse of Seckford Bridge
John Potest of Ipswich
John Pretunley of Woodbridge
John Profett of Nayland
Richard Purser of Stoke-by-Nayland
John Robard of Stoke-by-Nayland
John Roote of Nayland
Nicholas Roote of Nayland
John Roper of Nayland
Richard Roper of Nayland
Robert Rynham of Hadleigh
Richard Seyman of Hadleigh
John Sheldrake of Stoke-by-Nayland
Robert Sheldrake of Nayland
Robert Sherman of Stoke-by-Nayland
John Shipman of Frere Street, Colchester
Robert Shipman of Frere Street, Colchester
Thomas Shott of Stoke-by-Nayland

Richard Skinner of Higham
Chamberleyne Smith of Nayland
Thomas Smith of Ipswich
John Smyth of Stoke-by-Nayland
John Sparlyng of Nayland
Thomas Sperys of Hadleigh
John Spore of Nayland
John Sporeman of Ipswich
John Standbanke of Ipswich
William Stonard of Hadleigh
John Stondard of Ipswich
Thomas Strotton of Ipswich
William Sugle of Hadleigh
Robert Sympson of Colchester
Thomas Taverner of Hadleigh
John Tayler, the fuller, of Stoke-by-Nayland
John Thornam of Woodbridge
Roger Tokelove of Woodbridge
William Tokelove of Woodbridge
John Toplyn of Hadleigh
Richard Turner of Stoke-by-Nayland
William Warde of Hadleigh
John Waryn of Nayland
William Wegenalle of Hadleigh
Richard Wellys of Stoke-by-Nayland
Thomas Wellys of Hadleigh
… Wheler of Bentley
John Whitefoot of Stoke-by-Nayland and Colchester, burgess
    of Colchester
John Wigan of Stoke-by-Nayland
Richard Yngolde of Stoke-by-Nayland

Notes

1. A Suffolk Gentleman

1. *CPR* 1452–1461, p. 678. Howard had on one previous occasion in 1452 been sent by Henry VI to promote friendship between his father-in-law, Lord Moleyns, and John Clopton: PL, vol. 2, pp. 79–80. He also served in the war in France 1452–53: CP, vol. 9, p. 610.

2. See C. Richmond, 'Mowbray, John [VI], third Duke of Norfolk' (*ODNB*).

3. A. Crawford, 'Howard, John' (*ODNB*); J. Ashdown-Hill, 'The Lancastrian Claim to the Throne', *Ric.* 13 (2003), pp. 27–38; J. Ashdown-Hill, *The Dublin King* (Stroud, 2015), p. 67.

4. 'One of the richest peers in the kingdom', Crawford, 'Howard, John' (*ODNB*, vol. 28, p. 390).

5. John de Vere, 12th Earl of Oxford (husband of Elizabeth Howard), and his eldest son, Aubrey, were executed in 1461. His younger son, John, was later allowed to succeed to the earldom, but was arrested and briefly imprisoned for plotting against Edward IV in 1468. The 13th earl subsequently seems to have been involved in the plots of the Earl of Warwick. In 1470 he joined Margaret of Anjou in France, returning to England on the restoration of Henry VI. He fled again when Edward IV returned. H. Castor, 'Vere, John de, twelfth Earl of Oxford'; S.J. Gunn, 'Vere, John de, thirteenth Earl of Oxford' (*ODNB*).

6. For details of the Moleyns family and their title see Θ, subsection 2.3.1.

7. J.M. Robinson, *The Dukes of Norfolk: a quincentennial history* (Oxford: OUP, 1982), p. 4. Robinson believes that he may have fought at Agincourt, though no evidence is cited for this opinion.

8. R. Archer, 'The Mowbrays, Earls of Nottingham and Dukes of Norfolk to 1432' (unpublished D. Phil thesis, Oxford, 1984), pp. 179–81, argues forcefully that Margaret Mowbray was the first Mowbray Duke of Norfolk's youngest daughter, the eldest being Elizabeth, Countess of Suffolk (who had no children and became a nun) while the second

was Isabel, Lady Ferrers (later Lady Berkeley). Archer's evidence for this conclusion seems to be chiefly the fact that in 1483, following the extinction of the direct Mowbray line, Richard III awarded 'the title which was of elder creation, namely the earldom of Nottingham' to the Berkeley co-heirs. Against this one must set the undoubted fact that the Howard co-heir was awarded the significantly higher rank of Duke of Norfolk, together with the hereditary post of Marshal of England, considerations which possibly leave room for continued speculation regarding the relative seniority of Margaret and Isabel.

9. Subsequently, following Sir Robert Howard's death, Lady Margaret remarried. Her second husband was an old family friend and connection, Sir John Grey of Ruthin. It is as Lady Grey that she appears in some of the Howard accounts.

10. Archer claims this inference is reinforced by the date of the marriage, which she states coincided with the dowager Duchess of Norfolk's last illness. This seems unlikely to be the case. The dowager Duchess of Norfolk died on 8 July 1425, but Robert and Margaret seem to have married three or four years earlier. The coolness (if it existed) could equally have been associated with Elizabeth Fitzalan's remarriages and the births of further children. Archer considers that Margaret Mowbray's first marriage may have been a love match: Mowbrays, pp. 179–81.

11. B. *OB*, p. 99.

12. On 10 January 1426/7 he is named without any title as the recipient of property, in a conveyance by William Clopton esquire of (Long) Melford: J. *Ch.*, p. 73.

13. J. *Ch.*, pp. 75–7; December 1430 – June 1432. See also Θ, section 2.

14. Robert also had a younger full-blood brother, Henry (b.c. 1389), who is mentioned in their mother's will of 13 October 1426, TNA, PROB 11/3, ff. 49–50.

15. J. Ch., p. 80.

16. In 1476–7, for example, John Howard, shipman, prosecuted Henry Purser for debt in the Colchester courts. His guarantor was Thomas Lalleford, a member of Lord Howard's affinity. ERO, D/B5 CR 76, m. 3r. See Θ, subsection 4.3.8.

17. This mention occurs in April 1453: PL, vol. 1, p. 249.

18. IRO, HA 246/B2/498; feoffment by William Argent of Chevington to Edward, Earl of March, John Howard esquire, William Bury, Robert Cumberton, Robert Bernard and Thomas Moleyns. Like Howard himself, Robert Bernard was a well-known member of the Mowbray affinity. On the other hand, Robert Cumberton and Thomas Moleyns were members of Howard's own affinity. Both men, in fact, were related to him – and to one another – by marriage (see Θ, section 2).

19. *PL*, vol. 2, p. 239.
20. Sir Robert Chamberlain and Sir Gilbert Debenham were certainly with the king in Flanders: J. Bruce, ed., *Historie of the Arrivall of Edward IV in England* (London: Camden Society, 1838), p. 2.
21. H. Kleineke, 'Gerard von Wesel's newsletter from England, 17 April 1471', Ric. 16 (2006), pp. 66–83 (p. 80).
22. Bruce, *Arrivall*, p. 2.
23. *PL*, vol. 2, p. 406.
24. Weever's engraving of the glass more closely resembles Henry Lilly's 1637 drawing of the stained-glass figure of Sir John Howard III (which was then in the windows of the parish church at Stoke) than other representations of the Stoke-by-Nayland glass image of his more famous grandson, the first Duke of Norfolk.
25. The representation of Howard reproduced here is taken from an engraving of Vertue's painting.
26. *PL*, vol. 2, p. 120. For John Jenney see also Θ, subsection 4.14.5.
27. A.J. Pollard, 'Fifteenth Century Politics and the Wars of the Roses', *The Historian* (spring 1998), pp. 26–8 (p. 27).
28. A. Crawford, 'The Private Life of John Howard: a study of a Yorkist Lord, his family and household' in P. Hammond, ed., *Richard III: Loyalty, Lordship and Law* (Richard III and Yorkist History Trust, 1986), pp. 6–24 (p. 17), remarks that John Howard's books do not provide evidence of religious devotion. That may be true, but he certainly supported local cult centres (see Chapter 15).

2. *Black and Blue*

1. Robinson, *Dukes*, pp. 1–4.
2. This summary of the origins of Howard's client network is necessarily very brief. The subject is treated more fully in Θ.
3. C.M. Woolgar, *The Great Household in Late Medieval England* (London, 1999), p. 9.
4. Although the cloth was usually issued as measured lengths rather than made up into garments.
5. Woolgar, *Great Household*, p. 9.
6. *MEJ*, p. 245. The livery of a lord could still be worn when serving overseas.
7. John Paston wrote: 'my Lord of Norffolk gave Bernard, Broom nor me no gownys at thys seson, wherfor I awaytyd not on hym; notwythstandyng I ofyrd my servyse for þat seson to my lady, but it was refusyd, I wot by avyse. Wherfor I purpose no more to do so': *PL*, vol. 1, p. 545.
8. C.M. Chattaway, 'When is a Livery not a Livery? Distributions of Clothing at the late fourteenth century Burgundian Court', lecture presented at the MEDATS Conference, *The Development of Liveries and*

Uniforms in Europe before 1600, London, 20 May 2006.

9. See below and *PPE*.
10. Green seems to have been the Talbot livery colour, at least in the early
    fifteenth century; B. Ross, *Accounts of the Stewards of the Talbot Household
    at Blakemere,* 1392–1425 (Shropshire Record Series: University of Keele
    2003), pp. 44–5 & *passim.*
11. The grain (or kermes – the latter name being derived from the
    species of evergreen oak tree upon which it lives) is the pregnant
    female of the insect *Coccus ilicis.* It was from the dried bodies of
    these creatures that a rich crimson dye was produced [*Middle
    English Dictionary* (http://quod.lib.umich.edu/cgi/m/mec/med-
    idx?type=id&id=MED39198), also *Dictionary.com* (http://dictionary.
    reference.com/)]. The result was so long-lasting that its qualities
    ultimately became proverbial: it is the reason why we still refer to
    the inveterate as 'ingrained'. There are records of the distribution of
    crimson livery fabric to Mowbray clients, probably in preparation for
    the coronation of Queen Elizabeth Woodville (BL, Add. MS 46349,
    ff. 8r–11r; HHB, part 1, pp. 162–8). Included in such distributions
    were fellow noblemen who were not close neighbours, including the
    brother and nephew of the Duchess of Norfolk (BL, Add. MS 46349,
    f. 9v; HHB, part 1, p. 165).
12. Crawford, 'Private Life of John Howard', p. 17.
13. BL, Add. MS 46349, f. 12r; *HHB,* part 1, pp. 169–70. The wardrobe
    accounts of Edward IV show the king providing murray and blue livery
    for royal servants: *PPE,* p. 163 & *passim.*
14. Woolgar, Great Household, p. 9.
15. *MEJ,* p. 196.
16. See, for example, J. Ashdown-Hill, 'The Red Rose of Lancaster?' *Ric.*
    10, no. 133 (June 1996), pp. 406–20, and A.F. Sutton & L. Visser-Fuchs,
    'The Device of Queen Elizabeth Woodville: A Gillyflower or Pink',
    Ric. 11, no. 136 (March 1997), pp. 17–24.
17. Gothic, p. 204 and illustration, p. 205, no. 68f (BM, MME 56, 7–1, 2111).
18. A signet seal of Elizabeth Talbot, bearing the head of an elephant wear-
    ing a chain, bears also a sprig of small, five-pointed flowers (WRO,
    L1/87). It seems likely that borage flowers are intended.
19. BM, MME 1933, 3–8, 3, seated talbot hound livery badge in lead, height
    4.4cm, illustrated in Gothic, p. 204, no. 68d.
20. 'John Mowbray, Duke of Norfolk, whose cognisance was a lion
    rampant argent, for the barony of Seagrave' was referred to in con-
    temporary verses as 'the lion', or 'the white lion': F. Madden, 'Political
    Poems of the Reigns of Henry VI and Edward IV', *Archaeologia,* 29, part
    2 (1842), pp. 318–47 (pp. 341 & 345).
21. Crawford, 'Private Life of John Howard', p. 21; *HHB,* p. xxvi.

22. Richard II of England and Philip the Bold, Duke of Burgundy, both made gifts of their personal devices in this way. C.M. Chattaway, 'Looking a Medieval gift horse in the mouth. The role of the giving of gift objects in the definition and maintenance of the power network of Philip the Bold', *Bijdragen en mededelingen betreffende de geschiedenis der Nederlanden*, 114 (January 1999), pp. 1–15 (p. 4).
23. The Dunstable 'Swan' jewel is one example.
24. *MFJ*, p. 249.
25. *MEJ*, p. 286. A device in this context means a jewelled collar.
26. For full details of this evidence see Θ, subsections 1.7 and 3.4.
27. Θ, appendix 6.7.
28. Botfield, *Manners and Household Expenses of England in the Thirteenth and Fifteenth Centuries*, pp. 582–6. Crawford's 1992 reprint of the Howard accounts reproduced Botfield's text unaltered, perpetuating the error.
29. Year eight (November 1468) is the only other possible reading. I am most grateful to Heather Warne, Archivist to His Grace the Duke of Norfolk, for her assistance in re-examining the Arundel MS, and for also kindly venturing a second opinion on the reading of this year date.
30. The evidence is examined much more fully in Θ, subsection 3.4.
31. Arundel Castle MS, f. 123r (numbered p. 131); HHB, part 1, p. 586.
32. Margaret's previous husbands were Nicholas Wyfold and John Norris.
33. I am grateful to Dr Anne Crawford for this suggestion.
34. Θ, appendices 7.5, 7.6.
35. See Θ, appendix 6.7, 'Origin' column.
36. BL, Add. MS 46349, f. 10r; HHB, part 1, p. 166. An alternative possibility in this case is that the colour was related to Hew's profession (he may have been a priest or a medical doctor).
37. BL, Add. MS 46349, f. 81r; HHB, part 1, p. 290.
38. BL, Add. MS 46349, f. 127r; HHB, part 1, p. 397.
39. *PPE*, pp. iii, 156. Only Howard was given black fabric by the king.
40. Θ, subsection 2.5.1.
41. 'Item, my Lord bout v. yerdes of blak velvet, prise of the yerd xij s. whereof my Lord sent to Mastres Jane Tymperley, by his servaunt Laurence, a lyvere iiij yerdes': Soc. Ant., MS 77, f. 18; HHB, part 2, p. 312.
42. Soc. Ant., MS 77, f. 54v; *HHB*, p. 385.
43. Soc. Ant., MS 77, f. 69; HHB, part 2, pp. 412–13. This purchase dates from 1483. No day or month is recorded but the entry post-dates Howard's elevation to the dukedom. Red cloth was also purchased on this occasion but, unlike the blue fabric, it is not specifically described as 'livery'. A purchase of blue fabric (together with some red and tawny cloth) is also recorded on 28 June 1483, but the word 'livery' does not occur in that entry: Soc. Ant., MS 77, f. 66; HHB, part 2, p. 407.

3. 'The High and Mighty Princess'

1. *PL*, vol. 2, pp. 54, 120, recording the Duke of York's support for Howard's election as knight of the shire for Norfolk in the 1450s.

2. Catherine often goes under the surname 'Swynford', but this was merely the name of her first husband. It is always preferable to refer to women by their maiden surnames if these are known.

3. J.L. Chamberlayne, 'A Paper Crowne: the Titles and Seals of Cecily Duchess of York', *Ric.* 10, no. 133 (June 1996), p. 430.

4. Chamberlayne, 'A Paper Crowne', p. 430, citing Waurin, *Chroniques*.

5. *PL*, vol. 1 (Oxford, 1971), p. 165.

6. CPR 1461–1467, p. 131. 'Erbury' cannot be identified under that name. Since other references in the Patent rolls regularly pair the manor of Hundon with that of Sudbury, it seems possible that a reference to Sudbury is intended, and that a copyist's error has occurred.

7. Chamberlayne, 'A Paper Crowne', pp. 430–1.

8. During this visit Edward IV issued a writ in favour of his mother's servant, Richard Mannyng of Halstead, Essex, dated *'apud Clare octavo die mensis octubris anno regni Regis Edwardi quarti post conquestum Anglie tercio'*: J. Ashdown-Hill, 'Suffolk Connections of the House of York', *Proceedings of the Suffolk Institute for Archaeology & History,* vol. 41, part 2 (2006), pp. 199–207; also W.G. Benham, ed., The Red Paper Book of Colchester (Colchester, 1902), p. 60. The original Red Paper Book is in the Essex Record Office. It has been subject to several systems of enumeration. Edward IV's writ is on the folio variously numbered 123v, CIIIv, or 84v.

9. BL, Add. MS 46349, f. 83r; HHB, part 1, p. 295.

10. BL, Add. MS 46349, f. 85r; HHB, part 1, p. 301.

11. J. Ashdown-Hill, 'Suffolk Connections of the House of York', pp. 201–2. See also Gothic, no. 209 & plate 7.

12. For Howard's interest in the cult of the Holy Cross, see Chapter 15, and also Θ. Further evidence of Cecily's possible interest in this cult may be the fact that her daughter, Margaret of York, is reputed to have been born at Waltham Abbey, home of the shrine of the Holy Cross of Waltham.

13. *Habet regere Regem sicut vult*: Chamberlayne, 'A Paper Crowne', p. 431.

14. J.L. Laynesmith, *The Last Medieval Queens* (Oxford: OUP, 2004), p. 209, citing G.C. Macaulay, ed., The English Works of John Gower, 1900–1, I, p. 148.

15. These are *Alma Redemptoris mater* (from Advent to Candlemas), *Ave Regina caelorum* (from Candlemas to the Wednesday of Holy Week), *Regina caeli* (from Easter Sunday until the Friday after Pentecost), and *Salve, Regina* (from the Saturday after Pentecost to the Friday before Advent).

16. *CPR* 1461–1467, p. 41.

17. 30 May 1465: CPR 1461–67, pp. 41–2.

18. Chamberlayne, 'A Paper Crowne', p. 432.

19. Laynesmith, Queens, p. 209.

20. *R3MK*, p. 99.

21. IRO, HA 246/B2/498: see Chapter 1.

22. Elizabeth's remains still lie in Suffolk to this day, for she was buried at her husband's side, beneath a fine alabaster effigy in a canopied tomb on the north side of the chancel of Wingfield Church.

23. BL, Add. MS 46349, f. 83r; *HHB*, part 1, p. 295.

24. BL, Add. MS 46349, f. 12v; HHB, part 1, pp. 170–1. The intended recipient of this letter is unknown.

25. For a fuller examination of John Howard's relationship with his lawyers, see Θ.

26. Lincoln's Inn, The Records of the Honourable Society of Lincoln's Inn: The Black Books, vol. 1, 1422–1586 (London, 1897), pp. 26, 30, 34, 37, 39, 40, 48, 50, 56, 60, 63.

27. Inexplicably, the 1992 published index to *HHB* treats John Sulyard's surname as identical to that of Thomas Suward or Syward. There is, in fact, no connection.

28. See below, and also J. Ashdown-Hill, 'Yesterday my Lord of Gloucester came to Colchester ...', Essex Archaeology and History, vol. 36 (2005), pp. 212–17.

29. Arundel Castle MS, ff. 25v, 27r, 42r, 42v, 44r; HHB, part 1, pp. 481, 484, 486, 500, 502, 508. For John Butler, see Θ.

30. BL, Add. MS 46349, f. 139r; HHB, part 1, p. 402.

31. The previous legisperitus was John Grene, who seems to have held the post from 1463–71 (or perhaps until 1472). Prior to 1463 no information on Colchester legisperiti is available, and the post may, in fact, have been newly created in 1463.

32. Θ, subsection 4.13.3.

33. For the full text of these letters, see Appendix 1.

34. The fifteenth-century records contain very diverse spellings of Guy's surname, including Fawefox and even *Fowler*, but *Fairfax* seems the most likely modern form.

35. In the event, Pigot did not serve in this instance. His name is found in other contexts, however, and he was a serjeant-at-law.

36. ERO, D/DCe L76.

37. R. Horrox & P.W. Hammond, eds, *British Library Harleian Manuscript 433*, vol. 3, *second register of Edward V and miscellaneous material*, (London: Richard III Society, 1982), p. 238 (f. 332r).

38. E. Foss, A Biographical Dictionary of the Judges of England, 1066–1870 (London, 1870).

39. Foss, *Judges.*
40. Θ, subsection 4.13.1.
41. Θ, subsection 4.13.1.
42. Harwich Town Council, archives: Bundle 53/5. Although John Howard is not mentioned in this quitclaim, the manor of Barnhams was subsequently acquired by Howard servants.
43. The reference (devoid of knightly title) is probably to William Catesby the younger: the 'Cat' of the well-known doggerel against Richard III.
44. Soc. Ant., MS 76, f. 26r; HHB, part 2, p. 18.
45. Lincoln's Inn, The Black Books, vol. 1, pp. 35, 36, 38, 40, 43, 45, 51, 55, 57, 62.
46. BL, Add. MS 46349, f. 10v; HHB, part 1, p. 167.
47. BL, Add. MS 46349, f. 104v; HHB, part 1, p. 328.
48. BL, Add. MS 46349, f. 126v; HHB, part 1, p. 371.
49. Arundel Castle MS, f. 2v; HHB, part 1, p. 462.
50. Arundel Castle MS, f. 120r (actually numbered p. 125); HHB, part 1, p. 581.
51. ERO, D/DCe L63r and L64r.
52. Horrox & Hammond, eds, BL Harleian Manuscript 433, vol. 1, p. 56 (f. 18v); vol. 3, p. 191, (f. 310r).
53. Soc. Ant., MS 76, f. 114r; HHB, part 2, p. 159.
54. R3MK, p. 99.
55. C. Halsted, Richard III as Duke of Gloucester and King of England (London, 1844), vol. 2, p. 513.
56. Laynesmith, Queens, p. 178.
57. Laynesmith, Queens, p. 213.
58. A.F. Sutton and L. Visser-Fuchs, The Hours of Richard III, Stroud 1990, p. 39.
59. Sutton and Visser-Fuchs suggest that the book was loot, found after the battle of Bosworth in Richard's tent, but actually there is absolutely no evidence of this, and in any case that would not preclude the possibility that it had then passed into the hands of Cecily Neville.

4. *Father Figure?*

1. See below.
2. BL, Add. MS 46349, f. 9v; HHB, part 1, p. 165.
3. L.L. Otis, *Prostitution in Medieval Society* (Chicago and London: University of Chicago Press, 1985), pp. 15–39, 111–13. For the situation in Colchester, see Θ.
4. R.M. Karras, *Common Women* (Oxford: OUP, 1996), pp. 35–43.
5. D.W. Robertson, *Chaucer's London* (New York: John Wiley & Sons, 1968), pp. 101–4.

6. A. McCall, *The Medieval Underworld* (London: H. Hamilton, 1979), pp. 182–5.

7. Robertson, Chaucer's London, pp. 22, 58, 104.

8. BL, Add. MS 46349, f. 10r; HHB, part 1, p. 166. Brandon's residence in Southwark possibly also provided a convenient excuse for visits to the stews.

9. Robertson, Chaucer's London, p. 58.

10. C. Reeves, Pleasures and Pastimes in Medieval England (Stroud, 1995), p. 204.

11. Although details of Catherine's symptoms are not recorded it seems possible that she suffered from a persistent cough, since 'suger candy', 'wyne' and 'water of honysoclys', as well as unspecified 'medesyns', were supplied to her in 1465: BL, Add. MS 46349, ff. 86v, 87r; HHB, part 1, p. 304.

12. He was to celebrate his twenty-first birthday with ostentatious ceremony in London in October 1465: PL, vol. 1, p. 530.

13. They probably married in about 1450, when John Mowbray was about six years old and Elizabeth Talbot about seven. See J. Ashdown-Hill, 'Edward IV's Uncrowned Queen', Ric. 9, no. 139 (December 1997), p. 170, and 'The Wills of John Talbot, first Earl of Shrewsbury, and of his sons, Lord Lisle and Sir Louis Talbot', *Transactions of the Shropshire Archaeological and Historical Society* (forthcoming).

14. PL, vol. 1, p. 248.

15. Θ, appendix 6.5.

16. He was more or less of an age with his cousin, John Mowbray, 4th Duke of Norfolk.

17. On 30 April 1472 the Paston correspondence, mistaking the bride's family name, reported 'Dame Ely'beth Bowghcher is weddyd to þe Lorde Howardys soone and heyre': PL, vol. 1, p. 448.

18. For further details of 'Richard', see Θ.

19. Research by M.A. Marshall, published at second hand by Rose Skuse, 'Richard III's Children', The Rose and Crown (magazine of the Beds & Bucks Group of the Richard III Society) no. 44, July 2008, pp. 6–7, suggests that John of Gloucester was born in June 1470, and Catherine Plantagenet in September 1471, but no evidence for these dates is cited.

20. On Gloucester's illegitimate children, see P.W. Hammond, 'The Illegitimate Children of Richard III', Ric. 5 (1979–81), pp. 92–6.

21. Crawford's suggestion that it refers to 1469 cannot be correct: A. Crawford, 'John Howard, Duke of Norfolk: a possible murderer of the princes?', *Ric.* 5, no. 70 (September 1980), pp. 230–35 (p. 233).

22. J. Ashdown-Hill, 'Yesterday my Lord of Gloucester came to Colchester'.

23. This phrase in parenthesis is an instruction to the clerk.

24. 'speak of', deleted.

25. 'and I', deleted.
26. 'not sorry', deleted.
27. Arundel Castle MS, f. 119v (numbered in MS p. 124); HHB, part 1, pp. 580–1.
28. He was created Baron Howard in 1469/70.
29. Botfield, 1841, p. 580.
30. By 1467–68 Thomas Howard was in his early twenties. None of the Howard children seem to have spent long periods away from their parental home while growing up.
31. G. Morgan, The Romance of Essex Inns (Letchworth, 1963), p. 26. Morgan cites no earlier source for this tradition.
32. BL, Add. MS 46349, ff. 143v – 146r; HHB, part 1, pp. 413–19. As we have seen, the Howard livery was not green. At this period it was black. It was later changed to blue. See Chapter 2.
33. The livery colour of the Duke of Gloucester at this stage of his career is unknown, but like his brother Clarence, he presumably had his own livery, which will have been different from that of the king. On the occasion of a royal visit to Coventry by the future Edward V, blue and green liveries were provided: M.D. Harris, *The Coventry Leet Book* (London, 1907–13), pp. 390–4.
34. At least, Clarence seems to have been thought to hold some sway with Norfolk: see PL, vol. 1, pp. 344–5, 403–4.
35. PL, vol. 2, index.
36. PL, vol. 1, pp. 447, 468; vol. 2, pp. 406, 432.
37. BL, Add. MS 46349, f. 16v; Arundel Castle MS, f. 26r; HHB, part 1, pp. 175, 482. The livery colours in question are not recorded.
38. R3MK, p. 26.
39. PL, vol. 1, p. 201.
40. For these conflicts, see PL, vol. 1, pp. 199, 392; vol. 2, pp. 235, 239.
41. PL, vol. 1, pp. 270, 282. The contents of the Paston correspondence are not invariably completely accurate.
42. PL, vol. 2, p. 277.

5. *'Trusty and Well-Beloved'*
1. *PL*, vol. 2, p. 393.
2. *CPR 1461–1467*, p. 28.
3. *CPR 1461–1467*, p. 203.
4. *CPR 1461–1467*, pp. 559, 568, 573. These included 22 March 1463: commission of array, Essex *CPR 1461–1467*, p. 277; 3 May 1464: commission of enquiry, *CPR 1461–1467*, p. 347; 11 June 1464: commission of enquiry, *CPR 1461–1467*, p. 348; 15 December 1464: commission of enquiry,

Norfolk and Suffolk, *CPR 1461–1467*, p. 390; 29 October 1466: commission to make arrests, *CPR 1461–1467*, p. 553.

5. *PL*, vol. I, p. 291.

6. *CPR 1467–1477*, p. 171.

7. 12 February: *CPR 1467–1477*, p. 199.

8. 4 March 1470: *CPR 1467–1477*, p. 204.

9. *PL*, vol. i, p. 441.

10. *CPR 1467–1477*, p. 387, present writer's italics. There was yet another pardon on 20 May 1475, *CPR 1467–1477*, p. 516.

11. *CPR 1467–1477*, pp. 494, 608, 613, 622, 631.

12. *CPR 1467–1477*, p. 605. 'Kyrklod' is probably Kirkley Roads, a 'natural' harbour between Yarmouth and Lowestoft. I am grateful to Dr Herbert Eiden for this suggestion. See H. Eiden, '*In der Knechtschaft werdet ihr verharren* – ': *Ursachen und Verlauf des englischen Bauernaufstandes von 1381* (Trier: Verlag Trierer Historische Forschungen), pp. 340–4; N. Saul, 'Local Politics and the Good Parliament' in *Property and Politics: Essays in Later Medieval English History*, ed. T. Pollard (Gloucester: Sutton, 1984), pp. 156–71, esp. p. 156.

13. 15 November: *CPR 1476–1485*, p. 22.

14. *CPR 1476–1485*, pp. 50, 111, 112, 183–4.

15. *PL*, vol. 2, pp. 117, 119–21.

16. Sir Thomas Tyrell of Heron (1442, 1445, 1447, 1449, 1459, 1470); William Tyrell junior, Esq., of Beeches in Rawreth (1449, 1450, 1455); Thomas Tyrell, Esq., of Heron (1478, 1483 – January 1484); Sir James Tyrell (1483 – June)

17. William Tyrell, Esq., senior, of Gipping.

18. *HP Biog*.

19. N. Bacon, *The Annalls of Ipswiche* (London, 1654; reprinted Ipswich, 1884), p. 121. This was recorded on 15 April 1463, so the reference is presumably to John Tymperley II. See Θ, subsection 2.5.1. Ipswich had something of a fifteenth-century tradition of electing Tymperleys: John Tymperley III was elected in 1483; his grandfather had been MP for Ipswich in 1455; and either his grandfather or his father had been elected in 1459, as well as to the Yorkist Parliament meeting in Coventry and to the Parliament of 1460.

20. See Appendix 2. No information survives in respect of Colchester MPs for the parliaments of 1469, January 1483, June 1483 and November 1483.

21. 'There were two types of sanctuary in medieval England.' Any church could offer some degree of protection, but 'some abbeys and minsters had special rites of sanctuary ... anyone who took refuge in such a sanctuary could remain there with impunity for life'. R.F. Hunnisett,

The Medieval Coroner (Cambridge: CUP, 1961; reprinted Florida 1986), p. 37. Colchester Abbey had been granted such extraordinary rights of sanctuary in 1109 [J.C. Cox, *The Sanctuaries and Sanctuary Seekers of Mediaeval England* (London: Allen, 1911), p. 197] but these rights seem to have been contested. Abbot Ardeley appealed to Henry VI for the abbey's rights of sanctuary to be confirmed, on the grounds that during the king's incapacity, the community at St John's had expended much time and effort in praying for his recovery, and on 13 May 1453 the king obliged: *CPR 1452–1461*, p. 80.

22. BL, Add. MS 46349, f. 25v; *HHB*, part 1, p. 186.

23. The surname Stansted is otherwise unrecorded in Colchester at this period, implying that the new abbot was born elsewhere, and indeed, Stansted, like Ardeley, could be a toponym, related to either Stanstead Mountfichet, in Essex, or Stansted in Suffolk. Of the two the latter seems the more likely point of origin for the new abbot. It is known that Sir John Howard had some connection with the manor of Stansted.

24. Howard himself, however, was summoned to this Parliament: Crawford, 'Howard, John' (*ODNB*). Abbot Stansted did sit in subsequent Yorkist Parliaments. It is a fact that some religious houses were partisan. Clare Priory, in Suffolk, for example, clearly favoured the house of York, and deployed the not inconsiderable writing talents of Friar Osbern Bokenham OSA in support of this cause.

25. 'Lovell our dog' of the famous 'Cat and Rat' rhyme.

26. The duchess (possibly for political reasons) did not mention St John's Abbey in her own will. However, her executor, the dean of her chapel, Richard Lessy, evidently acting upon her instructions, stipulated in his will of February 1498: 'In primis I owe to the hous of saynte Johannes sayntuare in Colchester for my Ladies dettis – whom god pardonn – xxj li the which summe I will be made and spent to the bieng of v chales to be geven to the saide hous of colchestre to praie for my Ladie and for me as procuratoure of this benifete so that the chalesis be Clerely worth xxj li. Beside the facioun the which my will is: to paie of my owne coste and charge': TNA, PROB 11/11 f. 200r. I am grateful to Marie Barnfield for drawing my attention to Lessy's will, throughout which 'my Lady' refers to the Duchess of York.

27. *CPR 1494–1509*, pp. 124, 126.

28. Thomas Montgomery was another: *PL*, vol. ii, p. 239.

29. *CPR 1461–1467*, p. 124.

30. *CPR 1461–67*, p. 10 (reiterated 23 February 1462, *CPR 1461–1467*, p. 119).

31. *CPR 1461–1467*, p. 27.

32. *CPR 1461–1467*, pp. 111, 187, 200, 323, 458.

33. *PL*, vol. ii, pp. 277, 376.

34. *CPR 1461–1467*, p. 527.

35. *CPR 1467–1477*, pp. 98, 132.

36. Before 4 March 1470: *CPR 1467–1477*, p. 204.

37. *CPR 1467–1477*, pp. 538, 545, 547.

38. www.heraldica.org/topics/orders/garterlist.htm (consulted September 2008).

39. 3 August 1478, grant to Lord Howard of the manor of Whymple, Devon (late of George, Duke of Clarence): *CPR 1476–1485*, p. 120.

40. 10 February 1479: *CPR 1476–1485*, p. 137.

41. A 'wardship' is the custody of the heir to an estate during his minority, with the guardian taking a share of the income of the estate. A 'marriage' is the right to arrange the marriage of such a minor heir.

42. *HHB*, pp. xxvi–xxvii.

43. Soc. Ant., MS 76, f. 130r; MS 77, f. 18r; *HHB*, part 2, pp. 181, 312.

44. BL, Add. MS 46349, ff. 32r, 48r; *HHB*, part 1, pp. 194, 222.

45. BL, Add. MS 46349, f. 145v; *HHB*, part 1, p. 418.

46. BL, Add. MS 46349, f. 126r; *HHB*, part 1, p. 371.

47. BL, Add. MS 46349, ff. 120v, 121r, 125r, 133v; Arundel Castle MS, f. 129r; *HHB*, part 1, pp. 362, 368, 389, 596. The record of 20 February 1466/7 probably looks back to the visit of the previous summer.

48. BL, Add. MS 46349, f. 141r–v; *HHB*, part 1, pp. 407–8.

49. C. Weightman, *Margaret of York, Duchess of Burgundy, 1446–1503* (Gloucester, 1989), p. 45. It is certain that Howard was a member of the wedding party (see below). This would account for the lack of personal accounts for him covering this period in the Household Books.

50. H. Beaune and J. d'Arbaumont, eds, *Mémoires d'Olivier de la Marche*, 4 vols, Paris 1883–88, vol. 3, p. 111. The name of John Howard ('Jehan Hauvart') is preceded by those of the queen's brothers, Lord Scales and Sir John Woodville, Sir Humphrey Talbot ('frere de la duchesse de Norfolck') and Sir Thomas Montgomery.

51. Weightman, *Margaret*, p. 59.

52. Arundel Castle MS, f. 123v; *HHB*, part 1, p. 587.

53. Arundel Castle MS, f. 93v; *HHB*, part 1, p. 557.

54. 11 December 1462: *PL*, vol. I, p. 523.

55. *PL*, vol. 2, pp. 234–5.

56. *PL*, vol. 1, pp. 199, 392.

57. *PL*, vol. 1, pp. 270, 274, 282.

58. *CPR 1467–1477*, p. 204.

59. *PL*, vol. 2, p. 406.

60. Θ, subsection 1.6.

61. Charles was killed at the battle of Nancy in 1477.

62. Charles the Bold had been Edward IV's brother-in-law and ally.

63. Soc. Ant., MS 76, pp. 7–13; *HHB*, part 2, pp. 9–13. All of the indentures with Howard are likewise for sixteen weeks.

64. *PL*, vol. 2, p. 442.
65. Soc.Ant., MS 77, ff. 102v, 103v; *HHB*, part 2, pp. 468, 470.
66. See Appendix 4.
67. Soc.Ant., MS 76, f. 105v; *HHB*, part 2, pp. 144–5.
68. With the exception of Frosdam [William Frodsham] who has eleven mentions, none of these men are named less than fifteen times in the extant Howard accounts. For Frodsham we know only that he served in the Scottish campaign and that he regularly received wages. Brief career details are given below for all the others with the exception of John Mersch. Mersch is omitted because more than one Howard servant seems to have borne this name, and it is difficult to disentangle the references. See, however, Θ, subsection 4.8.
69. BL, Add. MS 46349, f. 87r; *HHB*, part 1, p. 304. The sums varied, but a payment of 5s. was not unusual.
70. Norfolk and Norwich Archaeological Society, shelf 2, no. 6, quoted in *HHB*, p. xli. He also received clothing on occasions.
71. Payments to him are recorded in a list of naval expenses relating to Harwich in 1466: BL, Add. MS 46349, ff. 110v, 111r; *HHB*, part 1, pp. 338–9.
72. Bows were supplied on 18 April 1466, at or near Manningtree, on 2 June 1466, at Sandwich, and on 19 July 1467, probably in London: BL, Add. MS 46349, ff. 112v, 119r, 145r; *HHB*, part 1, pp. 343, 357, 417. There are further references to bows supplied to Wady in the Arundel Castle MS, f. 132r; *HHB*, part 1, pp. 600–1.
73. Arundel Castle MS, f. 86r; Soc.Ant., MS 76, ff. 7r, 42v; *HHB*, part 1, p. 548; part 2, pp. 6, 45.
74. Soc.Ant., MS 76, f. 200r; *HHB*, part 2, p. 267.
75. Soc.Ant., MS 77, f. 37r; *HHB*, part 2, p. 302.
76. Soc.Ant., MS 77, f. 115v; *HHB*, part 2, p. 490.
77. Arundel Castle MS, ff. 86r, 87r; *HHB*, part 1, pp. 549, 551.
78. Soc.Ant., MS 76, p. 4 (f. 7r), f. 165v; *HHB*, part 2, pp. 5, 240.
79. Soc.Ant., MS 77, f. 115v; *HHB*, part 2, p. 490.
80. Soc.Ant., MS 76, p. 4 (f. 7r), ff. 78r, 82r, 138r, 151r (London); MS 77, ff. 14v, 30r (Christmas 1482), 49v, 58r (London), 65r, 102v; *HHB*, part 2, pp. 5, 96, 101, 194, 220, 305, 333, 375, 392, 405, 469.
81. Soc.Ant., MS 76, ff. 39v, 201r; *HHB*, part 2, pp. 41, 267.
82. Soc.Ant., MS 77, ff. 13r, 87v, 94r, 97v; *HHB*, part 2, pp. 302, 444, 453, 460.
83. Soc.Ant., MS 76, p. 4 (f. 7r), ff. 115v, 185v, 187r, 187v, 200r; *HHB*, part 2, pp. 5, 161, 254, 256, 267.
84. Soc.Ant., MS 77, ff. 102v, 107v, 108v, 115r, 115v; *HHB*, part 2, pp. 468, 475, 478, 489, 490.
85. Soc.Ant., MS 76, ff. 37r, 129v; *HHB*, part 2, pp. 36, 181.

86. Soc. Ant., MS 76, p. 4 (f. 7r), ff. 39v, 65v, 192r; *HHB*, part 2, pp. 5, 40, 77, 260–1.
87. Soc. Ant., MS 76, f. 78v, 84v, 128v; MS 77, ff. 54v, 63r; *HHB*, part 2, pp. 96, 105, 179, 386, 401. Intriguingly, he was paid for carrying an unidentified child to Stoke on 12 June 1483: Soc. Ant., MS 77, f. 63r; *HHB*, part 2, p. 401.
88. Soc. Ant., MS 77, ff. 92r, 115v; *HHB*, part 2, pp. 451, 490.
89. Soc. Ant., MS 76, p. 4 (f. 7r); *HHB*, part 2, p. 5.
90. Soc. Ant., MS 76, ff. 39v, 49v, 97r, 126v, 202r; MS 77, ff. 13v, 17r, 19v, 30r, 50r, 58r, 65r, 103r; *HHB*, part 2, pp. 41, 55, 125, 177, 269, 303, 310, 314, 334, 376, 392, 405, 469.
91. Soc. Ant., MS 76, f. 147r; *HHB*, part 2, p. 211.
92. Soc. Ant., MS 76, f. 85r; MS 77, ff. 61v, 75v, 87v, 94r; *HHB*, part 2, pp. 106, 398, 424, 444, 453.
93. Soc. Ant., MS 76, f. 134v; MS 77, f. 67v; *HHB*, part 2, pp. 188, 410.
94. 'A peir brigandines, a peir splentes, a salate, a cheff of arowes, and a jaket and a standart, a gusset': Soc. Ant., MS 76, f. 192v; *HHB*, part 2, p. 261.
95. Soc. Ant., MS 77, f. 115v; *HHB*, part 2, p. 490.
96. Soc. Ant., MS 76, f. 25r; *HHB*, part 2, p. 17.
97. Soc. Ant., MS 76, ff. 25r, 38r, 96v, 132r, 158v; MS 77, ff. 9r, 21r, 22r, 73v, 103v, 109v; *HHB*, part 2, pp. 17, 37, 125, 185, 235, 295, 318, 319, 420, 470, 479.
98. Soc. Ant., MS 76, f. 56v; *HHB*, part 2, p. 65.
99. Soc. Ant., MS 76, p. 4 (f. 7r), ff. 27r, 52v, 81r, 129r, 151r, 151v; *HHB*, part 2, pp. 5, 20, 59, 100, 180, 220, 221.
100. CHM, p. 53, bundle 39, no. 22.
101. Soc. Ant., MS 76, p. 172r; *HHB*, part 2, p. 243.
102. Soc. Ant., MS 76, p. 4 [f. 7r]; *HHB*, part 2, p. 7.
103. Soc. Ant., MS 76, p. 25r; *HHB*, part 2, p. 17. Given the fact that Lullay was a musician, pypes may in this case mean musical instruments, not barrels of wine.

6. The First English Carvel

1. C. Richmond, 'English Naval Power in the Fifteenth Century', *History*, vol. 52, no. 174, pp. 1–15 (pp. 2, 6, 8).
2. Richmond, 'English Naval Power', p. 6 and *passim*; J.D. Mackie, *The Earlier Tudors, 1485–1558* (Oxford: Clarendon, 1952), 1983, p. 210. Richmond's list of fifteenth-century English vessels (pp. 12–15) fails to mention the *Edward*.
3. Soc. Ant., MS 76, pp. 7–13; *HHB*, part 2, pp. 9–13.
4. See Chapter 7.
5. Howard's accounts for the 1460s often refer simply to 'the carvel'. Such anonymous references are taken to relate to the *Edward*.

6. From the eleventh to the thirteenth century the area in the Port of London between London Bridge and the Tower of London was the focus of ship-building. Later, ships for Henry V's fleet had been built at Smallhythe in Kent: G. Milne, 'Joining the Medieval Fleet', *British Archaeology*, no. 61 (October 2001); www.britarch.ac.uk/BA/ba61/feat2. shtml (consulted January 2008).

7. Milne, 'Joining the Medieval Fleet'.

8. P. Marsden, *Sealed by Time, the loss and recovery of the Mary Rose* (Portsmouth: Mary Rose Trust, 2003), p. 139.

9. By 1471, however, the chapel of St Nicholas in Harwich was described as a parish church: *CHM*, p. 57, bundle 39, no. 44, will of Isabella Peyton, widow.

10. L. T. Weaver, *The Harwich Story* (Dovercourt, 1975), p. 9. Murage had previously been granted to Harwich by Edward III, but the grant was revoked because Ipswich protested.

11. BL, Add. MS 46349, f. 110r; *HHB*, part 1, p. 337.

12. M. R. Eddy and M. R. Petchey, *Historic Towns in Essex: an Archaeological Survey* (Essex County Council, Chelmsford, 1983), p. 60.

13. *Historic Towns in Essex*, p. 60. However, the *Harwich Town Assessment Report*, p. 11, considers that 'the location of [the ship-building yard] is uncertain, but it was probably sited at the northern end of the town, beside the quays, as the later ship-yards were'.

14. The later Navyard Wharf is still sited to the north-east of Harwich, eastwards of the modern Kings Quay Street.

15. Milne, 'Joining the Medieval Fleet'.

16. Illustrated in the Bayeux Tapestry and on thirteenth-century port seals. G. S. Laird Clowes, *Sailing Ships, their history and development*, part 1 (London: Science Museum, 1932), pp. 45–6.

17. Laird Clowes, *Sailing Ships*, part 1, p. 48. Fore-and-after castles and a stern-mounted rudder were established by the fourteenth century, as illustrated on Edward III's gold nobles.

18. Laird Clowes, *Sailing Ships*, part 1, pp. 52–3. English 'mizen' now means the after mast, but French 'misaine' means the foremast, and this is probably the meaning in the case of Henry V's ship: Marsden, *Sealed by Time*, p. 138 [citing I. Friel, 'Henry V's Grace Dieu and the wreck in the R. Hamble near Burlesdon, Hampshire', *International Journal of Nautical Archaeology*, 22 (1993), p. 17], states that this ship was clinker-built but had three masts.

19. Richard I of England is reported as having sunk a three-masted Saracen ship as early as 1191 (Laird Clowes, *Sailing Ships*, part 1, p. 53). At that period, however, even in the Mediterranean, three-masted vessels would have been extremely unusual.

20. Laird Clowes, *Sailing Ships*, part 1, p. 54.

21. BL, Add. MS 46349, f. 106v; *HHB*, part 1, p. 333. There is also reference to a payment of six shillings to Clayse Bolard 'for his musyn' on 24 April 1466 (BL, Add. MS 46349, f. 42r; *HHB*, part 1, p. 211). By this time *musyn* clearly referred to the after (mizen) mast.

22. Laird Clowes, *Sailing Ships*, part 1, p. 56.

23. BL, Add. MS 46349, f. 37v; *HHB*, part 1, p. 199.

24. Laird Clowes, *Sailing Ships*, part 1, pp. 61–2. Apart from the fact that warships carried guns, there was no clear distinction between them and merchant ships in the fifteenth century.

25. Laird Clowes, *Sailing Ships*, part 1, p. 60. Guns were not introduced along the sides of vessels until the sixteenth century.

26. The *Christopher* of London, owned by Thomas Rogers, and the *Mary Shirborne* of Calais, are two named examples. There are numerous references to unnamed carvels. Likewise, many ships which are named in the accounts are not characterised by their style of construction.

27. There are English references to carvel-built ships from the first half of the fifteenth century, but these relate to foreign vessels. The earliest specific mention of English carvel-built ships (*PL*, vol. 2, p. 340) relates to Richard Neville, Earl of Warwick, and dates to 1 June 1458 – just a few years before Howard began building a carvel for Edward IV.

7. Innovations

1. VCH Essex, vol. 10, p. 229.

2. Soc. Ant., MS 76, ff. 51r, 109r; *HHB*, part 2, pp. 57, 151.

3. Soc. Ant., MS 77, f. 4r; *HHB*, part 2, p. 287.

4. A. Emery, *Greater Medieval Houses of England*, 3 vols (Cambridge: CUP, 1996), vol. 2, East Anglia, Central England and Wales, pp. 25–7.

5. Soc. Ant., MS 77, f. 26r; *HHB*, part 2, p. 326.

6. J. Ridgard, *Medieval Framlingham, Selected Documents 1270–1524*, Suffolk Records Society, vol. 27 (1985), p. 133.

7. D. King & D. Sylvester, eds, *The Eastern Carpet in the Western World* (London: Arts Council, 1983), p. 14.

8. King & Sylvester, *Carpets*, p. 14.

9. Framlingham Castle inventory of 1524 in Ridgard, *Medieval Framlingham*.

10. Arundel Castle MS, f. 45r; *HHB*, part 1, p. 510.

11. Soc. Ant., MS 77, ff. 51v, 61v; *HHB*, part 2, pp. 379, 398.

12. Arundel Castle MS, f. 33v; *HHB*, part 1, p. 491; Soc. Ant., MS 77, f. 18v; *HHB*, part 2, p. 312.

13. Carpet manufacture seems to have been, in origin, an eastern craft, and many of the carpets found in medieval Europe were imported. King & Sylvester, *Carpets*, p. 11.

14. BL, Add. MS 46349, f. 91v; *HHB*, part 1, p. 317. A 'garnish' comprised a dozen platters, a dozen dishes and a dozen saucers.

15. VCH Essex, vol. 9, p. 25. The surname Beche continues in Colchester into the sixteenth century. The last Abbot of Colchester, Thomas Beche (*alias* Marshall), who opposed the religious policy of Henry VIII and was put to death for the stand he took, was possibly related to this family.

16. The name John Beche figures in the list of Colchester bailiffs in 1428, 1429, 1431, 1433, 1437, 1440, 1442, 1444, 1447 and 1456. In 1456 John Beche died during his period of office as bailiff. It seems probable that these entries, covering a span of twenty-eight years, all refer to a single individual, who might have been the father or the grandfather of John Howard's pewterer.

17. ERO, D/B5 CR 73, m. 1v, where he figures as a juryman.

18. It was stated in court that he regularly offered for sale *vasa electrina confecta de falso metallo vocata metallo allaium* ('pewter vessels made of a false metal known as alloyed metal'). ERO, D/B5 CR 73, m. 1v. For *electrina* and *allaium* see *Dictionary of Medieval Latin from British Sources*, Fascicules 1 and 3.

19. Apparently the prosecution of William Beche failed to put an end to the manufacture of substandard pewter in Colchester, for in 1474 the Pewterers' Company seized offending items (thus providing what was, until now, the earliest known evidence for the existence of the pewter industry in Colchester): J. Blair and N. Ramsey, *English Medieval Industries* (London, 2001), p. 68.

20. Soc. Ant., MS 76, f. 119v; *HHB*, part 2, p. 167.

21. Soc. Ant., MS 76, f. 45r; *HHB*, part 2, p. 49.

22. See Θ, appendix 11. 'Foreigner' in this context meant not originally from Colchester, but Austyn Wogayn may also have been a foreigner in the modern sense of the word.

23. By about 1450 the spring-driven clock had also been invented, but early spring-driven timepieces were very inaccurate. 'Iron clocks and lantern clocks, hanging on the wall from a hook and prevented from moving by two sharp spurs at the back of the clock, were the first general domestic clocks. The weights hung below them and generally had to be pulled up twice a day': E. Bruton, *The History of Clocks and Watches* (London: Orbis Books, 1979), p. 47.

24. Later brass was used, giving its name to 'lantern clocks' (the term is thought to be a corruption of 'latten clocks'). Fifteenth-century brass clocks do exist. An example from the Low Countries is displayed at the British Museum.

25. B. Mason, *Clock and Watchmaking in Colchester*, England (London: County Life, 1969), p. 42.

26. Mason, *Clock and Watchmaking in Colchester*, p. 43.

27. At the very least, one of their recent forebears must have been a clock-maker.

28. 'Item solut pro reparacione orlogij homini de Colchester, ijs. iiijd.' Saffron Walden Churchwarden's Accounts, 1439–90, f. 61, cited in Mason, *Clock and Watchmaking in Colchester*, p. 43.

29. Mason misdates the repair of Howard's clock to 1483, but the event took place on 9 March in year twenty-two of Edward IV: the regnal year which ran from 4 March 1482 to 3 March 1483.

30. This clock, from Ramsey Church, is mostly intact. It is preserved in Colchester's Clock Museum. There has been some debate as to whether it dates from so early as the fifteenth century, but Mason believes it does, and suggests it was probably made in Colchester.

31. Mason, *Clock and Watchmaking in Colchester*, pp. 47–50.

8. The Howard Lifestyle

1. In earnest of their agreement, Howard paid Hill 10s.: BL, Add. MS 46349, f. 107v; *HHB*, part 1, p. 336.

2. J.A. Jephcott, *The Inns, Taverns and Pubs of Colchester* (Colchester: Bowcott, 1995), p. 215. The present High Street façade of the Red Lion dates from the rebuilding scheme carried out by Howard's grandson in about 1510. By this time the house in Colchester was evidently redundant, and was transformed from a dwelling into business premises which were then let out for profit.

3. This was while he was Earl of Surrey during the lifetime of his father (John Howard V's son), the second Duke of Norfolk.

4. For more detailed evidence on this point, see Θ, section 5.

5. BL, Add. MS 46349, ff. 50r, 53r; *HHB*, part 1, pp. 226, 231.

6. Oliver van Cach's name appears in the 1472 Colchester fealty list (Θ, appendix 11). Isabel van Cacche, presumably his wife, issued a deed in favour of William Clopton and others in 1488–89 (B.OB, p. 137).

7. BL, Add. MS 46349, ff. 50r, 53r, 67r, 72r, 92v; Soc. Ant., MS 76, ff. 118v, 141r; Soc. Ant., MS 77, f. 43r; *HHB*, part 1, pp. 226, 231, 263, 274, 319; part 2, pp. 165, 199, 359.

8. BL, Add. MS 46349, ff. 67r, 92v, 105v; Arundel Castle MS, ff. 44r, 135v; *HHB*, part 1, pp. 263, 318–19, 331, 507, 608. Wadselle's name does not occur in the 1472 Colchester fealty list (appendix 11), but he may have been dead by then.

9. Arundel Castle MS, f. 122v; *HHB*, part 1, p. 584.

10. Soc. Ant., MS 77, f. 76v; *HHB*, part 2, p. 425.

11. BL, Add. MS 46349, ff. 50r, 53r; *HHB*, part 1, pp. 226, 231. 'Peyres of breganders' or 'brigandines' were cuirasses of leather to cover the breast

and back, reinforced with metal plates. Wilkinson, *Arms and Armour*, pp. 20, 60.

12. ERO, D/B5 CR 81, mm. 4v, 5v: case of Sir Laurence Reynsforth versus John Brown, armourer. John Brown is probably identical with the John Bron named in both the 1472 Colchester Fealty list (appendix 11), and in the Oath Book entry for 1475 – where his wife's name is given as Mathilda (B.OB, p. 130).

13. BL, Add. MS 46349, f. 50r; *HHB*, part 1, p. 226. Robyn and his 'fellow' each received three shillings. One shilling was paid to the 'man'.

14. BL, Add. MS 46349, f. 48v; *HHB*, part 1, p. 222. Clayson also supplied beer and timber.

15. The surviving Howard household accounts are not, of course, a complete record.

16. On James's identity, see Θ, appendix 14.

17. On 8 May 1464 Howard added a tip of 2d, and on 18 November 1465 'my master gave him to drink, 3d.': BL, Add. MS 46349, ff. 67r, 90v; *HHB*, part 1, pp. 262, 314.

18. 6 May 1464: BL, Add. MS 46349, f. 66v; *HHB*, part 1, p. 261. Isabelle was John Howard's eldest daughter by his first wife, Catherine de Moleyns. She would have been about sixteen years old in 1464.

19. 14 July 1464: BL, Add. MS 46349, f. 72v; *HHB*, part 1, p. 274. A pair of boots for Howard usually cost about a shilling.

20. See F. Grew and M. de Neergaard, *Shoes and Pattens* (London, 1988), pp. 91–2, 101.

21. The demarcation line between cordwainers (who basically made new shoes) and cobblers (who repaired old ones) had in theory been established by a ruling of 1409, which prohibited cobblers from using new leather to replace soles or quarters, though they were permitted to 'clout' them, by attaching a sole of new leather underneath an existing sole. Complete replacement of the sole with a new leather one was reserved to cordwainers: Grew and Neergaard, *Shoes and Pattens*, pp. 89–90.

22. There were specialist patten-makers in Colchester at this period: ERO, D/B5 Cr 78, m. 38r: complaint of Wm Vangelisburgh, 'patynmaker' (attorney John Algood).

23. BL, Add. MS 46349, ff. 51r, 65v, 83r, 138r, 141v; Arundel Castle MS, f. 26v; Soc. Ant., MS 76, ff. 81r, 85v, 92r, 96r, 97r, 136r, 149r; MS 77, ff. 31v, 46v; *HHB*, part 1, pp. 228, 258–59, 295, 400, 409, 485; part 2, pp. 100, 107, 116, 124, 126, 191, 216, 336, 368.

24. Soc. Ant., MS 77, f. 12r; also *HHB*, part 2, p. 300 (which, however, contains two small errors in the transcription).

25. Soc. Ant., MS 76, ff. 26r, 48v, 106r; *HHB*, part 2, pp. 18, 54, 146. Their names were William Hyll and Robert Pynchebek (both of whom came

from Clare), Robert Rys and John Porter. See also Richard Lullay, in Chapter 5.

26. Soc. Ant., MS 76, ff. 26v, 33r, 86v; *HHB*, part 2, pp. 19, 31, 108. Two of them were called Christopher and Valantine.

27. Soc. Ant., MS 77, f. 3v; *HHB*, part 2, p. 286. The choirboys of the 1480s are named in the accounts as Little Richard, singer of the chapel, Dick of the chapel (*alias* 'Great Dick'), Little Edward, Edward, Edmond and Harry of the chapel. Little Richard seems to have been particularly favoured (see below). In 1524, on the death of John Howard's son, Thomas, second Duke of Norfolk, there was 'a great book of vellum with masses and anthems pricked 2nd folio secundus counter tenor' in the chapel at Framlingham Castle. It was valued at 66s. 8d: Ridgard, *Medieval Framlingham*, p. 150. Most of the books in the chapel were more modern, and of printed paper, but it is possible that this book dated from John Howard's lifetime.

28. The Romans had used the word *lusores* ('players') to refer to both singers and actors. This broad Latin term continued in use into the Middle Ages, and the usage passed into the various vernaculars.

29. There is secondary evidence throughout the Middle Ages for the development of dramatic 'interludes' as aristocratic entertainment. Mummers from London entertained Richard II and his court in 1377. Early fifteenth-century texts survive of 'Prefaces' written by John Lydgate, a Dominican friar, which 'call not only for disguise of the persons involved, but for the use of substantial scenic properties' (C. Ricks, ed., *The Penguin History of Literature vol. 3: English Drama to 1710* [Harmondsworth, 1971], p. 26). It is possible that Chaucer's *Franklin's Tale* contains a reference to similar entertainments: L.D. Benson, ed., *The Riverside Chaucer* (Oxford: OUP, 1987), p. 183, lines 1142–49.

30. 'For a *boke* that my lady had of' Notbem, 6s 8d, *HHB*, part 1, p. 510. (It is necessary to distinguish carefully between entries relating to a book [*boke; booke; plural bokys*] and those relating to a buck [*buk*].)

31. On 4 May 1464 Howard 'payd to John Gyldre for ij bokys, a Frenshe boke, and a Yenglyshe boke called *Dives et Pauper* xiijs. iiijd.'. On 14 January 1464/5 he paid 6s 9d to Agnes Wright for a 'booke' and just over a month later, on 22 February 1464/5, the accounts record the purchase of 'a boke conteynynge vij quayres off fyne paper' at a cost of 2s 1d (BL, Add. MS 46349, f. 66r, Arundel Castle MS, ff. 27v, 83v; *HHB*, part 1, pp. 260, 487, 547). The last of these sounds like a blank book to be written in, similar to the surviving Howard account books. Both of the surviving account books for the 1460s must, however, have been purchased earlier than 1465.

32. The surname Lympnour is, of course, simply a version of 'limner' (illuminator).

33. BL, Add. MS 46349, f. 146v; *HHB*, part 1, p. 419. Illuminated manuscripts such as the Howard Hours were produced, by the fifteenth
century, not in monastic *scriptoria* but by lay enterprises located in
larger towns and cities which could attract a wealthy clientele. Bury St
Edmunds was a noted centre for such work.

34. Arundel Castle MS, f. 143v; *HHB*, part 1, p. 620, set out here as it
appears in the manuscript.

35. *Lorne*, past participle of lesen, 'to lose': Kurath, *Middle English Dictionary*.

36. Or possibly 'with a strange spear', since *yowtyne* (= *outen*) is written as a
separate word and may therefore be the adjective, meaning 'strange' or
'foreign': Kurath, *Middle English Dictionary*.

37. Or 'But yet I keep it up'. Storen stothe could mean 'to provide support'.
However, this line is, probably deliberately, somewhat enigmatic. Almost
certainly a sexual allusion is intended, since stothe – literally 'pillar' –
also has the secondary meaning 'penis': Kurath, Lewis et al., eds, *Middle
English Dictionary*.

38. BL, Add. MS 46349, f. 48r; *HHB*, part 1, p. 221.

39. ERO, D/B5 CR 79, m. 1v. Records of the Colchester tennis court date
back to at least 1425, see VCH Essex, vol. 9, p. 63. There is no indication as to its location, but it may have been in the vicinity of Bere Lane
(Vinyard Street), where other recreational facilities such as brothels and
bear-baiting were also on offer.

40. See, for example, Soc. Ant., MS 76, f. 95r; MS 77, f. 51r; *HHB*, part 2,
pp. 122, 378.

41. 28 July 1467. BL, Add. MS 46349, f. 146v; *HHB*, part 1, p. 420. Thomas
Lympnour also illuminated Howard's manuscript commission (see
above).

42. H. Grieve, *The Sleepers and the Shadows,* vol. 1 (Chelmsford, 1988), p. 85.

43. BL, Add. MS 46349, f. 4v; *HHB*, part 1, p. 156. We have seen already that
John Howard was much better-off than his young cousin. See also L.E.
Moye, 'The Estates and Finances of the Mowbray Family', p. 14.

44. BL, Add. MS 46349, f. 85v; *HHB*, part 1, p. 301. *Langam* could be an
alternative medieval spelling of Lavenham, or it may refer to Langham
(Essex).

45. On the Friday (18 September) after Holy Rood Day (the Feast of the
Exaltation of the Holy Cross – 14 September). Arundel Castle MS, f.
132r; *HHB*, part 1, p. 601.

46. BL, Add. MS 46349, f. 148v; *HHB*, part 1, p. 423.

47. In the grounds around what is now the University of Essex. Wivenhoe
was a former de Vere manor, which Howard had obtained as a result of
the attainder of the 12th Earl of Oxford.

48. Soc. Ant., MS 76, ff. 84v–86v; *HHB*, part 2, pp. 104–9.

49. Soc. Ant., MS 76, f. 91r & v; *HHB*, part 2, p. 115.

50. Harl. MS 433, 1, 155.

51. Harl. MS 433, 2, 111.

52. BL, Add. MS 46349, f. 146r; *HHB*, part 1, p. 419. Nothing further is known of Darcy.

53. Arundel Castle MS, f. 96 (actually numbered 92 in MS); *HHB*, part 1, p. 558.

54. Soc. Ant., MS 76, f. 149r; MS 77, f. 4v; *HHB*, part 2, pp. 216, 287.

55. Soc. Ant., MS 76, ff. 87r, 91v; *HHB*, part 2, pp. 109, 115.

56. Arundel Castle MS, f. 35r; *HHB*, part 1, p. 492.

57. Bells are attached to the hawk's legs with leather thongs called 'bewits'.

58. BL, Add. MS 46349, f. 153r; *HHB*, part 1, p. 431. An apparent reference to 'drinking at hawking' may be a further mention of this sport, although Lord Howard seems to have patronised a tavern run by a man called Hawkins in the 1480s and this entry could refer to him: Soc. Ant., MS 76, f. 34v; *HHB*, part 2, p. 32.

59. Soc. Ant., MS 77, f. 26v; *HHB*, part 2, p. 328.

60. Soc. Ant., MS 77, f. 43r; *HHB*, part 2, p. 360.

61. According to the Boke of *St Albans* the choice of falcon was entirely hierarchical. Only the emperor should use an eagle. Kings employed gyrfalcons, princes and dukes had peregrines, and so on: Reeves, *Pleasures and Pastimes*, pp. 113–14.

62. In 1368 Nicholas de Litlington, Abbot of Westminster, offered up prayers for the recovery of his sick hawk, accompanied by the presentation of a wax falcon as a votive offering: Reeves, *Pleasures and Pastimes*, p. 112.

63. BL, Add. MS 46349, f. 99v; *HHB*, part 1, p. 454. In September 1482 Howard purchased a 'lytell nagge' for 7s., but this sounds like a workhorse: Soc. Ant., MS 77, f. 6v; *HHB*, part 2, p. 291.

64. BL, Add. MS 46349, f. 139v; *HHB*, part 1, p. 403. This was possibly in connection with the forthcoming Anglo-Burgundian tournament at Smithfield. Crimson and black were the livery colours of Charles the Bold, heir to the dukedom of Burgundy.

65. Ridgard, *Medieval Framlingham*, pp. 157–8. Until her death in 1506, Earl Soham Lodge formed part of the dower holding of Elizabeth Talbot, widow of the last Mowbray duke. It was thus never held by John Howard.

66. A further half angel was paid to a bear-ward in December 1463: BL, Add. MS 46349, f. 5r & v; *HHB*, part 1, pp. 156–7.

67. For bear-baiting, see Reeves, *Pleasures & Pastimes*, p. 101; for the Colchester evidence, see J. Ashdown-Hill, *Mediaeval Colchester's Lost Landmarks* (Derby: Breedon Books, 2009).

68. ERO, D/B5 Cr75, m. 7v. The Colchester Berehalle and its garden stood in the vicinity of the modern Osborne Street car park.

Richard III's 'Beloved Cousyn'

69. BL, Add. MS 46349, f. 75r; *HHB*, part 1, p. 280.
70. Soc. Ant., MS 76, f. 81v; *HHB*, part 2, pp. 100–1.
71. BL, Add. MS 46349, f. 87r; Soc. Ant., MS 76, f. 30v; Soc. Ant., MS 77, f. 47r; *HHB*, part 1, pp. 304–5; part 2, pp. 25–6, 369–70.
72. BL, Add. MS 46349, f. 85r; Soc. Ant., MS 76, f. 28r; *HHB*, part 1, pp. 299–300; part 2, p. 22.
73. Arundel Castle MS, f. 45r; *HHB*, part 1, p. 509. This purchase of porpoise mentions no specific location, but occurs in the context of purchases at St Osyth.
74. Soc. Ant., MS 76, f. 145r; *HHB*, part 2, p. 208.
75. In 1498–99. B.OB, p. 141, and OB, f. 113r. Whether this John Carter was the lad who brought Howard the porpoise, or his father, is uncertain, since the first name of neither individual is given in the Howard accounts.
76. Honeysuckle flowers: Kurath, *Middle English Dictionary*.
77. Sweetmeats: Kurath, *Middle English Dictionary*.
78. Powdered sandlewood. Red sandlewood powder was used partly as a colouring agent: Kurath, *Middle English Dictionary*.
79. Confections or preserves, probably candied fruits: Kurath, *Middle English Dictionary*.
80. Soc. Ant., MS 76, ff. 34v, 41r; *HHB*, part 2, pp. 32, 42–3.
81. Soc. Ant., MS 76, f. 43v; *HHB*, part 2, p. 46.
82. Soc. Ant., MS 77, f. 3v; *HHB*, part 2, p. 286.
83. Presumably a Colchester hostelry. Colchester records do not mention *Nole(s),* but John *Noke* is listed as a taverner (*tavernarius*) and as an innkeeper (*hostillerus*) in 1476–78: ERO, D/B5 Cr 76, m. 11v; Cr 77, m. 2r.
84. Soc. Ant., MS 77, f. 26r; *HHB*, part 2, p. 327.
85. N. Orme, *Education and Society in Medieval and Renaissance England* (London: Hambledon, 1989), p. 309, citing VCH *Suffolk*, vol. 2, p. 340.
86. N. Orme, *English Schools in the Middle Ages* (London: Routledge, 1973), p. 306, citing VCH *Suffolk*, vol. 2, p. 325 ff. See also Bacon, *Annalls of Ipswiche*, pp. 140, 147.
87. Orme, *English Schools*, p. 304, citing VCH *Suffolk*, vol. 2, p. 325.
88. P. Morant, *The History and Antiquities of the County of Essex*, vol. 1 (London, 1768), p. 171.
89. Orme, *English Schools*, p. 317, citing *HHB*, part 1, pp. 179, 269.
90. See Chapter 4.
91. Soc. Ant., MS 76, ff. 81r (1481), 107r, 108r (1481/2), MS 77, ff. 12r, 33r (1482), 34v (1482/3); *HHB*, part 2, pp. 99, 147, 149, 300, 338, 341.

9. My Lord Chamberlain
1. They were married on 6 February 1460/1.
2. R. Horrox, 'Hastings, William first Baron Hastings' (*ODNB*).

3. *R3MK*, p. 28.
4. *Sed et privatarum voluptatum conscius ac particeps erat*. Mancini, pp. 68–9.
5. *R3MK*, p. 29.
6. *R3MK*, p. 27.
7. *R3MK*, p. 75.
8. Her sister was the Duchess of Norfolk; her uncle, the Earl of Warwick; her cousin by marriage, Sir Thomas Montgomery. Any of these could have introduced her to the king.
9. *R3MK*, p. 85.
10. J. Ashdown Hill, *Eleanor, the Secret Queen* (Stroud, 2009), p. 37.
11. Kleineke, 'Gerard von Wescl's newsletter from England', p. 80.
12. Horrox, 'Hastings' (*ODNB*).
13. Horrox, 'Hastings' (*ODNB*).
14. *R3MK*, p. 29.
15. *R3MK*, p. 123, citing the Great Chronicle.
16. *Sutton et al., Royal Funerals*, p. 10. The codicils do not survive, so we have only hearsay evidence as to their contents.

10. Secrets of the King's Bedchamber

1. Mancini as quoted in C. Ross, *Edward IV* (London, 1974), p. 315.
2. More as quoted in Ross, *Edward IV*, p. 315.
3. Ross, *Edward IV*, p. 315.
4. Josephine Tey, *Daughter of Time* (Harmondsworth, 1954), p. 82.
5. K. Dockray, 'Edward IV: Playboy or Politician?', *Ric*, vol. 10, no. 131 (December 1995), pp. 306–25 (p. 316).
6. K. Dockray, *Edward IV, a source book* (Stroud, 1999), p. 2.
7. *Cr. Chr.*, p. 151.
8. *Cr. Chr.*, p. 153.
9. Armstrong, Mancini introduction, p. 16; *R3MK*, p. 285.
10. Mancini, p. 67.
11. The first, second and last of these are often listed under married surnames: Butler, Lucy and Shore respectively. The last is also frequently but inaccurately referred to as 'Jane' rather than Elizabeth (see below, note 39). Buck, writing in the seventeenth century, claimed to identify for us a fifth partner of Edward IV, called Catharine de Claryngdon – but he is the only source to name her, and if Catharine existed, we know nothing whatever about her.
12. This appears not dissimilar to the pattern which Edward IV's grandson, Henry VIII, displayed later in his relationships.
13. See Ashdown-Hill, *Eleanor*.
14. J. Ashdown-Hill, 'The Go-Between', *Ric*. 15 (2005), pp. 119–21.

15. *CP*, vol. 9, p. 610.
16. BL, Add. MS 46349, ff. 3r, 20r, 58r, 106r; Arundel Castle MS, f. 26r; Soc. Ant., MS 76, f. 92r; *HHB*, part 1, pp. 153, 180, 240, 332, 482; part 2, p. 116.
17. Ashdown-Hill, *Eleanor*, chapters 11–17.
18. BL, Add. MS 46349, f. 2r; *HHB*, part 1, p. 151. The reference to 'my lord' in this and subsequent quotations is to John Mowbray, fourth Duke of Norfolk.
19. For detailed evidence on this point, see Ashdown-Hill, 'The Go-Between'.
20. BL, Add. MS 46349, f. 3v; *HHB*, part 1, p. 153.
21. BL, Add. MS 46349, f. 7r; *HHB*, part 1, p. 160.
22. Parker Library, *Liber Albus*, f. 72 (old foliation) or f. 51 (modern pencil foliation). The letter was published in Masters, *Corpus Christi*, appendix, p. 30. See also Ashdown-Hill, *Eleanor, The Secret Queen*, Appendix 1.
23. I am grateful to Dr E.S. Leedham-Green, Ancient Archivist at Corpus Christi College, for confirming this point.
24. Masters, *Corpus Christi*, p. 30.
25. Θ, appendix 5.
26. The title of 'highness' was undoubtedly applied to the Mowbray dukes of Norfolk (see, for example, *PL*, vol. 1, p. 66). Whether it was also applied to Eleanor is unknown, although Leland, in a probable reference to Eleanor's death at Kenninghall, spoke of her as 'a Quene or sum grete lady': L.T. Smith, *The Itinerary of John Leland, parts 6 and 7*, London 1907–10, p. 120.
27. BL, Add. MS 46349, f. 121r; *HHB*, part 1, p. 363. There were also Cottons in Cambridgeshire, one of whom was the receiver general of Margaret of Anjou.
28. M. Hicks, *Edward V: The Prince in the Tower* (London, Tempus, 2003), pp. 34–7.
29. Later, during the reign of Henry VII, he was allowed to change his surname to Plantagenet. He acquired the title of Viscount Lisle by marriage to the heiress (see below).
30. See Ashdown-Hill, 'The Elusive Mistress: Elizabeth Lucy and her Family', *Ric.* 11 (June 1999), pp. 490–505.
31. See Ashdown-Hill, 'The Elusive Mistress'; also *Eleanor*, p. 93.
32. Daughter of Elizabeth Talbot, Viscountess Lisle, by her husband, Edward Grey.
33. Arundel Castle MS, f. 26r; *HHB*, part 1, pp. 482–3.
34. BL, Add. MS 46349, f. 99v, Arundel Castle MS, f 26r; *HHB*, part 1, pp. 454 (and see note 2), 483.
35. Arundel Castle MS, f. 26r; *HHB*, part 1, p. 482.
36. Arundel Castle MS, f. 9r; *HHB*, part 1, p. 469.

37. A. Crawford, 'The Mowbray Inheritance', *Ric.* 5, no. 73 (June 1981), pp. 334–41 (p. 335).

38. Crawford, 'Mowbray Inheritance', p. 338.

39. After her Shore marriage was annulled, Elizabeth Lambert married Thomas Lynom. Despite this, contemporaries continued to call her 'Mistress Shore'. By the sixteenth century her real first name seems to have been forgotten, and in 1609, when Beaumont and Fletcher produced their play, *Knight of the Burning Pestle*, they could find no record of it, so they then invented for her the first name Jane: hence 'Jane Shore'.

40. F. Pedersen, *Marriage Disputes in Medieval England* (London, 2000), p. 117.

41. A.F. Sutton, 'William Shore, merchant of London and Derby', *Derbyshire Archaeological Journal*, 106 (1986), pp. 127–39 (p. 127).

42. Sutton, 'William Shore', p. 130.

43. Sutton, 'William Shore', pp. 130–1.

44. There are two references to William in the Howard accounts for 1481. One reason why Shore's name is not found more often is probably that for the decade of the 1470s, during which his business relationship with Howard was developing, no Howard accounts survive.

45. ERO, D/R 76, m. 3r.

46. On the Hervys, see Θ, subsection 4.15.4.

47. ERO, D/B5 CR 76, m. 17. Agard (presumably Shore's step-nephew) is not mentioned in the Howard accounts.

48. The quitclaim and grant are registered twice. Firstly on ERO, D/B5 CR 76, m. 20v, where the entry is deleted, with the note that the insertion was out of sequence and a scribal error. It was then reinserted on m. 24.

49. Or possibly a relative of the apprentice with the same name: Sutton, 'William Shore', p. 128, citing Mercers' Company: wardens' accounts 1463–64 and *Register of Freemen from 1347*.

50. Sutton, 'William Shore', p. 132.

51. ERO, D/B5 CR 76, mm. 22v, 25r, 26r, 27r.

52. Soc. Ant., MS 76, f. 39r; *HHB*, part 2, p. 39. Sutton dates this to July, as part of Howard's provisions for the Scots campaign, but the entry in the Howard accounts is certainly under April. Although no first name is recorded, and although Howard also had dealings with a John Shore of Colchester, this entry clearly refers to William, for John Shore was merely a sailor, serving at this time as a member of the ship's company of Howard's vessel, the *Anthony*: Soc. Ant., MS 76, p. 4 [f. 7r]; *HHB*, part 2, p. 7.

53. Soc. Ant., MS 76, f. 89r; *HHB*, part 2, p. 112.

54. Sutton, 'William Shore', p. 131.

55. Sutton, 'William Shore', p. 133.

56. Sutton, 'William Shore', p. 134. See figure 19.

11. The Death of Edward IV

1. Then his principal residence, at Stoke-by-Nayland, Suffolk.
2. Soc.Ant., MS 77, f. 6v; *HHB*, part 2, p. 291.
3. Soc.Ant., MS 77, ff. 8r, 9v; *HHB*, part 2, pp. 294, 296. Crawford's implication that Howard was in France at this time cannot be correct: *HHB*,
   p. xxvii.
4. The account for the occasion included 'a pownde of gounpowder'. Soc.
   Ant., MS 77, f. 33v; *HHB*, part 2, p. 339. 'Wyldffyre' had been manufactured for Lord Howard on previous occasions, BL, Add. MS 46349, f. 6v;
   HHB, part 1, p. 160. See also Θ, subsection 5.8.7.
5. Soc.Ant., MS 77, f. 33v; *HHB*, part 2, p. 340.
6. Soc.Ant., MS 77, f. 31v; *HHB*, part 2, p. 336. Since they are described
   specifically as 'pleyers', not as minstrels, these may have been actors.
7. Kendall, *Richard the Third*, p. 148.
8. *Cr. Chr.*, pp. 148–9.
9. M. Clive, *This Son of York* (London, 1973), p. 272; Mancini, p. 69.
10. See Chapter 5 – diplomacy.
11. Clive, *Son of York*, p. 274.
12. On 20 February the king granted relief to the burgesses of Lyme [now
    Lyme Regis] in Dorset, 'in consideration of the devastation of their
    town and port by the sea': *CPR 1476–1485*, p. 338.
13. Mancini, p. 59. Possibly the weather was bad throughout 1483. Storms
    and floods in Wales, and storms in Brittany, are recorded for October of
    that year: *R3MK*, p. 221.
14. Kendall, *R3*, p. 144.
15. Clive, *Son of York*, p. 275.
16. Soc.Ant., MS 77, f. 37v; *HHB*, part 2, p. 346. In the published transcript
    the date is erroneously given as 19 January.
17. Soc.Ant., MS 77, f. 38v; *HHB*, part 2, p. 348.
18. 'Remember, man, that you are dust, and to dust you will return.'
19. Kendall, *R3*, p. 150.
20. Kendall, *R3*, p. 162.
21. Soc.Ant., MS 77, f. 41v; *HHB*, part 2, p. 356.
22. Soc.Ant., MS 77, f. 42v; *HHB*, part 2, p. 358.
23. *CPR 1476–1485*, p. 346.
24. A.F. Sutton, L.Visser Fuchs and R.A. Griffiths, *The Royal Funerals of the
    House of York at Windsor* (Richard III Society 2005), p. 10.
25. E.E. Ratcliffe and P.A. Wright, *The Royal Maundy, a brief outline of its
    history and ceremonial* (The Royal Almonry, Buckingham Palace, seventh
    edition, 1960), pp. 6–9, citing a manuscript account in the College of
    Arms, describing the practice in the early Tudor period. The sovereign
    continued to perform the foot-washing in person until the deposition
    of James II.

26. Mancini, p. 59.
27. *Cr. Chr.*, p. 153. The codicils do not survive, so we cannot be certain what (if anything) was added to the king's will at this time.
28. Because of its speculation about the death of a Bishop of Ely, some writers have dated the note much earlier, in August 1478. This view is now generally discounted. Others, notably Hanham, have argued on the basis of the reference to the death of 'chamberlain' that the note dates to mid-June 1483 and expresses fears for the life of Edward V. (A. Hanham, ed., *The Cely Letters 1472–1488* [London, 1975], pp. 285–6). The present writer has suggested elsewhere that this dating is in error and that the note belongs to early April 1483. See also below.
29. Presumably Archbishop Thomas Rotherham.
30. John Morton. The report of his death was, of course, false.
31. Sic. The fact that Gloucester is not called Lord Protector surely rules out the possibility of any date later than early May 1483.
32. 'My lord prince' can only be the Prince of Wales (soon to be Edward V). Richard of Shrewsbury would have been designated as 'my lord of York'. For a fuller discussion of this point, see J. Ashdown-Hill, 'The Death of Edward V – new evidence from Colchester', *Essex Archaeology and History*, vol. 35 (2004), pp. 226–30.
33. Lord Howard was, in fact, safely at home in Suffolk.
34. Edwards, *The Itinerary of King Richard III*, p. 1; Kendall, *R3*, p. 153. It is canonically improper to offer a requiem mass for a living soul.
35. Mancini, pp. 58–9.
36. Soc. Ant., MS 77, f. 52r; *HHB*, part 2, p. 378. The messenger who brought the letter received half a gold angel.
37. Soc. Ant., MS 77, f. 53r; *HHB*, part 2, p. 383.
38. Soc. Ant., MS 77, f. 53r; *HHB*, part 2, p. 383. Howard certainly seems to have been in a hurry His journeys to the capital were usually slower, with more frequent stops.
39. *Edwards, Itinerary R3*, p. 1; 'This last nyght'. L. Lyell and F. Watney, eds, *The Acts of the Court of the Mercers' Company 1453–1527* (Cambridge, 1936), pp. 146–7, quoted in *Road*, p. 93.
40. Soc. Ant., MS 77, f. 53v; *HHB*, part 2, p. 384: 'for bot hyr the day befor xijd.'
41. Soc. Ant., MS 77, f. 63v; *HHB*, part 2, p. 402: eight boats to Westminster and back – 2s; one boat more 3d.
42. Mancini, p. 71.
43. Edward specified in his will that he should be buried at St George's Chapel, in the spot which he had identified to the Bishop of Salisbury: Sutton *et al.*, *Royal Funerals*, p. 96.
44. Sutton *et al.*, *Royal Funerals*, p. 11.
45. Sutton *et al.*, *Royal Funerals*, p. 13.

46. Soc. Ant., MS 77, f. 53v; *HHB*, part 2, p. 384: 'to a man that bare a letter to Stoke xijd.'

47. Road, p. 95; *Cr. Chr.*, pp. 154–5.

48. Kendall, *R3*, p. 173.

49. Soc. Ant., MS 77, f. 54r; *HHB*, part 2, p. 385.

50. The sources are unclear, stating 'Wednesday 17 April', which is impossible: Sutton *et al., Royal Funerals*, p. 35, n. 243. However, on p. 14 Sutton et al. nevertheless repeat the impossible date of Wednesday 17 April, and subsequent errors in their chronology ensue.

51. John de la Pole, the eldest son of Edward's sister, Elizabeth of York, Duchess of Suffolk.

52. 'as the nyght weyned': Sutton *et al., Royal Funerals*, p. 37, citing College of Arms, MS I.7, ff. 7–8v.

53. Mancini, p. 120, n. 63.

54. Soc. Ant., MS 77, f. 54v; *HHB*, part 2, p. 385.

55. Soc. Ant., MS 77, ff. 54v, 55r; *HHB*, part 2, p. 386.

56. Mancini, p. 71; *Cr. Chr.*, pp. 154–5.

57. *Cr. Chr.*, pp. 154–5.

58. Kendall, *R3*, p. 164.

59. *Edwards, Itinerary* R3, p. 1.

60. *Cr. Chr.*, pp. 154–5.

61. Kendall, *R3*, p. 173.

62. *CPR 1476–1485*, pp. 350–1. Guy Fairfax had served the Duke of Gloucester and his mother in a legal capacity in the past.

63. Mancini, p. 121, n. 64. See also below.

64. Kendall, *R3*, p. 164. There seems to be no contemporary record of such a message from Rivers to Gloucester, but someone must have done something to coordinate the subsequent meeting in Northampton on 29 April.

65. Kendall, *R3*, pp. 164, 173; Edwards, *Itinerary R3*, p. 1.

66. According to the *Crowland Chronicler*, Buckingham and Gloucester met at Northampton. *Cr. Chr.*, pp. 154–5.

67. *CPR 1476–1485*, p. 354.

68. Kendall, *R3*, p. 178.

69. The French threat would certainly account for Edward Woodville's sailing. The fact that he took with him a significant part of the contents of the royal treasury is perhaps less easily explained.

70. Mancini, p. 81.

71. Soc. Ant., MS 77, f. 55v; *HHB*, part 2, p. 388.

72. Road, p. 95; *Cr. Chr.*, pp. 154–5.

73. For a plausible explanation of the reason for this, see A. Hanham, 'The Mysterious Affair at Crowland Abbey', *Ric.* 18 (2008), pp. 1–20.

74. *Cr. Chr.*, pp. 154–5.

75. *Cr. Chr.*, pp. 154–5.
76. *Cr. Chr.*, pp. 154–5 (present writer's italics).
77. Kendall, *R3*, p. 176; Edwards, Itinerary *R3*, p. 2.
78. *Road*, p. 99.
79. Kendall, *R3*, p. 179. The Crowland chronicler says 'the following night', which could conceivably mean the night of 1–2 May.
80. *Cr. Chr.*, pp. 156–7.
81. Soc Ant., MS 77, f. 56r; *HHB*, part 2, p. 389.
82. A 'month-mind' was a mass celebrated for the repose of the soul of a recently deceased person about one month after his or her demise.
83. Edwards, *Itinerary R3*, p. 2.
84. Kendall, *R3*, p. 182.
85. Edwards, Itinerary *R3*, p. 2.
86. Road, p. 99; *Cr. Chr.*, pp. 156–7.
87. Soc. Ant., MS 77, f. 57r; *HHB*, part 2, p. 390.

12. 'Bastard King'

1. *Cr. Chr.*, pp. 156–7.
2. *Cr. Chr.*, pp. 156–7.
3. *Mancini*, p. 121, n. 65.
4. *Mancini*, p. 122, n. 67.
5. Kendall, *R3*, p. 188.
6. *Cr. Chr.*, pp. 158–9; Mancini, p. 123, n. 72.
7. R. Horrox and P.W. Hammond, eds, *British Library Harleian Manuscript 433*, vol. 1, (Richard III Society, 1979), pp. 7–8. The grant is reiterated later: pp. 72 and 117.
8. Mancini, p. 122, n. 67.
9. Nichols, *Grants &c ... Edward V*, pp. 3–4.
10. Soc. Ant., MS 77, f. 57v; *HHB*, part 2, pp. 391–2.
11. From 29 May 1482 to 28 May 1483 the date letter of the London Hall Mark for gold and silver items was 'E': *Hall Marks and Date Letters* (N.A.G Press, London, 1944), pp. 6, 21.
12. See also below: 'June'.
13. Kendall, R3, p. 191, citing *CPR*; Nichols, *Grants &c ... Edward V*, pp. 5–11.
14. *CPR 1476–1485*, pp. 349, 356.
15. Nichols, Grants &c ... *Edward V*, p. 11.
16. *CPR 1476–1485*, p. 349.
17. Soc. Ant., MS 77, f. 58v; *HHB*, part 2, p. 393; Kendall, *R3*, p. 185.
18. Soc. Ant., MS 77, ff. 59v, 63r, 63v; *HHB*, part 2, pp. 395, 401, 402.
19. Kendall, *R3*, p. 185; *Cr. Chr.*, pp. 158–9. Simon Stallworthe, in a letter to

Sir William Stonor, speaks of 23 June, but this is probably an error on his part (see below: 9 June).

20. Nichols, *Grants &c ... Edward V*, p. 15.
21. Nichols, *Grants &c ... Edward V*, p. 17.
22. Edwards, *Itinerary R3*, p. 2.
23. *Cr. Chr.*, pp. 156–7.
24. *CPR 1476–1485*, p. 348.
25. Mancini, p. 123, n. 72.
26. Nichols, *Grants &c ... Edward V*, pp. 31–7.
27. Mancini, pp. 124–5, n. 74.
28. Nichols, *Grants &c ... Edward V*, pp. 49–50.
29. *CPR 1476–1485*, p. 349.
30. *CPR 1476–1485*, p. 349.
31. Kendall, *R3*, p. 201, citing *Stonor Letters and Papers*, II, pp. 158–60, and *Ex. Hist.*, p. 16.
32. Soc. Ant., MS 77, f. 62r; *HHB*, part 2, p. 399.
33. *Cr. Chr.*, pp. 158–9. After the arrival of Edward V in London the chronology of the Crowland chronicler, hitherto meticulous, becomes rather approximate, and he glosses over the month from 13 May to 12 June almost without comment. Thus his reference is not very precisely timed, but it falls within this period.
34. Soc. Ant., MS 77, f. 62v; *HHB*, part 2, p. 399.
35. Lord Berkeley petitioned for his share of the Mowbray inheritance, though the date of the petition is not precisely known. No trace survives of a similar petition from Lord Howard. Crawford, 'Mowbray Inheritance', p. 338.
36. Nichols, *Grants &c ... Edward V*, pp. 56–7; *CPR 1476–1485*, pp. 351–2.
37. *Road*, pp. 102–3, citing Facsimiles of National Manuscripts, part 1, Southampton 1865, item 53.
38. Kendall, *R3*, pp. 205–6.
39. *Road*, p. 104, citing *Paston Letters*, vol. 3, p. 306.
40. Kendall, R3, p. 207. Kendall dates these meetings to Thursday 12 June.
41. *Road*, p. 105, citing R. Firth Green, 'Historical Notes of a London Citizen 1483–8', *English Historical Review*, vol. 96 (1981), p. 588. The extant copy of this account probably dates from the early sixteenth century, but is believed to reproduce earlier material: R3MK, p. 289.
42. *Cr. Chr.*, pp. 158–9.
43. Mancini, pp. 90–1.
44. *Road*, p. 103.
45. *Cr. Chr.*, pp. 158–9.
46. Mancini, pp. 88–9.
47. Mancini, pp. 62–3.

48. f. 107r (old enumeration, p. 156). As it stands, this entry was written up in September 1483.
49. Ashdown-Hill, 'The Death of Edward V', p. 229.
50. *Cr. Chr.*, pp. 158–9.
51. *Road*, p. 113.
52. Edwards, Itinerary R3, p. 3.
53. *CPR 1476–1485*, p. 360.
54. Edwards, *Itinerary R3*, p. 4. Carson states (*R3MK*, p. 99) that Richard was actually residing at his rented accommodation: Crosby's Place, but using his mother's home as his headquarters.
55. See Chapter 14.
56. Kendall, R3, p. 227. The Patent rolls record only Howard's appointment as earl marshal: *CPR 1476–1485*, p. 358.
57. Horrox & Hammond, eds, Harl. MS 433, vol. 1, pp. 72, 117.
58. *CPR 1476–85*, p. 363; Harl. MS 433, vol. 1, pp. 80–2 (undated in Harley).
59. Horrox & Hammond, eds, Harl. MS 433, vol. 1, pp. 74, 80–2, 91; *CPR 1476–1485*, pp. 359, 362, 365. While some of these grants are undated in Harley, they must all belong to late June or early July 1483.
60. *CPR 1476–1485*, p. 360.
61. J. Kirby, ed., *The Plumpton Letters and Papers*, Cambridge 1996, pp. 59–60.
62. Soc. Ant., MS 77, f. 65v; *HHB*, part 2, p. 406.
63. Edwards, *Itinerary R3*, p. 4.
64. *Road*, p. 118.
65. Soc. Ant., MS 77, f. 67v; *HHB*, part 2, p. 410. Kendall, *R3*, p. 228.
66. Soc. Ant., MS 77, f. 67v; *HHB*, part 2, p. 410.
67. Edwards, *Itinerary R3*, p. 4.
68. CP, vol. 9, p. 612, citing Lord Chamberlain's Records, 9/50, ff. 103, 105.
69. *CPR 1476–1485*, p. 361. Edward V had made this grant on 21 May (see above).
70. *CPR 1476–1485*, p. 363. Edward V had made this grant on 20 May (see above).
71. Edwards, *Itinerary R3*, p. 4.
72. *CPR 1476–1485*, pp. 361, 365.
73. *CPR 1476–1485*, p. 362.
74. Edwards, *Itinerary R3*, p. 4.
75. *CPR 1476–1485*, p. 403.
76. *Cr. Chr.*, pp. 162–3.
77. Edwards, *Itinerary R3*, p. 5.
78. Edwards, *Itinerary R3*, p. 5.
79. Soc. Ant., MS 77, f. 68r; *HHB*, part 2, p. 411.
80. Edwards, *Itinerary R3*, p. 5.
81. This building survives, in part, though it was moved to Chelsea in 1908–10. Incidentally the house is variously known in modern texts

as 'Crosby Place' and 'Crosby Hall', but the fifteenth-century Howard accounts invariably refer to it as 'Crosby's Place'.

82. *CPR 1476–1485*, p. 365.

83. *CPR 1476–1485*, p. 366.

84. *CPR 1476–1485*, pp. 359, 363, 365.

85. Soc.Ant., MS 77, f. 71v; *HHB*, part 2, p. 416.

86. Edwards, *Itinerary R3*, p. 5.

87. Edwards, *Itinerary R3*, p. 5.

88. TNA, C81/1392 No. 1; Catalogue for the NPG exhibition of 1973, p. 98 (punctuation modernised); see also A.J. Pollard, *Richard III and the Princes in the Tower* (Stroud, 1991), p. 109. Kendall, not Herbert, was Richard III's usual secretary. I am grateful to Annette Carson for drawing my attention to this letter.

89. Catalogue for the NPG exhibition of 1973, p. 55.

90. *Cr. Chr.*, pp. 162–3.

91. R. Horrox and P.W. Hammond, eds, *British Library Harleian Manuscript 433*, vol. 1 (Gloucester, 1979), pp. 87, 121, 143, 209; vol. 4 (Gloucester, 1983), p. 141.

92. On 1 March 1484; R. Horrox and P.W. Hammond, eds, *British Library Harleian Manuscript 433*, vol. 2 (Gloucester, 1982), p. 190.

93. Soc.Ant., MS 77, f. 73r; *HHB*, part 2, p. 419.

94. Soc.Ant., MS 77, f. 73v; *HHB*, part 2, p. 420.

95. Soc.Ant., MS 77, f. 75v; *HHB*, part 2, p. 423.

96. Soc.Ant., MS 77, f. 76r; *HHB*, part 2, p. 424.

97. M. Hicks, 'Unweaving the Web: The Plot of July 1483 against Richard III and its Wider Significance', *Ric.* 9, no. 114 (September 1991) pp. 106–9 (p. 107).

98. J. Stow, *Annales, or a General Chronicle of England* (London: A.M. for R. Meighen, 1631), p. 459.

99. M. Hicks, 'Unweaving the Web: The Plot of July 1483 against Richard III and its Wider Significance', *Ric.* 9, no. 114 (September 1991), p. 107, citing J. Stow, *Annales of England* (London, 1631), p. 459.

13. Ducal Progress

1. The Itinerarium is the traditional order of prayer for those setting out on a journey.

2. J. Ashdown-Hill, 'Norfolk Requiem: the passing of the house of Mowbray', *Ric.* 12, no. 152 (March, 2001), pp. 198–217.

3. The first example of a dukedom being bestowed on a royal bastard was Henry VIII's elevation of his illegitimate son, Henry Fitzroy. Everyone knew that Fitzroy was a bastard at the time when his title was conferred

on him. Later still, under Charles II, ducalising royal bastards became almost the norm.

4. *Calendar of Papal Registers*, vol. 11, *Papal Letters 1455–1464* (London, 1921), p. 232, and vol. 12, *Papal Letters 1458–1471* (London, 1933), p. 672.

5. Born in 1444, the fourth Mowbray Duke of Norfolk was a few weeks past his seventeenth birthday when his father died (and his wife was probably already eighteen). There is no record of any appointment of a legal guardian for him, and Edward IV immediately began appointing the new duke to commissions even during his minority.

6. See Θ, section 3.

7. Soc. Ant., MS 77, ff. 62r – v; *HHB*, part 2, p. 390. See Chapter 12.

8. See Chapter 12, note 96.

9. Edwards, Itinerary R3, p. 5.

10. H. Ellis (ed.), Three Books of Polydore Vergil's English History comprising the reigns of Henry VI, Edward IV and Richard III (London: Camden Society, 1844), p. 194.

11. Edwards, *Itinerary R3*, p. 5.

12. Edwards, *Itinerary R3*, p. 5.

13. Edwards, *Itinerary R3*, pp. 5–6.

14. *CPR 1476–1485*, p. 365.

15. It is traditional for major feasts of the Catholic Church to be prolonged for an octave (eight days). Nowadays only the feasts of Christmas and Easter are celebrated with octaves, but in the Middle Ages the Feast of the Assumption also had an octave.

16. Soc. Ant., MS 77, f. 100r; *HHB*, part 2, p. 464.

17. Soc. Ant., MS 77, f. 89r; *HHB*, part 2, p. 445.

18. Soc. Ant., MS 77, f. 91r; *HHB*, part 2, p. 450: 20*d* 'for my Lordys offering at owir Lady'. This reference is almost certainly to Our Lady of Sudbury, for no other Marian shrine lay in the immediate vicinity of Lavenham and Stoke-by-Nayland. Moreover, as we have seen, apart from Sudbury Howard either visited or sent offerings to every other Marian shrine in the eastern counties at this time.

19. Soc. Ant., MS 77, ff. 91v–93r; *HHB*, part 2, pp. 451–2.

20. Edwards, *Itinerary R3*, p. 6.

21. Edwards, *Itinerary R3*, p. 6.

22. Edwards, *Itinerary R3*, p. 6.

23. Edwards, *Itinerary R3*, p. 6.

24. Hicks, *Richard III*, 2000, p. 138. Hicks (p. 157) assumes that Buckingham was 'with the king as far as Pontefract on 27 August, the date of his Hereford warrant', but offers no evidence in support of this contention, against which, see above '2 August'.

25. *R3MK*, pp. 140 and 200, citing *CPR 1470–85*, pp. 165–6 and TNA, C 66/556, m. 7v.

26. *R3MK*, p. 138.
27. *R3MK*, p. 201, n. 2, citing Harl. MS 433, vol 1, pp. 3–4.
28. Edwards, *Itinerary R3*, p. 6.
29. Edwards, *Itinerary R3*, p. 7.
30. Edwards, *Itinerary R3*, pp. 7–8.
31. *R3MK*, p. 212.
32. The issues around this entry are complex. For a fuller discussion, see Ashdown-Hill, 'The Death of Edward V'.
33. Regis *Edwardi pueros: Cr. Chr.*, pp. 162–3.
34. *R3MK*, p. 153, citing L. Toulmin-Smith, ed., *The Maire of Bristowe is Kalendar* (1872).
35. *R3MK*, p. 211.
36. C.S.L. Davies, 'A Requiem for King Edward', *Ric.* 9 (September 1991), pp. 102–5.

Davies debates whether this could have been a belated requiem for Edward IV, but on balance this seems improbable (see below).

37. In the case of Edward IV, news of his death had reached the Curia by May 1483. Thus it seems highly unlikely that the September requiem in Rome could have been a delayed commemoration for him.
38. *PL*, vol. 2, Oxford 1976, pp. 442–3.
39. *PL*, p. 443.
40. Kendall, *R3*, p. 271.
41. Edwards, *Itinerary R3*, p. 8.
42. Edwards, *Itinerary R3*, p. 8.
43. Kirby, *Plumpton Letters*, pp. 60–1.
44. Edwards, *Itinerary R3*, p. 9.
45. *CPR 1476–1485*, p. 370.
46. *CPR 1476–1485*, p. 371. Richard's phrase 'called Shore's wife' is noteworthy. As Richard was clearly aware, the Shore marriage had been annulled, so Elizabeth Lambert no longer had any real right to use Shore's surname. On the problem of her name in general, see Chapter 10, note 39.
47. Edwards, *Itinerary R3*, p. 9.
48. *CPR 1476–1485*, p. 368. The appointment was recorded later in the Patent rolls, amongst the entries for the following month.

14. 'The King's Kinsman'

1. *CPR 1476–85*, p. 411; Horrox & Hammond, eds, Harl. MS 433, vol. 1, p. 116 (undated in Harley).
2. This entry in the household accounts has been taken to refer to the Tower of London, and the work has been seen by some as evidence

of Howard's complicity in the unnatural death of Edward IV's sons. However, the 'Tower *of London*' is not specified, and it seems incredible that the two boys could have died as early as May 1483: Crawford, 'John Howard, Duke of Norfolk: a possible murderer of the princes?', p. 232.

3. *Harl. MS 433*, vol. 3, pp. 235, 238.
4. *Harl. MS 433*, vol. 2, p. 110.
5. *CPR 1476–85*, p. 465.
6. *Harl. MS 433*, vol. 2, p. 111.
7. *Harl. MS 433*, vol. 1, p. 155; vol. 2, p. 111.
8. *Harl. MS 433*, vol. 1, p. 220.
9. *CPR 1476–85*, pp. 397, 399, 400.
10. R3MK, p. 235.
11. For more on this see J. Ashdown-Hill, *The Dublin King* (Stroud 2015), chapters 3 and 4.
12. Horrox & Hammond, eds, *Harl. MS 433*, vol. 1, p. 3 (punctuation modernised). There is no year date given in the letter itself, but the only occasion when Richard III was at Pontefract in June was in 1484: Edwards, *Itinerary R3*, p. 20.
13. *Harl MS 433*, vol. 2, p. 157.
14. *Harl MS 433*, vol. 3, pp. 151–5, 193.
15. *CPR 1476–85*, p. 501; *Harl MS 433*, vol. 1, p. 229 (undated in Harley).
16. *CPR 1476–85*, pp. 489–90,
17. *Rerum Britannicarum Medii Aevi Scriptores*, or Chronicles and Memorials of Great Britain and Ireland during the Middle Ages, *Letters and Papers illustrative of the Reigns of Richard III and Henry VII* (London: Rolls House, 1857), p. 64.
18. R3MK, p. 258.
19. The time of the solar eclipse was recorded at Augsburg (where the eclipse was total): http://ls.kuleuven.ac.be/cgi-bin/ wa?A2=ind0103&L=vvs&P=1445, citing Achilli Pirmini Gassari: *Annales Augustburgenses*. According to NASA, its central duration was 4 minutes 53 seconds: http://sunearth.gsfc.nasa.gov/eclipse/SEsaros/ SEsaros121.html (both websites consulted April 2008).
20. Psalm 54 (55), verse 4.
21. *R3MK*, pp. 259–60.
22. This letter was misunderstood by Buck, who took it to relate to a proposed marriage between Richard III and his own niece. Carson (*R3MK*, p. 259), citing Kincaid, shows how the lack of punctuation in medieval writing could account for this error. The insertion of a single comma would have made the real meaning plain.
23. *CPR 1476–85*, p. 510; *Harl. MS 433*, vol. 1, pp. 263, 266.
24. *CPR 1476–85*, pp. 497, 541; *Harl. MS 433*, vol. 1, p. 267.
25. *PL*, vol. 2, p. 444.

26. E. Hall, *Chronicle* (1550, facsimile reprinted 1970). Shakespeare used a slightly different version of this rhyme in his play *Richard III*.
27. Halsted, *Richard III*, vol. 2, pp. 471–2, quoting Grafton, *Great Chronicle* (1569).
28. M. Bennett, *The Battle of Bosworth* (Stroud, 1985), p. 186, fn. 18, citing Beaumont 'Bosworth Field', in Nichols, *Leicestershire*, vol. 4, p. 561.
29. Bennett, *Bosworth*, p. 186, fn. 18, citing Molinet, *Chroniques*.
30. R.A. Griffiths and R.S. Thomas, *The Making of the Tudor Dynasty* (Stroud, 1985), p. 163.
31. J. Nichols, *The History and Antiquities of the County of Leicestershire*, 4 vols, London 1811, vol. 4, part 2, p. 561.

15. John Howard's Religious Life

1. Library of Magdalene College, Cambridge, published in H.M. Gillett, *Walsingham* (London, 1946), pp. 78–81.
2. Two magnificent cathedrals – Arundel Cathedral and the Cathedral of St John the Baptist in Norwich – were both the gift of a later Duke of Norfolk.
3. Pollard, *North-Eastern England*, p. 182.
4. Pollard, *North-Eastern England*, p. 173.
5. Pollard, *North-Eastern England*, p. 185, citing M.G.A. Vale, *Piety, Charity and Literacy among the Yorkshire Gentry, 1370–1480* (York: Borthwick Paper 50, 1976), p. 15. See also Ashdown-Hill, Eleanor, chapter 15.
6. Pollard, *North-Eastern England*, p. 183.
7. Pollard, *North-Eastern England*, p. 179, citing C. Richmond, 'Religion and the Fifteenth-Century Gentleman' in R.B. Dobson, ed., *The Church, Politics and Patronage in the Fifteenth Century* (Gloucester, 1984), p. 199.
8. Soc. Ant., MS 77, ff. 54r, 56r; *HHB*, part 2, pp. 385, 389.
9. BL, Add. MS 46349, f. 25v; *HHB*, part 1, p. 186. This refers to Abbot John Canon, who was appointed to the abbacy in 1464 and died in 1468.
10. See Chapter 5. Howard also paid other visits. On 27 December 1482 he was accompanied by his second wife. On that occasion Lord and Lady Howard made standard offerings: 4d to the abbey, 1d to the image of Our Lady, and 2d in alms.
11. St Leonard's Church has a chancel and north aisle dating from about 1330. Most of the tower is of about 1380, though the top part has been rebuilt in comparatively modern times. The south arcade of the nave is of about 1425–50, while the clerestory was added in about 1500. The living was held by St John's Abbey: C. Cockerill & D. Woodward, *The Hythe, Port and Church* (Colchester: privately published, 1975), pp. 21–2; Benham, *Guide*, p. 145.

12. Soc. Ant., MS 77, f. 47r; *HHB*, part 2, p. 370.
13. BL, Add. MS 46349, f. 64v; *HHB*, part 1, p. 256.
14. BL, Add. MS 46349, f. 69v; *HHB*, part 1, p. 268.
15. At Corpus Christi the consecrated Host is traditionally carried in procession, displayed in a monstrance; in rural areas the fields were blessed.
16. Soc. Ant., MS 76, f. 43r; *HHB*, part 2, p. 45.
17. Θ, subsection 5 x x.
18. Soc. Ant., MS 76, f. 30v; *HHB*, part 2, pp. 25–6.
19. The bill was settled on 6 March: BL, Add. MS 46349, f. 105v; *HHB*, part 1, p. 331.
20. BL, Add. MS 46349, f. 51r; *HHB*, part 1, p. 228. The published version of this entry has been rather mangled by the editor.
21. BL, Add. MS 46349, f. 71r; *HHB*, part 1, pp. 271–2. This may have been for motives which were not religious, since Prittlewell Priory held the living at Stoke-by-Nayland.
22. BL, Add. MS 46349, f. 151v; *HHB*, part 1, p. 428.
23. BL, Add. MS 46349, f. 153v; *HHB*, part 1, p. 432.
24. 14 September: the Feast of the Exaltation of the Holy Cross. BL, Add. MS 46349, f. 149r; *HHB*, part 1, pp. 423–4.
25. For details of his patronage of this shrine, see below.
26. BL, Add. MS 46349, f. 152v; *HHB*, part 1, p. 430. The original editor of the Howard accounts identified the day in question as the Feast of All Saints (1 November), a view with which Hutton, by implication, concurs (Hutton, *Merry England*, p. 45). Both are likely to be in error, however. Cheney (*Handbook of Dates*, p. 61) identifies 'Soulmas Day' as 2 November. Duffy (*Stripping the Altars*, p. 47) likewise characterises 2 November as 'the focus of the late medieval cult of the dead'. Certainly the modern Catholic liturgical calendar distinguishes sharply between 1 November (All Saints' Day), which celebrates the saints in heaven, and 2 November (All Souls' Day), when prayers are offered for the souls of the dead in purgatory. On balance Sir John Howard's 'Soulmas Day' was almost certainly 2 November.
27. BL, Add. MS 46349, f. 5v; *HHB*, part 1, p. 158.
28. Soc. Ant., MS 77, f. 3v; *HHB*, part 2, p. 286.
29. Soc. Ant., MS 76, f. 122r; *HHB*, part 2, p. 170. It sounds as though the organs may have been damaged by choirboys or others who were up to mischief, for 'the same tyme my Lord toke Sir William Davyes, the pryst, to pay for a lok to the orgenys, 4*d*.'
30. The Castle inventory of 1524 records 8 albs for children and 8 hymnals among the chapel furnishings: Ridgard, *Medieval Framlingham*, pp. 149, 153.
31. Soc. Ant., MS 76, f. 113v; *HHB*, part 2, p. 157.
32. Presumably prepared for use in some way. Possibly the transaction refers to the addition of the standard dedicatory inscription which often figures on chalices: *Ora(te) pro* [donor's name] *offerens sacrificium*.

33. Soc. Ant., MS 76, f. 42r; *HHB*, part 2, p. 44.
34. W.M. Copinger, *The Manors of Suffolk*, vol. 1 (London, 1905), pp. 215–16.
35. Probably one pair for each of the two side altars and one pair for processional use.
36. Rigard, *Medieval Framlingham*, pp. 129–58. It is also interesting to note items of equipment which the chapel did not possess. There was no monstrance, and no reliquaries are recorded.
37. The modern practice makes green the normal colour. This is changed to red for martyr feast days, to white or gold for major feasts, and to purple for the penitential seasons of Advent and Lent. Either purple or white is used for funerals and commemorations of the dead. Prior to the 1960s black was used in connection with the dead and for Good Friday, but black vestments are now rarely seen.
38. Ridgard, *Medieval Framlingham*, pp. 129–58.
39. Copes were and are worn for processions, and for solemn celebrations of the Divine Office.
40. This is still the case today in churches of the eastern rites, and seems to have been normal in the western church in the Middle Ages. See, for example, 'The Procession of St Gregory', from the *Très Riches Heures du Duc de Berry*.
41. Only one of each is listed in the Framlingham Castle vestry, in black (presumably mainly for use at solemn requiem masses). Even given that the mixing of colours may have been acceptable fifteenth–century practice, the fact that only one dalmatic and one tunicle was provided means that they cannot have been required very often. Examples of these vestments were also entirely absent from the V&A exhibition of 1930. MacLagan, *English Medieval Art*.
42. Of the two, anniversary foundations were more ostentatious and 'intrusive', repeating publicly, sometimes with notable ceremony, the entire funeral liturgy. For the important differences between chantry and anniversary foundations, see C. Burgess, 'A service for the dead: the form and function of the anniversary in late medieval Bristol', *Transactions of the Bristol & Gloucestershire Archaeological Society*, vol. 105 (1987), pp. 196–7.
43. It proved immediately popular, and processions, modelled on those that already took place at Palm Sunday, grew up to mark it. These processions at Corpus Christi were expressions of popular piety, for they were never formally laid down by the church authorities as a requirement.
44. A trend which has arguably continued to the present day.
45. He was at Canterbury, for example, in 1482: Soc. Ant., MS 76, f. 133v; *HHB*, part 2, p. 186.
46. Soc. Ant., MS 76, f. 39r; *HHB*, part 2, p. 39.
47. Soc. Ant., MS 77, f. 33v; *HHB*, part 2, p. 339.

48. On 23 September 1464, for example, 'my mastyr rode to Walsyngeham': BL, Add. MS 46349, f. 75r; *HHB*, part 1, p. 281.

49. For the pilgrimage of 1469, see J. Ashdown-Hill, 'Walsingham in 1469: the Pilgrimage of Edward IV and Richard, Duke of Gloucester', *Ric.* II, no. 136 (March 1997), 2–16; for that of 1482: Soc. Ant., MS 77, ff. 6v, 8r, 9v; *HHB*, part 2, pp. 291, 294, 296.

50. See Chapter 13.

51. The tour included the Marian shrines of Ipswich, Walsingham, Thetford and Sudbury.

52. The original focus of the cult was the 'Holy House', said to be a copy of the Virgin Mary's house in Nazareth. There was a secondary focus on two adjacent holy wells. In the thirteenth century, however, an image of Our Lady of Walsingham had been introduced to the shrine, and by John Howard's time this cult image, rather than the Holy House in which it stood, was the main focus of pilgrims' devotion. There were also a number of lesser attractions, including a relic called 'Our Lady's milk'.

53. Soc. Ant., MS 76, f. 45r; *HHB*, part 2, p. 49.

54. In October 1463. BL, Add. MS 46349, f. 51v; *HHB*, part 1, p. 228.

55. Soc. Ant., MS 77, f. 68v; *HHB*, part 2, p. 412.

56. This shrine's existence 'was first recorded in 1297, when it would appear to have [already] been an established shrine': S. Smith, *The Madonna of Ipswich* (Ipswich: East Anglian Magazine, 1980), p. 20. Later the cult received royal patronage, and eventually that also of Sir Thomas More and of Cardinal Wolsey (who was, of course, a native of Ipswich). Edward I's daughter, Elizabeth, was married at the shrine; Henry IV's daughter, Blanche of Lancaster, came on pilgrimage; and so, later, did Henry VIII and Catherine of Aragon. Elizabeth of York, daughter of Edward IV and queen of Henry VII, patronised Our Lady of Ipswich, though no record survives of a personal visit by her: Smith, *Madonna of Ipswich*, pp. 24–5; *PPE*, p. 3.

57. The West Gate crossed the western end of the modern Westgate Street, and was perhaps the most widely used of the four main gates which gave access to the town of Ipswich.

58. An eighteenth-century visitor to Ipswich, Mr Grove of Richmond, stated in 1761: 'It stood on one side of Lady Lane, a little way out of St Matthew's Gate [West Gate] on the left hand … [but] there is not scarce one stone left upon another.' Fragments of medieval masonry excavated from Westgate Street in the twentieth century, and now in Ipswich Museum, may have formed part of the shrine chapel. A medieval English wooden image of the Virgin and Child, preserved since the mid-sixteenth century at Nettuno in Italy (where it is venerated under the title of Nostra Signora delle Grazie – 'Our Lady of Graces'),

is reputed to be that of Our Lady of Ipswich, rescued by sailors from the iconoclasm of Henry VIII, and carried to Italy for safe-keeping (see figure 28): Smith, *Madonna of Ipswich*, pp. 15, 18, 23, 70.

59. Soc. Ant., MS 76, f. 55r; *HHB*, part 2, p. 62.

60. BL, Add. MS 46349, f. 47r; Soc. Ant., MS 76, f. 55, 110v; MS 77, f. 89r; *HHB*, part 1, p. 219; part 2, pp. 62, 153, 445.

61. For example, Soc. Ant., MS 76, ff. 30v, 31v, 44r, 45r; *HHB*, part 2, pp. 27, 28, 47, 49.

62. Soc. Ant., MS 76, f. 51r; *HHB*, part 2, p. 57.

63. Soc. Ant., MS 77, f. 100r; *HHB*, part 2, p. 464. The image was presumably of Howard himself. In a similar way, after the battle of Stoke, Henry VII sent a thank-offering to Our Lady of Walsingham in the form of a silver image of himself kneeling in prayer. Such a statuette placed in the vicinity of the cult image symbolised the perpetual devotion of the donor.

64. Woolpit History Group, *St Mary's Church, Woolpit*, [n.d.] pp. 2, 3. On this shrine see also C. Paine, 'The Chapel and Well of Our Lady of Woolpit', *PSIAH*, 38, part 1 (1993), 8–12; N. Pevsner, *Suffolk* (Harmondsworth: Penguin, 1961), p. 503.

65. Woolpit History Group, *St Mary's Church, Woolpit*, p. 3, citing the wills of Simon Brown (1390) and John Petyt (1442). The shrine chapel site at Woolpit is now partially occupied by a nineteenth-century vestry, but traces of a demolished larger building remain (see fig. 34).

66. Soc. Ant., MS 76, f. 119v; *HHB*, part 2, p. 166. The Dovercourt entry (see below) is equally vague, but its meaning is not in doubt.

67. Soc. Ant., MS 77, f. 91r; *HHB*, part 2, p. 450: Θ, subsection 3.3.

68. BL, Add. Ms 46349, ff. 59v–60r; *HHB*, part 1, pp. 243–4.

69. BL, Add. MS 46349, f. 47v Soc. Ant., MS 76, f. 55v; *HHB*, part 1, p. 220; part 2, p. 64.

70. Weaver, *Harwich Papers*, p. 26. The rood was burned in February 1532/3 by over-enthusiastic iconoclasts from Dedham and East Bergholt who were later hanged for their trouble. However, it was recalled, after its destruction, in an Elizabethan comedy, *Grim, the Collier of Croydon*, and in the play it is reported that the Holy Rood of Dovercourt was wont to speak: J.S. Farmer, ed., *Early English Dramatists: Five Anonymous Plays* (1908), cited (in an edition of 1966) by Weaver, *Harwich Papers*, pp. 26–7. See J. Ashdown-Hill, 'The Shrine of the Holy Rood of Dovercourt', *The Essex Journal*, Spring 2009, pp. 4–9.

71. TNA, PROB 11/24 151/81, will of Richard Strowgth, vicar of Dovercourt, 1531. The piscina of this chapel survives.

72. ERO, D/ACR2 199, will of Agnes Smyth, widow, 1526. Agnes left money for the repair of the highway from the Cross House, and also for a votive light to burn before the Holy Rood.

73. This event has traditionally been dated to February 1532, but the will of Henry Browne, curate of Dovercourt (dated 1 August 1532, and referring to the rood loft) shows that this date should be understood as February 1532/3. ERO, D/ACR2 252.

74. Soc. Ant., MS 76, f. 115r; *HHB*, part 2, p. 160. Thomas Dalamar entered Howard's service in about 1467, and is one of the four main compilers of the accounts. The identity of Hew Wryte is unclear. The vicar of Dovercourt at this time was Thomas Thornton, but wills of the early sixteenth century indicate that there were several curates at Dovercourt at about this period, in addition to the vicar.

75. BL, Add. MS 46349, f. 114r; *HHB*, part 1, p. 347.

76. Hutton suggests that 'Hocking' took place on the second Monday and Tuesday after Easter: R. Hutton, *The Rise and Fall of Merry England* (Oxford, 1996), p. 26. Cheney also believes that Hockday fell on the second Tuesday after Easter: C.R. Cheney, ed., *Handbook of Dates for Students of English History* (Cambridge: CUP, 1996), p. 52. Nevertheless, it is clear from the Howard accounts that in 1464 the Hocking at Stoke-by-Nayland and at Sudbury took place on the quindene day itself (Sunday), though at Harwich in 1466 Hocking was on the second Tuesday after Easter (see below).

77. BL, Add. MS 46349, f. 65r; *HHB*, part 1, p. 258.

78. BL, Add. MS 46349, f. 114r; *HHB*, part 1, p. 348. In 1466 Easter Day was 6 April, and in this case the Hocking did take place on the second Tuesday following.

79. P. Northeast, ed., *Wills of the Archdeaconry of Sudbury, 1439–1474*, vol. 1 (Woodbridge: Boydell Press, 2001), p. 43. No. 112. By his will of 13 August 1440 John Watlok of Clare left 20d to the Guild of St John the Baptist.

80. Copinger, *Suffolk Manors*, vol. 1, pp. 215–16.

81. See below.

82. BL, Add. MS 46349, f. 87r; *HHB*, part 1, p. 304.

83. Arundel Castle MS, f. 43v; *HHB*, part 1, pp. 504–05.

84. On 26 October 1465. BL, Add. MS 46349, f. 88v; *HHB*, part 1, p. 309.

85. BL, Add. MS 46349, f. 90r; *HHB*, part 1, p. 312.

86. BL, Add. MS 46349, f. 90r; *HHB*, part 1, p. 313.

87. BL, Add. MS 46349, f. 90r; *HHB*, part 1, p. 313.

88. 10 January 1465/6. BL, Add. MS 46349, f. 102r; *HHB*, part 1, p. 325.

89. BL, Add. MS 46349, f. 145v; *HHB*, part 1, p. 418.

90. Copinger, *Suffolk Manors*, vol. 1, pp. 215–16.

16. Post-Mortem Moves

1. CP, vol. 9, p. 612.

2. Edwards, 'Notes', pp. 2 and 6; L. Stone and H. Colvin, 'The Howard

Tombs at Framlingham, Suffolk', *The Archaeological Journal*, vol. 122 (May 1966), p. 161.

3. Stone and Colvin, 'Howard Tombs', p. 162.

4. BL, Add. MS 19193, *Papers Relating to Suffolk*, vol. 9, item 6, ff. 8–11, pub. as J. Ashdown-Hill, 'The Opening of the Tombs of the Dukes of Richmond and Norfolk, Framlingham, April 1841: the Account of the Reverend J.W. Darby', *Ric.* 18 (2008), pp. 100–7.

5. IRO, FC 101/E6/6: draft petition to the Lord Bishop of Norwich for a faculty to carry out the proposed renovations, dating from February/March 1888. There is no surviving record at the IRO of the grant of the required faculty, but work appears to have commenced later in 1888, the nave being tackled first.

Appendix 1

1. 1474.

2. 'late of London, with other' crossed out.

3. The meaning of this slightly oddly worded negative phrase seems to be that they had no option other than to enforce the laws.

4. ERO, D/DCe L63r.

5. In the bond he is named as Guy Fowler.

6. As we know from the draft bond issued by Catesby and Townshend, Pigot did not serve in this instance. His name is found in other contexts, however, and he was one of the serjeants-at-law confirmed in post by Warwick upon the restoration of Henry VI in 1470: N. Neilson, ed., *Year Books of Edward IV, 10 Edward IV and 49 Henry VI, ad 1470* (London: Selden Society, vol. 47, 1930), p. xiv; Θ, subsection 4.14.2.

7. Tentatively dated by the ERO to March 1475/6, but in the light of the preceding letter a date in March 1474 seems more likely: ERO, D/DCe L64r.

Appendix 2

1. HP *Biog*.

2. Bailiff of Colchester 1463, 1468, 1475, 1478, 1482: VCH Essex, vol. 9, p. 377.

3. Bailiff of Colchester 1454, 1459, 1461, 1465, 1468, 1470, 1473, 1478, 1483. Earlier generations of the Ford family had also served as Colchester bailiffs: John Ford I from 1350 to 1374, John Ford II from 1399 to 1418, John Ford III from 1451 to 1466 and Robert Ford from 1352 to 1379: VCH *Essex*, vol. 9, p. 377.

4. Bailiff of Colchester 1469, 1471, 1473, 1475: VCH *Essex*, vol. 9, p. 377.

5. Bailiff of Colchester 1464, 1466, 1470:VCH *Essex*, vol. 9, p. 377.
6. Bailiff of Colchester 1471, 1479, 1486, 1493:VCH *Essex*, vol. 9, p. 377.
7. Bailiff of Colchester 1469, 1472, 1476, 1479:VCH *Essex*, vol. 9, p. 377.

Appendix 3

1. Candlemas.
2. Ash Wednesday; beginning of Lent.
3. Anniversary of the accession of Edward IV.
4. Feast of St Edward the Confessor. King Edward IV's name-day.
5. Palm Sunday.
6. Feast of the Annunciation (Lady Day). Start of the new year according to the medieval English calendar.
7. Good Friday.
8. Easter Sunday.
9. Death of Edward IV; accession day of Edward V.
10. St George's Day.
11. Ascension Day.
12. Feast of Pentecost (Whit Sunday).
13. Trinity Sunday.
14. Feast of Corpus Christi.
15. Feast of the Nativity of St John the Baptist.
16. Accession day of Richard III.
17. Feast of St Anne; Queen Anne Neville's name-day.
18. Feast of the Assumption.
19. Feast of St Michael the Archangel.
20. First Sunday of Advent.
21. Christmas Day.

Bibliography

Manuscript Sources

Arundel Castle MS of John Howard's Accounts

BL, Add. MS 19193, *Papers Relating to Suffolk*, 9

BL, Add. MS 46349

HM, bundle 39, no. 44 (will of Isabella Peyton, widow)

HM, bundle 53/5

ERO, D/ACR2 199 (will of Agnes Smyth, widow, 1526)

ERO, D/ACR2 252

ERO, D/B5 CR 73

ERO, D/B5 CR 76

ERO, D/B5 CR 79

ERO, D/B5 CR 81

ERO, D/DCe L63r

ERO, D/DCe L64r

ERO, D/DCe L76

I.H. Jeayes, ed., *Descriptive Catalogue of a Collection of Charters sometime preserved at Gifford's Hall in Stoke-by-Nayland, Co. Suffolk*, unpublished, IRO, S 347, p. 73

IRO, FC 101/E6/6: draft petition to the Lord Bishop of Norwich for a faculty to carry out the proposed renovations, dating from February/March 1888

IRO, HA 246/B2/498

IRO, S 347

CCCC, Parker Library, *Liber Albus*

Soc. Ant., MSS 76 and 77

TNA, C81/1392 No. 1

TNA, PROB 11/11 f. 200r

TNA, PROB 11/24 151/81 (will of Richard Strowgth, vicar of Dovercourt, 1531)

Published Primary Sources

Armstrong, C.A.J. (ed.), Mancini D, *The Usurpation of Richard III*
(Gloucester, 1984) Bacon, N., *The Annalls of Ipswiche* (London, 1654;
reprinted Ipswich, 1884)

Beaune, H. and d'Arbaumont, J. (eds), *Mémoires d'Olivier de la Marche*, 4 vols.
(Paris, 1883–88)

Benham, W.G. (ed.), *The Red Paper Book of Colchester* (Colchester, 1902)
––––– *The Oath Book or Red Parchment Book of Colchester* (Colchester, 1907)

Botfield, B. (ed.), *Manners and Household Expenses of England in the Thirteenth
and Fifteenth Centuries* (Roxburghe Club, 1841)

Bruce, J. (ed.), *Historie of the Arrivall of Edward IV in England* (London:
Camden Society,

1838)

Calendar of Muniments in the possession of the Borough of Harwich (London,
1932), Calendar of Papal Registers, vol. 11, Papal Letters 1455–1464
(London, 1921)

Calendar of Papal Registers, vol. 12, Papal Letters 1458–1471 (London, 1933)

Calendar of Patent Rolls 1452–1461; 1461–1467; 1467–1477; 1476–1485;
1494–1509

Crawford, A., *Howard Household Books* (Stroud, 1992)

Davis, N. (ed.), *Paston Letters and Papers of the Fifteenth Century*, 2 vols
(Oxford: Clarendon, 1971 and 1976)

Ellis, H. (ed.), *Three Books of Polydore Vergil's English History comprising the
reigns of Henry VI, Edward IV and Richard III* (London: Camden Society,
1844)

Hall, E., *Chronicle* (London, 1550; facsimile reprinted 1970)

Hanham, A. (ed.), *The Cely Letters 1472–1488* (London, 1975)

Harris, M.D., *The Coventry Leet Book* (London, 1907–13)

Horrox, R. & Hammond, P.W. (eds), *British Library Harleian Manuscript 433*,
vol. 1; vol. 2; vol. 3, *second register of Edward V and miscellaneous material*
(London: Richard III Society, 1982)

Jeayes, I.H. (ed.), *Descriptive Catalogue of a Collection of Charters sometime
preserved at Gifford's Hall in Stoke-by-Nayland, Co. Suffolk* (unpublished,
Suffolk Record Office, Ipswich Branch)

Kirby, J. (ed.), *The Plumpton Letters and Papers* (Cambridge, 1996)

Rerum Britannicarum Medii Aevi Scriptores, or Chronicles and Memorials of
Great Britain and Ireland during the Middle Ages, *Letters and Papers
illustrative of the Reigns of Richard III and Henry VII* (London: Rolls
House, 1857)

Lincoln's Inn, *The Records of the Honourable Society of Lincoln's Inn: The Black
Books*, vol. 1, 1422–1586 (London, 1897)

Lyell, L. and Watney, F. (eds), *The Acts of the Court of the Mercers' Company 1453–1527* (Cambridge, 1936)

Madden, F., 'Political Poems of the Reigns of Henry VI and Edward IV', *Archaeologia*, 29, part 2 (1842), 318–47

Mancini – see Armstrong

Neilson, N. (ed.), *Year Books of Edward IV, 10 Edward IV and 49 Henry VI, ad 1470* (London: Selden Society, vol. 47, 1930)

Nichols, J.G. (ed.), *Grants &c from the Crown during the Reign of Edward V* (London, 1854)

Nicolas, N.H. (ed.), *Privy Purse Expenses of Elizabeth of York & Wardrobe Accounts of Edward IV* (London: W. Pickering, 1830; reprinted London: F. Muller, 1972)

Northeast, P. (ed.), *Wills of the Archdeaconry of Sudbury, 1439–1474*, vol. 1 (Woodbridge: Boydell Press, 2001)

Pronay, N. and Cox, J. (eds) *The Crowland Chronicle Continuations 1459–1486* (London, 1986)

Ridgard, J. (ed.), *Medieval Framlingham, Select Documents 1270–1524* (Woodbridge: Suffolk Records Society, 1985)

Ross, B., *Accounts of the Stewards of the Talbot Household at Blakemere, 1392-1425* (Shropshire Record Series: University of Keele, 2003)

Smith, L.T., *The Itinerary of John Leland, parts 6 and 7* (London, 1907–10)

Stow, J., *Annales, or a General Chronicle of England* (London: A.M. for R. Meighen, 1631)

Toulmin-Smith, L. (ed), *The Maire of Bristowe is Kalendar* (1872).

Vergil – see Ellis

Secondary Material – Books and Booklets

Ashdown-Hill, J., *Eleanor, the Secret Queen* (Stroud: The History Press, 2009)
——— *Mediaeval Colchester's Lost Landmarks* (Derby: Breedon Books, 2009)
Beaumont and Fletcher, *Knight of the Burning Pestle* – see Wheeler, C.B.
Benham, M., *Guide to Colchester and its environs* (Colchester, 1874)
Bennett, M., *The Battle of Bosworth* (Stroud, 1985)
Benson, L.D. (ed.), *The Riverside Chaucer* (Oxford: OUP, 1987)
Blair, J. & Ramsey, N. (eds) *English Medieval Industries* (London, 2001)
Bruton, E., *The History of Clocks and Watches* (London: Orbis Books, 1979)
Buck, G., *The History of the Life and Reign of Richard III* (London 1646; reprinted 1973)
Carson, A., *Richard III, the Maligned King* (Stroud: The History Press, 2008)
Castiglione – see Cox, V.
Cheney, C.R. (ed.), *Handbook of Dates for Students of English History* (Cambridge, 1996)

Clive, M., *This Son of York* (London, 1973)

Cockayne, G.E., *The Complete Peerage* (London, 1910–59)

Cockerill, C. and Woodward, D., *The Hythe, Port and Church* (Colchester: privately published, 1975)

Copinger, W.M., *The Manors of Suffolk*, vol. 1 (London, 1905)

Cox, J.C., *The Sanctuaries and Sanctuary Seekers of Mediaeval England* (London: Allen, 1911)

Cox, V. (ed) *Castiglione, Count Baldassare, The Book of the Courtier* (London, 1994) *Dictionary of Medieval Latin from British Sources*, Fascicules 1 and 3 (London, 1975–) Dockray, K., *Edward IV, a source book* (Stroud: Sutton Publishing, 1999)

Duffy, E., *The Stripping of the Altars* (London, 1992)

Eddy, M.R. and Petchey, M.R., *Historic Towns in Essex: an Archaeological Survey* (ECC: Chelmsford, 1983)

Edwards, R., *The Itinerary of King Richard III 1483–1485* (London, 1983)

Emery, A., *Greater Medieval Houses of England*, 3 volumes (Cambridge: CUP, 1996), vol. 2, East Anglia, Central England and Wales.

Farmer, J.S. (ed.), *Early English Dramatists: Five Anonymous Plays* (1908; reprinted New York, 1966).

Foss, E., *A Biographical Dictionary of the Judges of England, 1066–1870* (London, 1870) Gillett, H.M., *Walsingham* (London, 1946)

Grew, F. and de Neergaard, M., *Shoes and Pattens* (London, 1988)

Grieve, H., *The Sleepers and the Shadows*, vol. 1 (Chelmsford, 1988)

Griffiths, R.A. & Thomas, R.S., *The Making of the Tudor Dynasty* (Stroud, 1985)

Hall Marks and Date Letters (N.A.G Press: London, 1944)

Halsted, C., *Richard III as Duke of Gloucester and King of England*, vol. 2 (London, 1844)

Hammond, P.W. & Sutton, A.F., *Richard III, the Road to Bosworth Field* (London, 1985)

Harwich Town Assessment Report, ECC Planning – Archaeology Section (February 1999)

Hicks, M., *Richard III* (Stroud, 2000)

———— Edward V: *The Prince in the Tower* (London: Tempus, 2003)

Hunnisett, R.F., *The Medieval Coroner* (Cambridge: CUP, 1961; reprinted Florida 1986)

Hutton, R., *The Rise and Fall of Merry England* (Oxford, 1996)

Jephcott, J.A., *The Inns, Taverns and Pubs of Colchester* (Colchester: Bowcott, 1995)

Karras, R.M., *Common Women* (Oxford: OUP, 1996)

Kendall, P.M., *Richard the Third* (London, 1955; 1976)

King, D. and Sylvester, D. (eds), *The Eastern Carpet in the Western World* (London: Arts Council, 1983)

Kurath, H., Lewis, R.E. et al. (eds) *Middle English Dictionary* (Michigan: University of Michigan, 1952

Laird Clowes, G.S., *Sailing Ships, their history and development*, part 1 (London: Science Museum, 1932)

Laynesmith, J.L., *The Last Medieval Queens* (Oxford: OUP, 2004)

Lightbown, R.W., *Mediaeval European Jewellery*, V&A (London, 1992)

Mackie, J.D., *The Earlier Tudors, 1485–1558* (Oxford: Clarendon, 1952; 1983)

MacLagan, E. (ed.), *Victoria & Albert Museum Exhibition of English Medieval Art* (London, 1930)

Marks, R. & Williamson, P. (eds), *Gothic, Art for England 1400–1547* (London: V&A, 2003)

Marsden, P., *Sealed by Time, the loss and recovery of the Mary Rose* (Portsmouth: Mary Rose Trust, 2003)

Mason, B., *Clock and Watchmaking in Colchester, England* (London: County Life, 1969)

Masters, R., *History of the College of Corpus Christi* (Cambridge, 1753)

McCall, A., *The Medieval Underworld* (London: H. Hamilton, 1979)

Morant, P., *The History and Antiquities of the County of Essex*, vol. 1 (London, 1768)

Morgan, G., *The Romance of Essex Inns* (Letchworth, 1963)

Nichols, J., *The History and Antiquities of the County of Leicestershire*, 4 vols (London, 1811)

Orme, N., *Education and Society in Medieval and Renaissance England* (London: Hambledon, 1989)

——— *English Schools in the Middle Ages* (London: Routledge, 1973)

Otis, L.L., *Prostitution in Medieval Society* (Chicago and London: University of Chicago Press, 1985)

Pedersen, F., *Marriage Disputes in Medieval England* (London: Hambledon, 2000)

Pevsner, N., *Suffolk* (Harmondsworth: Penguin, 1961)

Pollard, A.J., *Richard III and the Princes in the Tower* (Stroud: Sutton Publishing, 1991)

——— *North-Eastern England during the Wars of the Roses: Lay Society, War and Politics 1450–1500* (Oxford, 1990)

Ratcliffe, F.E. & Wright, P.E., *The Royal Maundy, a brief outline of its history and ceremonial* (The Royal Almonry, Buckingham Palace, seventh edition, 1960)

Reeves, C., *Pleasures and Pastimes in Medieval England* (Stroud, 1995)

Richard III Exhibition Catalogue (NPG, 1973)

Ricks, C. (ed.), *The Penguin History of Literature vol. 3: English Drama to 1710* (Harmondsworth, 1971)

Robertson, D.W., *Chaucer's London* (New York: John Wiley & Sons, 1968)

Robinson, J.M., *The Dukes of Norfolk: A Quincentennial History* (Oxford: OUP, 1982)

Ross, C., *Edward IV* (London, 1974)

Smith, S., *The Madonna of Ipswich* (Ipswich: East Anglian Magazine, 1980)

Sutton, A.F. and Visser-Fuchs, L., *The Hours of Richard III* (Stroud: Sutton, 1990)

———, with Griffiths, R.A., *The Royal Funerals of the House of York at Windsor* (London, 2005)

Talbot, H., *The English Achilles, An Account of the Life and Campaigns of John Talbot, 1st Earl of Shrewsbury, 1383–1453* (London, 1981)

Tey, J., *Daughter of Time* (Harmondsworth, 1954)

Victoria County History, *Essex*, vol. 9 (London, 1994); vol. 10 (London, 2001)

Wedgwood, J.C. & Holt, A.D., *History of Parliament 1439–1509*, 2 vols (London, 1936–8)

Weaver, L.T., *The Harwich Story* (Dovercourt, 1975)

——— *Harwich Papers* (Dovercourt, 1994)

Weightman, C., Margaret of York, *Duchess of Burgundy, 1446–1503* (Gloucester, 1989)

Wheeler, C.B., *Six Plays by Contemporaries of Shakespeare* (Oxford, 1915; 1937 edition), pp. 203–95: Beaumont and Fletcher, *The Knight of the Burning Pestle*

Woolgar, C.M., *The Great Household in Late Medieval England* (London, 1999)

Secondary Material – Articles and Papers

Ashdown-Hill, J., 'The Red Rose of Lancaster?' *Ric.* 10, no. 133 (June 1996), pp. 406–20

——— 'Edward IV's Uncrowned Queen; The Lady Eleanor Talbot, Lady Butler', *Ric.* 11, no. 139 (December 1997), pp. 166–90

——— 'The Elusive Mistress: Elizabeth Lucy and her Family', *Ric.* 11, no. 145 (June 1999), pp. 490–505

——— 'Norfolk Requiem: the passing of the house of Mowbray', *Ric.* 12, no. 152 (March 2001), pp. 198–217

——— 'The Inquisition Post Mortem of Eleanor Talbot, Lady Butler, 1468', *Ric.* 12, no. 159 (December 2002), pp. 563–73

——— 'The Lancastrian Claim to the Throne', *Ric.* 13 (2003), pp. 27–38

——— 'Lady Eleanor Talbot's other husband', *Ric.* 14 (2004), pp. 62–81

——— 'The Death of Edward V – new evidence from Colchester', *Essex Archaeology and History*, vol. 35 (2004), pp. 226–30

————— 'Yesterday my Lord of Gloucester came to Colchester …', *Essex History*, vol. 36 (2005), pp. 212–17

————— 'The Go-Between', *Ric.* 15 (2005), pp. 119–21

————— 'The Suffolk Connections of the House of York', *Proceedings of the Suffolk Institute for Archaeology & History*, vol. 41, part 2 (2006), pp. 199–207

————— 'The Opening of the Tombs of the Dukes of Richmond and Norfolk, Framlingham, April 1841: the Account of the Reverend J.W. Darby', *Ric.* 18 (2008), pp. 100–7

————— 'The Shrine of the Holy Rood of Dovercourt', The Essex Journal (Spring 2009), pp. 4–9

————— 'The Wills of John Talbot, first Earl of Shrewsbury, and of his sons, Lord Lisle and Sir Louis Talbot', *Transactions of the Shropshire Archaeological and Historical Society* (forthcoming)

Burgess, C., 'A service for the dead: the form and function of the anniversary in late medieval Bristol', *Transactions of the Bristol & Gloucestershire Archaeological Society*, vol. 105 (1987), pp. 196–7

Castor, H., 'Vere, John de, twelfth Earl of Oxford', *ODNB*

Chamberlayne, J.L., 'A Paper Crowne: the Titles and Seals of Cecily Duchess of York', *Ric.* 10, no. 133 (June 1996), pp. 429–35

Chattaway, C.M., 'Looking a Medieval gift horse in the mouth. The role of the giving of gift objects in the definition and maintenance of the power network of Philip the Bold', *Bijdragen en mededelingen betreffende de geschiedenis der Nederlanden*, 114 (January 1999), pp. 1–15

————— 'When is a Livery not a Livery? Distributions of Clothing at the late fourteenth century Burgundian Court', lecture presented at the MEDATS Conference, *The Development of Liveries and Uniforms in Europe before 1600*, London, 20 May 2006

Crawford, A., 'John Howard, Duke of Norfolk: A Possible Murderer of the Princes?', *Ric.* 5, no. 70 (September 1980), pp. 230–4

————— 'The Mowbray Inheritance', *Ric.* 5, no. 73 (June 1981), pp. 334–40

————— 'The Private Life of John Howard: a study of a Yorkist Lord, his family and household', in P. Hammond (ed.), *Richard III: Loyalty, Lordship and Law* (Richard III and Yorkist History Trust, 1986), pp. 6–24

————— 'Howard, John', *ODNB*

Davies, C.S.L., 'A Requiem for King Edward', *Ric.* 9 (September 1991), pp. 102–5

Dockray, K., 'Edward IV: Playboy or Politician?', *Ric.* 10, no. 131 (December 1995), pp. 306–25

Eiden, H., '*In der Knechtschaft werdet ihr verharren –* ' : *Ursachen und Verlauf des englischen Bauernaufstandes von 1381* (Trier: Verlag Trierer Historische Forschungen), pp. 340–4

Gunn, S.J., 'Vere, John de, thirteenth Earl of Oxford', *ODNB*

Hammond, P.W., 'The Illegitimate Children of Richard III', *Ric.* 5, 1979–81, pp. 92–6

Hampton, W.E., 'The Ladies of the Minories', *Ric.* 4, no. 62, (September 1978), pp. 15–22

Hanham, A., 'The Mysterious Affair at Crowland Abbey', *Ric.* 18 (2008), pp. 1–20

Harper-Bill, C., 'Cecily Neville', *ODNB*

Hicks, M., 'Unweaving the Web: The Plot of July 1483 against Richard III and its Wider Significance', *Ric.* 9, no. 114 (September 1991), pp. 106–9

Horrox, R., 'Hastings, William first Baron Hastings', *ODNB*

Kloincke, Gerard von Wesel's newsletter from England, 17 April 1471', *Ric.* 16 (2006), pp. 66–83

Madden, F., 'Political Poems of the Reigns of Henry VI and Edward IV', *Archaeologia*, 29, part 2 (1842), pp. 318–47

Milne, G., 'Joining the Medieval Fleet', *British Archaeology*, no. 61 (October 2001); www. britarch ac.uk/BA/ba61/feat2.shtml (consulted January 2008)

Paine, C., 'The Chapel and Well of Our Lady of Woolpit', *PSIAH*, 38, part 1 (1993), pp. 8–12

Pollard, A.J., 'Fifteenth Century Politics and the Wars of the Roses', *The Historian* (spring 1998), pp. 26–8

Richmond, C., 'English Naval Power in the Fifteenth Century', *History*, vol. 52, no. 174 (February 1967), pp. 1–15

——— 'Mowbray, John [VI], third Duke of Norfolk', *ODNB*

Saul, N., 'Local Politics and the Good Parliament', in Pollard, T. (ed.), *Property and Politics: Essays in Later Medieval English History* (Gloucester: Sutton, 1984), pp. 156–71

Stone, L. & Colvin, H., 'The Howard Tombs at Framlingham, Suffolk, *The Archaeological Journal*, no. 122 (May 1966), pp. 159–71

Skuse, R., 'Richard III's Children', *The Rose and Crown* (magazine of the Beds & Bucks Group of the Richard III Society) no. 44 (July 2008), pp. 6–7

Sutton, A.F., 'William Shore, merchant of London and Derby', *Derbyshire Archaeological Journal*, 106 (1986), pp. 127–39

Sutton, A.F. & Visser-Fuchs, L., 'The Device of Queen Elizabeth Woodville: A Gillyflower or Pink', *Ric.* 11, no. 136 (March 1997), pp. 17–24

Woolpit History Group, *St Mary's Church, Woolpit* [n.d.]

Internet Sources

Dictionary.com http://dictionary.reference.com/ (June 2006)

http://ls.kuleuven.ac.be/cgi-bin/wa?A2=indo103&L=vvs&P=1445 (April 2008)

http://sunearth.gsfc.nasa.gov/eclipse/SEsaros/SEsaros121.html (April 2008)

Middle English Dictionary http://quod.lib.umich.edu/cgi/m/mec/ med-idx?type=id&id=MED39198 (June2006)

Milne, G., 'Joining the Medieval Fleet', British Archaeology no. 61 (October 2001). www. britarch.ac.uk/BA/ba61/feat2.shtml (January 2008); www. heraldica.org/topics/orders/ garterlist.htm (September 2008)

Unpublished Theses

Archer, R., 'The Mowbrays, Earls of Nottingham and Dukes of Norfolk to 1432' (unpublished D. Phil. thesis, Oxford, 1984)

Ashdown-Hill, L.J., 'The client network, connections and patronage of Sir John Howard (Lord Howard, first Duke of Norfolk) in north-east Essex and south Suffolk', unpublished PhD thesis, University of Essex, 2008

Index

Kings, ruling archdukes and dukes (Austria; Burgundy) and popes are listed by first name. For queens and all other individuals see surname. Married women are listed under maiden surname, if known. Where appropriate, entries are cross-referenced.